JOHN GERARD LEWIS

Catholic Voting and Mortal Sin

How You Vote Can Endanger Your Salvation

For my wife, Dana, a woman of infinite love, patience and support.

Contents

About the Author

John Gerard Lewis is the founder of VotingCatholic.com, which guides Catholics on how to vote according to the teachings of Catholic bishops. He is the former Board Chairman of the 1st Amendment Partnership, a Washington, D.C.-based nonprofit and nonpartisan organization dedicated to protecting religious freedom for Americans of all faiths. Mr. Lewis is also president of Lewis Legal News, Inc., which owns business and legal publications and also processes legal advertisements in several Midwestern states. He has been a regular columnist for SeekingAlpha.com and "The Trading Deck" at MarketWatch.com and has appeared as a guest on Fox Business News. Mr. Lewis's professional activities are summarized at JohnGerardLewis.com. He lives with his wife, Dana, in suburban Kansas City.

1

A Teaching Fatally Ignored

This is a book about gambling. It's a book about Catholics playing the odds about a specific Church teaching, as conveyed by the successors of Christ's apostles. That particular teaching from those successors, the bishops, is that it is sinful to not vote for the candidate who most adheres to the Church's teaching on abortion.

In fact, a number of bishops have gone as far as to say that not only is it sinful, but that it can be a mortal sin.

"Whoa!" you say. "Are you kidding me? Since when? I go to Mass every Sunday, and I haven't heard that."

I'm sure you haven't. But ignorance isn't a blanket excuse for Catholics. They have a duty to learn the tenets of the faith, and to do so with dedication. "Bishops, with priests as co-workers, have as their first task 'to preach the Gospel of God to all men,' in keeping with the Lord's command."[1] And here is what a number of bishops have said explicitly:

*Voting for the candidate who least adheres to the Church's teaching on abortion can be a mortal sin.**

It's that simple. It's what bishops, in increasing numbers, are publicly confirming. Here I do not argue whether these bishops are correct (although I accept their teaching); instead, I merely present the factual record: that a meaningful number of apostolic successors have declared that such voting behavior can be a mortal sin, and that a significant number of Catholics are ignoring their teaching. The posit that many Catholics are gambling cannot be successfully challenged, because they indisputably are. Those are the facts.

Now, it's also a fact that not all bishops have unambiguously made this declaration. To be sure, a very few are so tepid in their declared opposition to abortion that one might legitimately wonder if they truly oppose it. In the context of authentic Church doctrine, they can only be described as extremists. A larger segment of bishops assign "social justice" and "quality of life" issues the same importance as the holocaust of unborn innocents. But most American bishops have now made, or signed on to, statements placing abortion as the top issue for Catholics in the voting booth.

Thus, what we have among the bishops is not material discord about a Catholic's duty to vote for the most anti-abortion candidate, but the question of whether, or the degree to which, it is sinful not to do so.

(By the way, in this book I avoid the term, "pro-life" a much as possible, because it is often co-opted – and corrupted – by advocates of "seamless garment" propaganda to dilute the primacy of the abortion issue for Catholics. More on that later in the book. And, for convenience, all references to "abortion" as an "intrinsic evil" for Catholics also encompass the other current non-negotiable issues in play today: euthanasia, embryonic stem-cell research, human cloning, homosexual "marriage," and religious freedom.)

The prospect of sinning merely by casting a vote is a question that most American Catholics are never stirred to ponder. It's a free society, right? And, anyway, the Church can't legally tell us for whom to vote. "Separation of church and state." It's right there in the Constitution, right? (Wrong.) That's why priests and bishops don't talk strongly about politics – because politics and religion don't mix, right?

Well, that's what we're told, by both the political class and the Church, itself. Apparently, we can vote for whomever we want, and that seems to be fine with the Church. No worries, apparently.

But many priests and bishops are, in fact, starting to speak out and, notably, not in contravention of the Constitution or campaign laws. They have long possessed every right to discuss politics and even to tell you *how* to vote, as long as they don't tell you *for whom* to vote. But today's historic threat to religious freedom in America has compelled bishops and priests to push back and break their relative silence on serious moral issues. They are aggressively denouncing the evils of the day, especially those that are currently "in play" in the United States, namely the Six Non-Negotiables.

The "non-negotiables" were identified in the early 2000s by Catholic Answers, the largest Catholic lay apologetics apostolate in the United States. They have since been endorsed by bishops and priests worldwide. The original five non-negotiable issues – abortion, homosexual marriage, human cloning, embryonic stem cell research and euthanasia – were cited as high-profile, high priority, contemporary issues that a Catholic must never support. Indeed, while Catholics could disagree on many other issues, such as how best to help the poor or how to address environmental matters, these non-negotiable issues do not allow for disagreement among Catholics. They involve intrinsic evil, and on these serious moral issues Catholics must adhere to Church teaching.

(A sixth non-negotiable, religious freedom, was added in 2015, amid the rapid rise of once-unthinkable legislation and court rulings that suddenly began removing Christians' free exercise of their religion. This was most notoriously seen in the oppression of Christian small-business owners for refusing to provide services for homosexual weddings.)

For purposes of speaking out, the bishops winnowed the issues further, and it is perfectly logical that the dominant life-and-death issue, abortion, became the focus of their sermons, inside the churches and without. Abortion is the diabolical cataclysm of our day, they said. Euthanasia and embryonic stem cell research are as destructive to human life, but they are not as pervasive in society. There are more than 2,300 abortions in the United States every day.[2] Among today's moral atrocities, abortion is the greatest.

And so the bishops began their outcry, one by one and collectively. And they stated in strong and sometimes severe terms that Catholics must vote for anti-abortion candidates, for the good of society and for the health of their own spiritual lives. Some were bold enough to warn of such personal spiritual jeopardy in no uncertain terms. One by one, and emboldened by their growing line of predecessors, Bishops Paprocki, Chaput, Jenky, Sheridan, Ricken and others declared that failing to vote for the most anti-abortion candidate could be a mortal sin.

(Where prelates and clergy are quoted in this book, their office and location are those at the time of the quote.)

Of course, theirs remain voices in the wilderness among many of the faithful. That is to say that they've *convinced* themselves that they're faithful – Catholics, including clergymen, don't want to hear it. Why? The reasons are legion, but here are three common ones: 1) some priests don't want to deal with the pushback from liberal parishioners or from local media who will surely object to such a "radical," politically-incorrect pronouncement; 2) some priests simply have no desire to become embroiled in politics or societal issues; and 3) some priests simply disagree altogether about the sinfulness of voting for a pro-choice candidate. (Again, a ground rule for nomenclature: in this book, "pro-choice" and "pro-abortion" are one and the same, because either term provides for the murder of children. Murder is murder. Death is death. There is no gradation.)

And there we have the spectrum among Catholic clerics: Those who have perspicuously enunciated a doctrinaire teaching on one end, and, on the other, clergy and laymen who after decades of poor, undisciplined Catholic formation cannot abide the orthodoxy of: 1) the bishops' teaching authority, and 2) the teaching, itself.

Both steadfast orthodox and resolute liberal Catholics have long populated the pews, and their respective states of implacability are, of course, unlikely to change. But there is a very large segment in the middle. According to the 2014 Pew Religious Landscape Study, 41% of American Catholics identify themselves as neither conservative or liberal. Because Catholic voting patterns have proven to be reflective of society at large, at least in recent U.S. presidential elections, we can plausibly conclude that there is a large percentage of Catholics who are simply not political ideologues. That is, they are politically persuadable at election time, and probably don't much think about politics until then. They are the reason that since 1972 a majority of Catholics have voted for the winning presidential candidate, whether Republican or Democrat, including the pro-abortion Barack Obama twice. [3]

Many priests don't even bother to say to parishioners, "Vote for anti-abortion candidates." Instead, they retreat to safe ground: "Well, there are many issues to take into consideration as a good Catholic," they drone. "The environment, the poor, the elderly, abortion, immigration, fair housing, employment," and on and on until 10 minutes, sufficient for a Sunday homily (it's in no fashion a sermon), have passed, and they conclude that they've adequately performed their election-season duty.

But they don't stratify the issues. Abortion is just lumped in there somewhere in the middle, as if it's just another thing to consider in the voting booth. Never mind that the U.S. Conference of Catholic Bishops has explicitly averred that abortion "is not one issue among many."[4] Never mind that Pope Benedict XVI declared that "Not all issues have the same moral weight as abortion and euthanasia."[5] "Nah," the priest says to himself, "my week will be hell if I highlight abortion." Given his enormous pastoral responsibility, oughtn't he consider whether his own fate will be hell if he doesn't?

Perhaps such priestly capitulation to comfort will diminish in light of the aforementioned probity recently demonstrated by many bishops. But given the stakes at hand – eternal life or eternal death – why would priests and laity take the ultimate gamble by ignoring the bishops' profound declaration that voting contrary to Church teaching on matters of intrinsic evil can be a mortal sin?

In philosophy there is an argument, known as Pascal's Wager, that holds it to be an indisputably better bet to believe that there is a Christian God and lose nothing if there isn't, than to disclaim such belief and risk losing everything if there is. In other words, better to be safe than sorry. "I should be much more afraid of being mistaken and then finding out that Christianity is true than of being mistaken in believing it to be true," said Blaise Pascal, a 17th century French philosopher, mathematician and physicist. [6]

As to the rather weighty question of eternal bliss vs. eternal suffering, the only sane choice would be to side with Pascal, would it not?

French philosopher and Nobel Prize winner Albert Camus, who after long professing atheism appeared to have been gravitating to Christianity before his sudden death in a 1960 car wreck, put it this way: "I would rather live my life as if there is a God and die to find out there isn't, than live as if there isn't and to die to find out that there is."

Contemporary Catholic author Peter Kreeft recounts the story of an atheist who demanded proof of the existence of God from the great rabbi and philosopher Martin Buber. Buber refused but asked the atheist, "But can you be *sure* there is no God?" Forty years later, the man wrote, "I am still an atheist. But Buber's question has haunted me every day of my life." Pascal's Wager, Kreeft says, "has just that haunting power."[7]

If one accepts the teaching authority of the bishops, as a Catholic is obliged to do, then the salvific gravity of their teaching is of ultimate consequence. Catholic doctrine holds that God gave the Church to man as His teaching authority on earth and that the bishops, as successors to the apostles, are assigned to convey that teaching. Now, the bishops do not agree to the last man on every teaching (they are allowed to differ on matters of prudential judgment), but that is because they indeed are men, subject to human individuality. It is the same with popes, some of whom have taught doctrine well and some of whom have butchered it.

We thus see demonstrated the faithfulness, over 2,000 years, of the Holy Spirit who has sustained God's promise to never abandon His Church, even, as the retired Pope Benedict XVI put it, "when the boat has taken on so much water as to be on the verge of capsizing."[8]

Given the consensus, if not absolute unanimity, of the bishops on the mortal sinfulness of not voting for the most anti-abortion candidate, what is the Catholic's faithful response in the voting booth? Because some bishops are not completely on board, may a Catholic vote for whomever he wishes?

That would be the high-risk choice. Given that some bishops have said that not voting for the most anti-abortion candidate can be a mortal sin, then, proceeding from the logic of Pascal's Wager, the only rational choice for a Catholic voter is to act in his own salvific interest. It is an indisputably better bet to believe that those bishops are correct and lose nothing if they aren't, than to disclaim such belief and risk losing everything if they are.

Of course, it is a shame that one of philosophy's lowest arguments for living a virtuous life – eternal damnation – need be pulled out to encourage Catholics to do so. It bespeaks their ignorance of authentic Church teaching, specifically that they are required to put their faith and hope in that teaching. But it also affirms God's mercy. After all, God wants all of our love, but he allows mere fear of hell to be sufficient for sacramental absolution. His love for us is infinite, His standard for us infinitesimal.

* (Throughout this book, references to "most anti-abortion candidate" or "candidate who least adheres to the Church's teaching" also include the "most electable candidate" meeting these criteria. No Catholic is obligated to waste his vote on a clearly unelectable candidate, unless all of the other candidates hold decidedly unacceptable positions on abortion.)

2

Does a Catholic Voting Bloc Even Exist?

I s there a Catholic voting bloc in America today? Good heavens, no. Has there ever been? Oh yes. It was born of social and political repression in the mid-19th century and ended 100 years later as Catholics assimilated into American society.

Revolutions in 1848 had spurred German, Austrian and Bohemian Catholics to emigrate to America. They were joined by hundreds of thousands of Irish fleeing the potato famine. From 1840 to 1860, the American Catholic population swelled from 663,000 to 3.1 million.[1] The Democratic Party recognized this suddenly meaningful voting segment and began nominating Catholic candidates for local offices in urban areas. The Catholic vote thus became mostly a Democratic vote,[2] so much so that it contributed to the party's stranglehold on machine politics in cities like New York, Chicago, Philadelphia and Kansas City. "To encourage voters to support the Democratic ticket," wrote Thomas J. Craughwell, in *Our Sunday Visitor*, "the machine helped immigrants find jobs; picked up the tab for weddings, funerals and other family functions; paid doctor's bills or heating bills; and even handed out turkeys to the indigent at Thanksgiving and Christmas, thereby building up the immigrants' loyalty to the Democrats in urban areas. Wisely, as waves of new immigrants arrived in America – Slavs, Italians, Jews, French Canadians – (the) most(ly) Irish-dominated machine extended their help to the newcomers, ensuring that most of these future

American citizens would be loyal Democrats, too."

Catholic voters would be identified with the Democratic Party for decades, and in 1928 Al Smith became the first Catholic to be nominated for president by a major party. The former Democratic governor of New York lost the election to Herbert Hoover, but he didn't lose the Catholic vote – he got 80 percent.[3]

Four years later, Catholics were harboring resentment that Franklin Roosevelt had eclipsed Smith as the party's standard bearer. But after trying to snatch the nomination for himself during the Democratic national convention, Smith ultimately campaigned for FDR and likely helped deliver Catholic voters by estimates ranging from 70 to 81 percent.[4] Many Catholics were also influenced by the endorsements of Catholic leaders like Cardinals George Mundelein of Chicago and Patrick Hayes of New York, who were supportive of Roosevelt's New Deal programs.

The remarkable outcome of the 1948 election likely turned, at least in part, on the Catholic vote. Democrat Harry Truman had become an unpopular president and thus a decided underdog to Republican Thomas Dewey. In an historic upset, Truman defeated Dewey 49.4 to 45 percent in the popular vote. But Truman's share of the Catholic vote was 65 percent, owing both to preexisting party loyalty and to Catholics' appreciation for Truman's longstanding support of them and their values.

A Catholic voting bloc was, at least ostensibly, still intact, but erosion was looming. Many blue-collar Catholics were repelled by the prospect of a growing centralized government that had emerged from the New Deal and that was embraced by Democratic presidential candidate Adlai Stevenson in 1952. "Catholics deserted the Democrats in numbers that had not been seen since the election of 1920," wrote George Marlin in *The American Catholic Voter: 200 Years of Political Impact*.[5] Republican Dwight Eisenhower took 56 percent of the Catholic vote in 1952, but just 51 percent in 1956. In 1960, John Kennedy pulled an impressive 78 percent of Catholics back to the Democrats, but most likely because, he himself, was a Catholic and one who exuded extraordinary charisma.[6] Indeed, 38 years earlier, a more conservative Democrat, Al Smith, captured more of the Catholic vote than the golden boy of 1960 did.

After candidate Kennedy's watershed campaign speech (discussed in the next chapter), the one wherein he firmly ensconced his Catholic faith beneath his presidential ambition, a loosening moral culture and an American church that did little to oppose it served to further dissolve any remnant of a cohesive Catholic voting bloc. As society bifurcated into opposing conservative and liberal divisions, so did Catholics, including their bishops and priests. The social tumult of the 1960s positively begged for priests to respond to the issues of the day with authentic Catholic teaching. But many cowered under the threat, of all things, of the wholly mundane matter of tax exemption. Democratic Sen. Lyndon Johnson, the shrewdest politician of the last century, slipped the "Johnson Amendment" into the Internal Revenue Code of 1954 in order to keep nonprofit organizations, i.e., *churches,* from endorsing or opposing political candidates. Johnson understood the electoral consequences of an ecclesiastical stem-winder or even mere spiritual guidance. And ever since that law's enactment, a petrified, quailing American Catholic Church has effectively forbidden priests to talk politics from the pulpit and has thereby prioritized a tax break ahead of preaching truth – and saving souls.

Of course, the true prohibition enacted in the Johnson Amendment does not at all proscribe talking politics, despite the de facto policy imposed by the American bishops. Rather, it simply prohibits the explicit endorsement or non-endorsement of an identifiable candidate. It doesn't prohibit a priest from factually explaining the positions of a particular candidate vis-à-vis Catholic teaching, even if identifying that candidate by name. Priests rarely, but certainly should, add that, "Catholics should not vote for a candidate who holds these positions." Campaign-finance activists, i.e. liberal speech cops, would (falsely) accuse the priest of breaking the law, probably embroiling him and his bishop in a political mess. If that happened, what should the priest and bishop do? Well, they should courageously thrust themselves into the fight. But what do they almost always do when thusly accused? Well, they don't get accused, because such sermons are hardly ever given.

You see, the American bishops demoted their faith in favor of a secular interest, much as Kennedy did. Still today, the bishops, and their subordinate priests, effectively compartmentalize their witness to the faith by avoiding opportunities to evangelize in the public square. Kennedy's was an act of opportunism. The bishops' is as well, ostensibly to avoid controversy, a craven enough reason, but ultimately to preserve a lucrative tax break. This is not out of respect to the demarcation set forth in our Lord's instruction to "render unto Caesar." Rather, it's simply transacting business with Caesar.

As shameful as this is, it takes only a modicum of cynicism to wonder about yet another motivation for the bishops' avoidance of politics from the pulpit. The U.S. Conference of Catholic Bishops, as a body, has a history of tilting left on social issues. To allow priests to sermonize about which candidates best represent orthodox Catholic teaching would undoubtedly lead to some advocacy for conservative candidates, because conservative candidates are typically anti-abortion and adhere to traditional values. Liberal bishops and priests, of course, don't want to see conservatives elected, even if they're correct on the abortion issue, so they're happy to adopt and use as a pretext the incorrect interpretation of the Johnson Amendment. And there are so many of them that they easily silence their fellow clerics by spreading that agitprop. Most Catholic clerics have come to believe this lie about what they can and cannot say from the pulpit about politics.

The paucity of orthodox Catholic teaching over the decades has exacerbated the disintegration of any discernible Catholic unity in politics. Here's why: Prudential-judgment issues are those on which the church takes no absolute stand. But issues of intrinsic evil, according to church doctrine, are non-negotiable – there is unconditional right and wrong about such issues. And today's Catholic is not being taught the difference between right and wrong by the very institution created by Christ to teach it. Thus, in the political sphere today's American church verily abandons the souls under its care, refusing to provide salvific guidance in the face of the mortally sinful risks inherent in voting. Hence, the Catholic vote is grounded in nothing other than that of society at large. It's amorphous, unhinged from doctrine, composed of citizens who happen to be Catholic, but who do not behave as Catholic citizens.

"Four decades after John Kennedy," lamented Denver Archbishop Charles Chaput just ahead of the 2000 presidential election, "too many American Catholics no longer connect their political choices with their religious faith in any consistent way."[7] He then took direct aim at the intolerant liberalism of the Democratic Party:

"And a prolife Democrat like the late Governor Bob Casey – who was Irish and Catholic, just like John Kennedy – finds himself barred from speaking at his own party's convention in 1992, and ignored by his party's leadership until his death.

"That's the legacy of accommodating our Catholic faith to politics, instead of forming and informing our politics through our faith. Forty years later – despite the excitement and pride so many of us felt after John Kennedy's election – it's difficult, if not impossible, for a person who is publicly loyal to the Catholic faith on 'sanctity-of-life' issues to hold any major national leadership position in John Kennedy's own party."

Of course, as will be shown herein, Kennedy, himself, was significantly, integrally responsible for that, and consequently Catholics' "excitement and pride" for him was not well placed.

Notes political observer Michael Barone in Marlin's book: "American Catholics are as numerous as ever, more prosperous than ever, more diverse in their opinions than ever; but they are less of an identifiable bloc than they were well within living memory, when America had not elected a Catholic president."[8] In other words, a Catholic being elected president ironically resulted in a weaker, less unified Catholic electorate.

Political analyst John Morgan notes the categorization of contemporary Catholic voters:

• Urban, ethnic blue-collar types found in the north east and Midwest. They are typically democratic but socially conservative.

• Suburban Catholics who for the most part are third generation Irish and Italian. They are found in Long Island and outside of Chicago, Cleveland in Milwaukee and St. Louis. They are more attached to the Republican party.

• Midwest German and Polish Catholics who are very conservative but not wedded to the Republican Party. They serve as swing voters in Wisconsin,

Iowa, Minnesota, Michigan, Ohio, and Missouri.

• Hispanics, who are basically Democratic. In Marlin's judgment, for Republicans to attract Hispanic votes, they should appeal to their more socially conservative side.

• Cafeteria Catholics who, for the most part, have fallen away from the church. Marlin estimates that 20% of Catholics fall into this category. [9]

It's one man's conclusion, and certainly not an implausible one. But how does one reconcile this ordering, which, overall, suggests a conservative lean, with the fact that, using just one example, Catholics gave the far-left Barack Obama a majority of their votes twice? Certain demographic segments of Catholics may be "socially conservative" or "attached to the Republican party," but they vote as they wish. Their political viewpoints may be influenced by their Catholic faith, but their voting choices are certainly not governed by it. The reason for this is that at the insistence of the liberal, relativist culture – in society and in the church – they dutifully sever their faith from their politics, just as John Kennedy did, and they actually believe it is their obligation to do so. "Separation of church and state!" – the sophism rings in their ears, displacing their walk with Jesus. They have been taught, erroneously, that their vote is theirs alone and that not even the one holy, Catholic and apostolic church may accompany them into the voting booth. It's none of the Church's business, and therefore it's none of God's business. One recalls from the Lorica of St. Patrick:

"Christ with me, Christ before me, Christ behind me, Christ in me, Christ beneath me, Christ above me, Christ on my right, Christ on my left."

But stay over there, Lord, while I'm voting.

3

His Greatest Seduction: The Kennedy Capitulation

Foremost among John F. Kennedy's many reputed seductions (in case you haven't heard, "He was nearly a pathological philanderer," notes historian Michael O'Brien[1]) was the whole of American Catholics, and it resulted, not only ironically but accidentally, from a speech delivered to a group of Protestant leaders in 1960.

Two months before he was elected president that November, Kennedy stood before the Greater Houston Ministerial Association and told 300 Protestant ministers that he believed in an America "where no Catholic prelate would tell the president (should he be Catholic) how to act ... where there is no Catholic vote, no anti-Catholic vote, no bloc voting of any kind." And just to cement his then-novel dissociation of his public life from the magisterial dictates of the Church created by Almighty God, Himself, Kennedy tossed in his declared stand "against an ambassador to the Vatican" and government aid to parochial schools.

With clever semantic skill, he not only addressed Protestants' fears but also managed to not seriously alienate the existing Catholic voting bloc while doing so. It was a fortuitous result for Kennedy, because this novel separation of personal values from public policy seemed to work as a reasonable compromise for a Catholic politician. And coming just a few weeks before election day, Catholics had little time to debate whether such a pronouncement was acceptable or heresy. It caused barely a ripple among them. The stunningly charismatic, handsome young candidate was carrying a Catholic torch, and he had laid down a new "interpretation" to which many Catholics couldn't resist acceding. That he had to fudge a bit on his allegiance to the Church was viewed as, well, a negligible, easily-forgotten trade-off. Kennedy went on to receive 78% of the Catholic vote nationally, and over 80% in the valuable electoral states in the Northeast and Midwest, despite his precedent-setting denunciation of Catholic influence on his past and future career as a public servant.

But the Houston phenomenon also indelibly bifurcated the stolid Catholic precept of living one's faith in every worldly respect, and it thereby undermined the noble and edifying concept of a true Catholic voting bloc, a bloc that theretofore had reliably voted according to Catholic teaching.

Archbishop Charles Chaput, of Denver, in his own address to a Houston audience of Protestants in 2010, said Kennedy's speech caused a moral disaster. It "left a lasting mark on American politics," Chaput said. He added that Kennedy was "wrong about American history and very wrong about the role of religious faith in our nation's life. And he wasn't merely 'wrong.' His Houston remarks profoundly undermined the place not just of Catholics, but of all religious believers, in America's public life and political conversation. Today, half a century later, we're paying for the damage." [2]

Fr. Mark Massa, S.J., dean of the Boston College School of Theology and Ministry, said Kennedy "'secularized' the American presidency in order to win it ... he had to 'privatize' presidential religious belief – including and especially his own – in order to win that office." Massa noted that Kennedy's "near total privatization of religious belief" was so extreme that "religious observers from both sides of the Catholic/Protestant fence commented on its remarkable atheistic implications for public life and discourse." [3]

Not only did Kennedy's Houston address forevermore provide cover for elected officials to take public actions contrary to their professed faith, but it also exacerbated the U.S. Supreme Court's repeated and deliberate misconstruction of Thomas Jefferson's sentiments about the

First Amendment.

"I believe in an America where the separation of church and state is absolute," Kennedy declared.[4] The "church and state" reference was derived from an 1802 letter that Jefferson had penned to the Danbury Baptist Association in Connecticut: "I contemplate with sovereign reverence," he wrote, "that act of the whole American people which declared that their legislature should 'make no law respecting an establishment of religion, or prohibiting the free exercise thereof,' thus building a wall of separation between Church & State." [5]

But the "church and state" terminology is Jefferson's alone, has been carelessly taken out of context, and been disinguously misapplied over time. The First Amendment, the pertinent Constitutional provision here, makes no mention of any "wall of separation." Moreover, subsequent political and judicial interpretations have corrupted Jefferson's intended meaning, although Jefferson should have known that his rather sloppy ambiguousness left his words open to unremitting interpretive abuse.

As Daniel L. Dreisbach, professor of justice, law and society at American University, explained, "Jefferson's wall, as a matter of federalism, was erected between the national and state governments on matters pertaining to religion and not, more generally, between the church and *all* civil government. ... The wall's primary function was to delineate the constitutional jurisdictions of the national and state governments, respectively, on religious concerns, such as setting aside days in the public calendar for prayer, fasting, and thanksgiving."[7]

Thus, we see that Jefferson's "wall of separation" spoke exclusively to the limits of government to exert religious influence on the citizenry and was not describing a wall to "protect" government from religion. The latter was not Jefferson's wall, but merely an invention of others and therefore a mythical wall. But that fact was, perhaps negligently though probably willingly, lost on the courts.

In *Reynolds v. United States (1879)*, the U.S. Supreme Court dug deep to effectively, and quite awkwardly, shoehorn the Danbury letter into the Constitution of the United States. The letter, the justices said seven decades after it was written, "may be accepted almost as an authoritative declaration of the scope and effect of the [first] amendment." Jurisprudence, it therefore seems, would be so different today if only Jefferson had simply written more letters.

After another seven decades had passed, Justice Hugo Black brazenly pronounced in *Everson v. Board of Education (1947)* that the mythical wall not only existed but had somehow become "high and impregnable." Black thereby built a newer wall that looked even less like Jefferson's.

It was at that moment, Dreisbach says, that the Supreme Court bastardized the First Amendment. "A barrier originally designed, as a matter of federalism, to separate the national and state governments, and thereby to preserve state jurisdiction in matters pertaining to religion, was transformed into an instrument of the federal judiciary to invalidate policies and programs of state and local authorities," Dreisbach wrote. "As the normative constitutional rule applicable to all relationships between religion and the civil state, the wall that Black built has become the defining structure of a putatively secular polity."

And Black set the stage perfectly for John Kennedy's duplicitous landmark speech 13 years later. The highest court in the land had appropriated a line from a personal letter, written 145 years earlier, and used it to euthanize the quiddity of personal integrity. Now, Kennedy could conveniently argue, the Constitution actually *required* an officeholder to be of two characters: one that acts privately according to his true beliefs, and one that acts publicly within prevailing secular strictures. This newfound "constitutional requirement" would give Kennedy, and legions of politicians who would follow, license to perform public acts that were contrary to their *ostensible* personal moral standards and beliefs. (Of course, if they truly held God-given standards and beliefs they would never allow them to be compromised at all, even in the public sphere. Rendering unto Caesar is always subject to the laws of God.) Kennedy had thus taken the 1947 court's remarkable invention and injected it firmly into American politics.

To be sure, Kennedy tried to have it both ways in his Houston speech, largely succeeding politically, though contradicting himself in doing so. In the speech, he at once referenced a 1948 pastoral letter from America's Catholic bishops that vigorously supported democracy and religious freedom, but which also refuted Justice Black's church-and-state construal in *Everson*. Indeed, Archbishop Chaput notes that Kennedy "neglected to mention that the same bishops, in the same letter, repudiated the new and radical kind of separation doctrine he was preaching."[8]

And as if to show that he hadn't completely abandoned his allegiance to Catholicism – a look that the Protestant ministers would not respect – he was quick to aver that he would not "disavow my views or my church in order to win this election." But that's exactly what he was doing in the speech. "It began the project of walling religion away from the process of governance in a new and aggressive way," Chaput says. "It also divided a person's private beliefs from his or her public duties. And it set 'the national interest' over and against outside religious pressures or dictates."

Catholic scholar Robert Royal observes that "it was a strange concession for Kennedy or any Christian, let alone a Catholic," to say that in America no religious body should seek "to impose its will directly or indirectly" on public matters. Such a call for the sidelining of faith, he says, would be more suited to Nazi Germany, the old Soviet Union or modern France. He notes that most Americans take their moral bearings from their faith. "It is impossible to understand the basis of American democracy, or something like the civil rights movement, without religion."[9]

But the aftereffect of Kennedy in Houston would be so long-lasting as to seem permanent.

Had he lost the election, perhaps it would not be so. The politicization of Jefferson's words and Black's corruption of them might have, at least, been delayed. But Kennedy did win. Michael Barone, principal author of the annual *Almanac of American Politics,* concludes that Kennedy's election was "a victory for Catholicism."[10] But he is wrong. The "victory" was illusory, as Catholicism, particularly American Catholicism, would suffer greatly for it. Catholic voters were charmed by the first post-war Catholic presidential nominee, a youthful, handsome and rich war hero (though "war hero" is now a highly disputed descriptor of JFK). But over time they would find that their Catholic values were receding as a bulwark against immorality in American culture. While the Houston speech built on Black's wall of separation, it broke down the Catholic wall against rising decadence, which was accelerating. In 1960, the birth-control pill was approved for contraceptive use; within five years, the decades-long "sexual revolution" began, and just 13 years after the Houston speech the Supreme Court legalized abortion in *Roe v. Wade.*

The Catholic Church no longer played so much on the conscience or in the political calculations of American policymakers, Catholic or not. And Catholic office-seekers and officeholders could now put on two faces.

"Looking back, this was one of the watersheds of public life in our country," says Chaput. "Kennedy created a template for a generation of Catholic candidates: 'Be American first; be Catholic second.'"[11]

Indeed, the elation among Catholics, for having finally seen one of their own move into the White House, began to subside as the societal effects of the popularly-known "Kennedy Compromise" began to creep in. Many longtime Catholic Democrats, particularly in ethnic neighborhoods, became concerned "about the elitist, left-wing drift of the party," writes George Marlin.[12]

"The first signs of this," he says, "were detected in 1960's election returns. Even though 78 percent of Catholics had cast their votes for Kennedy, the total was still below the 80 percent that Al Smith had received in 1928. In fact, Kennedy had enjoyed greater popularity with Jews, who gave him 82 percent of their votes – and this was quite obviously because he was a liberal."

The loosening of the Democratic Party's grip on Catholics had begun earlier and was particularly manifested in the Dwight Eisenhower/Adlai Stevenson presidential contest eight years before Kennedy's Houston address. "The 1952 election results indicated that Catholic attitudes were changing," Marlin writes. "Catholics who moved to suburbia were no longer dependent on inner-city Democratic machines and did not feel the need to remain loyal to the party of their parents. Germans, Poles, and other Eastern European ethnics who watched their former homelands fall under the Iron Curtain were disenchanted with Democratic foreign policy initiatives. As for the Irish, by 1950 only 10 percent of their population was first-generation. Third and fourth generation upwardly mobile Irish were losing the affection their forebears had had for the Democratic Party of the 'good old days.' Mrs. Emily Smith Warner, daughter of Gov. Al Smith, exemplified this change of attitude when she endorsed and campaigned for Eisenhower."[13]

Republican candidate Eisenhower captured the votes of 73% of German Catholics and over 50% of Poles and Irish. Four years later, Marlin notes, "Catholic Poles, Germans, Irish, Italians, and Eastern Europeans cast over 50 percent of their votes for Eisenhower. He carried the heavily Catholic populated cities of Chicago, Buffalo, Baltimore, and Jersey City. Michael Barone observed that 'in 1956 (Eisenhower) made his biggest gains among Catholic voters.'"[14]

But this pronounced disaffection of Catholics for the Democratic Party did not betray a waning of the strength of Catholicism in American life in the 1950s, which, Marlin recounts, was actually a "Golden Age" in the words of Catholic historian Michael Perko. "Politically and economically powerful, the Church exercised a role in American life previously unknown," Perko writes. "No longer exclusively the preserve of a prosperous but insignificant minority, or of destitute immigrants, it had become a significant force of American society." [15]

Kennedy briefly brought Catholics back to the Democratic Party, winning 78% of their vote. [16] Lyndon Johnson mostly kept them in the fold in 1964, getting 76% of the Catholic vote. But in 1968, Catholics went for Democratic nominee Hubert Humphrey by just 59% to Republican nominee Richard Nixon's 33%. Nixon won that race and, in turn, aggressively went after Catholic voters in 1972, endorsing aid for parochial schools and opposing abortion funding. It worked. Nixon captured 59% of the Catholic vote, a new record for a Republican, Marlin said. [17]

The election of Jack Kennedy in 1960 was a momentary departure from the party-preference trend line for Catholics. It was an anomaly caused by the first nomination of a Catholic presidential candidate in more than three decades. And the shiny Kennedy charisma was, after all, thoroughly intoxicating for Catholics. But they would soon revert.

The "Kennedy Compromise," as the Houston speech would become known, ultimately proved to have been a "Kennedy Capitulation" that began to severely impair not just Catholic, but religious, influence on American culture altogether. Indeed, the speech, which was designed to, and surely to some extent did, allay Protestant fears about a prospective Catholic president, ironically served up a doctrine that would also diminish the historical preeminence of Protestantism in American politics as well as Christian influence, altogether, on society. Thus, writes Father Massa of Boston College, "the raising of the [Catholic] issue itself went a considerable way toward 'secularizing' the American public square by privatizing personal belief. Their very effort to 'safeguard' the [essentially Protestant] religious aura of the presidency ... contributed in significant ways to its secularization."[18]

Bishop Filipe J. Estevez, of St. Augustine, Fla., to some degree gave Kennedy the benefit of the doubt as to whether he understood what he was unleashing, according to Patti Maguire Armstrong in *The Remnant* newspaper. "In the early Sixties, religion and society were not hostile to one another as seems to be increasingly the case today in the United States," Estevez said. "I suspect that President Kennedy never meant that our faith and beliefs should not have any influence on how we act or how we vote."[19]

More likely, he never gave that piece of his legacy a second thought – or even a first. Archbishop Chaput contends that, even had the ambitious candidate foreseen the resulting damage to the American Church, it "was an easy calculus for Kennedy, who wore his faith loosely anyway."[20] Chaput concludes that Kennedy "created a model of accommodation which then helped to shape a whole generation of Catholic officeholders ... all of whom found a way to live comfortably with the canyon that opened up between their private religious convictions and their public service."[21]

Today, Chaput and a growing number of cardinals, bishops and priests are proclaiming, not merely suggesting, that the spiritual depth of that canyon, for these politicians and those who vote for them, may be fatally infinite and eternal.

4

The JFK Aftermath: Suddenly Like Everyone Else

The Kennedy Capitulation gave license not only to Catholic politicians, but also to rank-and-file Catholic Democrats for whom they served as contemporary models. Hard upon the election of Kennedy and the utter radiance of his mythical Camelot reign, fawningly imputed to him because of his purported affection for the 1960 Broadway musical (he, indubitably, was King Arthur), came the Second Vatican Council, which changed not only how Catholics practiced their faith, but also much of what they believed.

The Latin Mass, with its mystical aura, reverence and majestic hymns, was scrapped in favor of the vernacular, very busy "audience" participation, lots of hugging, and folk music that strained to shoehorn rewritten Gospel excerpts into awful melodies. Laypeople began to crowd the altar, statues of saints were taken down, and new churches were built in the style of concert arenas. The Mass had become a show, a performance. Chatting in the pews, before and during Mass, began to creep in, as did clapping – for first communicants, newlyweds, or a particularly riveting drum solo. "It's all so wonderfully participatory now!" people would say, "and we can eat meat on Friday, too! (Give me another hug!)"

And as they departed the church after Sunday Mass (the official Church assured us it was still Mass), they took their newfound, laid-back Catholicism into a world that was more than ready to receive and then adulterate it.

"Young Catholic married couples in the 1950s, enjoying postwar prosperity, had very large numbers of children," wrote Michael Barone in the introduction to George Marlin's book. "Then quite suddenly in the early 1960s, coinciding with the introduction of the birth-control pill, Catholic family size dropped sharply. It was at this same time that the number of vocations, of young Catholics choosing to become priests and nuns, dropped suddenly too. Now Catholics seemed much more like other Americans." They were, Barone says, "far less distinctive in American society."[1]

For liberal Catholics, and "good" Catholics who were swept up in the confusion, the assimilation and corresponding dilution of Catholic practices in everyday life did not result so much in an abandonment of the Church, itself, but rather a rejection of certain of its teachings. "Such people," wrote John Zmirak, author of *The Politically Incorrect Guide to Catholicism*, "focused on the parts of the Church's mission that still appealed to them, such as looking out for the poor and rebuking unjust discrimination."[2]

Thus was the modern "cafeteria Catholic" born.

Zmirak notes that this evolved Catholic took the Church's worthy tradition of helping the oppressed, such as in the 1960s' Civil Rights movement, in the wrong direction. The Church's new apparent informality provided scant resistance to Catholics wanting to join other social crusades of the time, such as homosexual and feminist movements, that contained decidedly un-Catholic teaching. Many Catholics "with left-wing sympathies and deep roots in the Democratic Party began to exert their energies on behalf of these new movements," Zmirak says, "assuring themselves that they were acting as Jesus had when he denounced the scribes and Pharisees."[3]

Some of them believed, or merely used the excuse, that they were still the ethnic Catholic outsiders that their parents and grandparents had been in our predominantly Protestant nation, Zmirak says, and in the fervor of the times they were therefore not particularly discriminating about joining other "outsider" groups.

"So Catholics who'd once taken part in Freedom Rides for black Americans got swept up in a 'Women's Liberation' movement that sought to dismantle legal definitions of marriage, laws restricting abortion, and finally the traditional family itself," Zmirak writes. "That movement's greatest success was *Roe v. Wade*, which gave the U.S. the laxest abortion laws on earth – outside of Communist countries – and resulted in the deaths of more than a million American unborn children every year since 1973."[4]

The Church picked a lousy time to sabotage itself. Church revolutionaries embraced the lure of the radically changing outside world, brought it into the parishes, and the Church simply didn't fight the invasion. The emboldened liberals therefore didn't feel compelled to leave a Church that was becoming ever so accommodating to them. But Mass attendance, in general, nosedived, Zmirak notes, as many Catholics no longer recognized their church and weren't compelled to stay there. Some decided to live as secularists, some joined Latin Mass congregations – like the Society of St. Pius X – that became estranged from Rome, and some simply fled to Protestant churches.

Inside and outside the church walls, many disaffected Catholics were reacting, including many Democrats for whom the euphoria of a Catholic presidency was subsiding as the mid-1960s approached. Ethnic Catholics in Rust Belt and Northeastern cities, especially, were "upset over many of the Great Society's social programs," Marlin writes. "And while most of them remained registered with the Democratic Party surveys showed that their loyalty was weakening. ... Myopic reform Democrats could not see that working-class ethnic Catholics in the sixties no longer felt wanted in the Democratic Party."[5]

Surely their vision would improve after the 1972 election, when Republican Richard Nixon, who had garnered just 33% of the Catholic vote in 1968, rebounded to capture 59% four years later.

A personal recollection by Father Peter Stravinskas, author of a dozen books on Catholic doctrine, illustrates what doubtlessly occurred in many Catholic households at that time:

"As the grandson of immigrants, I was raised to think that to be Catholic automatically meant being a Democrat," Stravinskas recounted in a homily delivered a few weeks before the 2016 presidential election.

"After all, it was the Democratic Party that had been so involved in assisting the newly-arrived with possibilities for financial security and upward mobility.

"The first presidential election in which I could vote (as a seminarian of twenty-one) was that of 1972. Looking at the positions of Richard Nixon and George McGovern, I determined that the Democratic platform would lead us into a serious moral downward spiral.

"When I informed my parents that I intended to vote for President Nixon, they responded with shock and dismay: 'How can you even think of voting for a Republican?' In great detail and with consummate patience, I explained my rationale to my parents, who gave no response.

"On election day, as I entered the voting booth and prepared to pull the lever for Nixon, I experienced something close to spasms in my arm, knowing that I was the first member of my family in half a century to sever the bond with the Democratic Party. Later that day, my mother asked, "'Well, how did you vote?'

"'I told you I would vote for Nixon, and I did.'

"'So did your father and I,' came her response."[6]

Nixon's successor, Gerald Ford, was rather equivocal on the abortion issue. But he did appreciate the importance of the Catholic vote, especially after the 1976 Republican National Convention, where Ronald Reagan's ascendant forces embedded into the platform a plank, urged by the National Conference of Catholic Bishops, supporting a Constitutional ban on abortion. That factor, plus a subsequent Ford pledge to enact tax breaks for parents who would send their children to parochial schools, swayed many Catholics and helped to narrow Ford's polling deficit against Democrat Jimmy Carter in the months before the election.

But Ford's infamous debate gaffe in October, in which he asserted that there was no Soviet domination of Eastern Europe, was a decisive gift to Carter. "Election analyst Robert Teeter," notes George Marlin, "concluded that the defection from the GOP ticket of Eastern European Catholics had cost Ford the election."[7]

Once again, however, it was but a brief departure from trend. Carter had reclaimed Catholics for the Democratic Party with 57% of their vote, but it would not hold when Ronald Reagan, who spent the next four years blazoning his traditional American bona fides, finally succeeded in becoming the Republican torchbearer.

"With his shirt sleeves rolled up," Marlin writes, "Reagan began his race for the White House by appealing directly to the ethnic-Catholic voters," portraying himself "as the antithesis of cultural liberalism."[8]

"Many Catholic voters sent a strong message in 1980 that they had had it with the Democratic Party's radical social agenda, appeasement policies towards the Communists, and failed economic policies," Marlin says.[9] Reagan captured 49% of the Catholic vote, to Carter's 42%, and would remain popular with Catholics, partly because of his bold endorsement of their values: opposition to abortion and communism as well as support for a constitutional amendment for school prayer and tax credits for parochial school tuition.

According to Gregory Allen Smith in his book, *Politics in the Parish*, the 1982-84 Notre Dame Study of Catholic Parish Life revealed that 29% of Catholics reported that they were Democrats and only 9% said they were Republicans.[10] But Reagan won a whopping 61% of the Catholic vote in 1984, according to Gallup, beating the old Republican record by nine percentage points.[11]

The Democrats' stranglehold on Catholic voting had been broken, but over the next five elections a series of uninspiring, less conservative Republican candidates – Bush I, Dole, Bush II, McCain and Romney – would allow the Catholic vote to sometimes drift back to the Democratic column. George H.W. Bush won 51% of it in 1988, but lost it in 1992, as did Bob Dole four years later.[12] George W. Bush narrowly lost Catholics in the disputed election of 2000, and the polls disagree about whether they went for him in 2004. Democrat Barack Obama won Catholics in 2008 and 2012.[13] And Donald Trump, in the face of virulent opposition by Catholic intellectuals and many churchmen, won the Catholic vote in the remarkable election of 2016, at least according to most analysts.[14]

5

The Anti-Antiabortion Democratic Party

T he Democratic Party did not set out 50 years ago to become known as "The Party of Death," as some now refer to it. While the Kennedy Capitulation opened the door for Catholic politicians to pretend to be of two minds on abortion, the Democratic Party thereafter developed into the unapologetic party of abortion, one that today even includes a right to abortion in the official party platform. How did this happen?

It began less than a year after President Kennedy was felled by the assassin's bullet. The hyper-political Kennedy family busily began mapping a way forward on the stickiest sticking point faced by liberal Catholic politicians – abortion. Although it was not a major issue in the mid-1960s, a "right" to abortion was emerging as a liberal cause célèbre, and the two major parties were going to have to address it. The Republicans could defer that task for a while, but the more liberally-populated Democratic Party could not. The Kennedy family, the Democratic Catholic bastion of the time, and a faction of liberal Catholic clerics went to work.

In his 2010 book, *The Faithful Departed: The Collapse of Boston's Catholic Culture,* Philip Lawler recounts how a watershed gathering at the Kennedy family compound in July 1964 cleared a path for Catholic liberals while they waited for their ultimate political bulwark: *Roe v. Wade,* the Supreme Court decision that legalized abortion on demand:

"Ostensibly the meeting had been called to provide advice for Robert

28

Kennedy, who was running for a New York Senate seat. But a candidate was not likely to face questions about abortion in 1964; the Kennedy planners had the more distant future in mind.

"The participants in that Hyannisport meeting composed a Who's Who of liberal theologians, most of them Jesuits. Father Robert Drinan was there, as was Father Charles Curran (the leader in the dissent against *Humanae Vitae;* his writings on moral issues were later condemned by the Vatican). Father Joseph Fuchs, a Jesuit professor at Rome's Gregorian University, was on hand; so were the Jesuits Richard McCormick, Albert Jonsen, and Giles Milhaven. Milhaven was later instrumental in the early public work of "Catholics for a Free Choice"; McCormick would become the Rose Kennedy professor of the Kennedy Institute for Bioethics at Georgetown University, and spent years teaching theology at Notre Dame.

"For two days the theologians huddled in the Cape Cod resort town as guests of the Kennedys. Eventually they reached a consensus, which they passed along to their political patrons. Abortion, they agreed, could sometimes be morally acceptable as the lesser of two evils. Lawmakers should certainly not encourage abortion, but a blanket prohibition might be more harmful to the common good than a law allowing abortion in *some* cases. And a danger to the common good would very likely arise if the political leaders sought to impose their own private views on public policy.

"The conference at Hyannisport offered a rare example of teamwork between academic theologians and practical politicians. The skillful operatives of the Kennedy family would round up the votes to end restrictions on abortion and eventually to provide public subsidies. The Jesuit theologians would provide protective cover for that effort, ensuring that Catholic colleges, universities, and theological journals gave a sympathetic reading to the politicians' public statements.

"Thus the basic lines of 'pro-choice' rhetoric were sketched out by Catholic theologians, at the residence of America's most famous Catholic family, nine years before the *Roe v. Wade* decision. The late President Kennedy had already laid the foundation for the argument that a Catholic politician must not attempt to enact his private religious views; now his brothers were prepared to take the next step forward. They were ready to explain that they were personally opposed to abortion, but..."

And that concocted reasoning, tinged with a pretense of ecclesiastical imprimatur, became the standard response for American Catholic liberals, who were recalcitrant even when their bishops pleaded with them to outlaw abortion. During his 10-year reign as Speaker of House that ended in 1987, Lawler notes, "Tip O'Neill – a Catholic Democrat from Massachusetts and a Kennedy ally – saw to it that not a single vote was taken on any measure to restrict abortion." And seven of those 10 years were during the tenure of the most overtly anti-abortion president in the nation's history. But even Ronald Reagan was unable to usher in meaningful restrictions on abortion, mostly because of opposition from Democrats – and their Catholic leadership.

But Catholics did reward Reagan for trying. Catholics at large supported Reagan for his unapologetic stance on abortion, but also because he reflected their "bedrock values of faith, family, work, neighborhood, peace, and freedom," as expressed in his 1984 State of the Union address and four years earlier in kicking off his general election campaign at the Statue of Liberty. On that Labor Day 1980, Reagan spoke to Catholics without ever calling them by name. They were a constituency he deliberately pursued, because it was obvious to him that 1) they were alienated by the Democratic Party's socialistic bent, and 2) that party's positions on moral values had long since diverged from the core values of the Catholic Church.

"Beginning in January of 1981, American workers will once again be heeded," Reagan said that day. "Their needs and values will be acted upon in Washington. I will consult with representatives of organized labor on those matters concerning the welfare of the working people of this nation.

"I happen to be the only president of a union ever to be a candidate for President of the United States."

Catholics listened to Reagan's message of economic hope and prosperity, bereft of socialistic solutions, for working-class families, and they identified with his traditional American ideas. And they were further attracted to the cultural vision that he propounded that day. Restoring the American dream, he said, "requires more than restoring a sound, productive economy, vitally important as that is. It requires a return to spiritual and moral values, values so deeply held by those who came here to build a new life. We need to restore those values in our daily life, in our neighborhoods and in our government's dealings with the other nations of the world."

What Catholic Democrats heard him saying was: Follow me, a former Democrat, into the Republican Party. And many of them did, alienated by the Democratic Party's pro-abortion agenda and President Jimmy Carter's abysmal economy. George Marlin observed that Carter "was so unpopular in Catholic circles that at the prestigious Al Smith Dinner, he was booed by New York's leading Catholics."[1]

Reagan's overture to Catholics would set the template for Donald Trump's own successful effort 36 years later. In fact, Reagan ended his Statue of Liberty speech with "so help us God, we will make America great again," the last four words of which became Trump's ubiquitous, ball-cap campaign slogan. For both of these Democratic Party defectors, a message of opportunity, reward through hard work instead of socialistic largesse, and the promotion of traditional Christian values won over the Catholic vote. They exposed the values of the two parties in sharp relief and revealed the Democratic Party as the party of abortion or "the party of death," as author Ramesh Ponnuru put it in the title of his 2006 book, *The Party of Death: the Democrats, the Media, the Courts, and the Disregard for Human Life*.[2]

Reagan captured 49% of Catholics in 1980. "Many Catholic voters sent a strong message in 1980 that they had had it with the Democratic Party's radical social agenda, appeasement policies towards the Communists, and failed economic policies," wrote George Marlin.[3] This constituted much of Trump's appeal to Catholics in 2016 when exit polls showed he won 52% of their vote.

Despite the seeming Catholic defection, the Democratic Party would not budge on its own particular brand of abortion values. The longer the pro-abortion policy remained in the party platform, the more embedded it became. It had become sacrosanct, and anti-abortion Democrats were ostracized by party leaders. This was particularly manifest at the 1992 Democratic National Convention, where Pennsylvania Gov. Bob Casey was not only denied an opportunity to present an anti-abortion minority plank, but was then stalked by a camera crew sent by the Democratic National Committee to further humiliate him. Such was the punishment for being an anti-abortion Democrat, and Casey could thank a fellow Irish Catholic family, the Kennedys, for it.

The party's anti-antiabortion intransigence has clearly damaged its ability to elect candidates, as proven by an aberration in 2006: In that year, the Democrats went off-script, and succeeded, by running anti-abortion candidates in certain nonpartisan congressional districts. "There's no way you would have had the success they had if they hadn't fielded (antiabortion and pro-family) candidates," said John J. DiIulio Jr., a political science professor at the University of Pennsylvania.[4] Those anti-abortion Democratic victors included Joe Donnelly, Brad Ellsworth and Baron Hill in Indiana; Jason Altmire and Chris Carney in Pennsylvania; Charlie Wilson in Ohio; and Heath Shuler in North Carolina. By 2011, all except Donnelly were out of office, falling prey to either local redistricting or the 2010 Republican Tea-Party tsunami. But Fordham University associate professor of theology Charles Camosy maintains that they were, in one way or another, "victims of a litmus test" – the party, in Camosy's view, was beginning to purge itself of anti-abortion candidates. And in so doing, it began purging itself of congressional officeholders. "In 2009," Camosy observed in a March 21, 2016 *Washington Post* column, "64 House Democrats voted against taxpayer funding for abortion; by 2015, only three did: In that time, Democrats lost 69 seats, leaving only 188 Dems to the 247 Republican majority."[5]

That there was a palpable effort to entrench a pro-abortion identity in the Democratic Party was especially evident in the virulent reaction of Catholic Democrats in 2007 to Pope Benedict's support for Mexican bishops who had warned politicians not to support abortion. Providing for "the killing of an innocent child is incompatible with receiving communion, which is receiving the body of Christ," Benedict said on a trip to Brazil. He further took note of the Church's authority in such cases to impose the ultimate penalty – excommunication.[6]

All of this served to send American Democrats over the edge. The very next day, 18 Catholic Democrats in the U.S. House of Representatives issued a statement railing against the pope, clinging to the illegitimate political thesis of the Kennedy Capitulation, as so many of their Democratic brethren had done before. Benedict's remarks, they thundered, "offend the very nature of the American experiment and do a great disservice to the centuries of good work the church has done."

In their telling, the pope ought to subordinate Catholic doctrine to an "American experiment" that, by the way, was crafted in the 18th century by Protestants. In their telling, obedience to the teachings of the Catholic Church, and therefore obedience to God, always applies – except when these 18 Catholic Democrats say that it doesn't. And they were willing to hold that position at the risk of their eternal salvation, granting, of course, that, after 50 years of heretical religious instruction, they may have been wholly ignorant of what they were risking. Regardless, given that the Catholic Church does not allow for dissent on certain of its teachings, support for abortion being one of them, these card-carrying dissidents thus classified themselves as nothing other than apostates.

"The fact is that religious sanction in the political arena directly conflicts with our fundamental beliefs about the role and responsibility of democratic representatives in a pluralistic America," these House Democrats said in their statement. "It also clashes with freedoms guaranteed in our Constitution."[7]

In other words, get out of the way, Bride of Christ, you're interfering with the freedoms guaranteed in our secular Constitution. The Catholic Church, it would seem, as the singular authority of God's laws, is just another political state in the eyes of these aberrant Catholic Democrats. They effectively say, "This is the United States of America, where even God's laws are subject to, and therefore overridden by, the true supreme authority: the United States Constitution."

Bishop Arthur J. Serratelli, of Patterson, N.J. brought an adult perspective to the matter. "In no way did the Pope's statement offend American pluralism," he said. "In a pluralistic society, people disagree. It is arrogant to insist that the Church does not have the right to her own teaching. Certainly, a politician has the freedom to reject Church's teaching. But let's be honest. To choose to be pro-choice is to reject the Gospel of life. It is to be not faithful to Church teaching."[8]

What these apostate Democrats were really saying was that the Catholic Church, God's highest teaching authority and the instrument that He uses to help its members get to Heaven by professing His immutable laws and occasionally imposing doses of healthy "Catholic guilt," in fact has no right to help its members get to Heaven by professing God's immutable laws or to ever make its members feel guilty. Ironically, their tantrum was caused by precisely that – guilt. They could not avoid it. Like petulant children, they were convicted by the pope's statement, felt guilty and reflexively lashed out. Otherwise, they'd have accepted or, at most, been indifferent to the words uttered by the Holy Father, and they would have simply ignored them.

As we can clearly see, even when they demanded that the Church leave them alone, God, through his Church, was pricking their consciences. They could not escape God. They devoutly venerate the falsely construed church-and-state construct, but God Almighty does not. He gives Himself primacy of place, and the First Commandment demands that all people, even Democrats, not place any other god before Him.

Over recent years, God has seemed to occasionally open some Democrats' eyes a bit, if only briefly. Some Democratic leaders have considered softening their antipathy towards anti-abortion activists, perhaps only for pragmatic, not moral, reasons. They're fully aware that the party's pro-abortion advocacy is a net vote loser, and they know it would be smart to politically reposition themselves on the issue. Said leading Democratic strategist Donna Brazile after the 2004 election defeat of her party's presidential candidate, John Kerry: "Even I have trouble explaining to my family that we are not about killing babies."[9] Prominent liberals Harry Reid (who sometimes expressed opposition to abortion), Nancy Pelosi, Charles Schumer and even Kerry himself were also saying that the Democratic Party needed to become more accommodating to anti-abortion members.

But any purported accommodation has been a deceit, a mockery to which anti-abortion Democrats, if they desired to stay in the party, have been forced to accede. The pro-abortionists who have run the party have long issued dissembling messages to its anti-abortion members. Former Vermont governor Howard Dean is the embodiment of the duplicity. "We ought not turn our back on pro-life people," Dean declared while campaigning for Democratic national chairman in 2004.[10] But in March of 2017, as the national campaign was heating up, he said on MSNBC that his party is "never going back to maybe making compromises on abortion."[11]

The party has in recent times tried to placate its few anti-abortion members by advocating a "reduction of the need" for abortion – increasing government funding for contraception and increasing welfare spending. Anything but *banning* abortion. And the cynic sees deeper skullduggery in this approach: that is, its strategic use to deliberately divide the small anti-abortion contingent in the party, rendering even weaker their protestations. Dean essentially admitted as much in explaining that there is a difference between an anti-abortion person and a Democratic Party-approved anti-abortion person. "If somebody is willing to stick with us who is pro-life, that means they are the right kind of pro-life person," Dean said.[12] (For the record, Dean was raised Protestant, but confessed in a *New York* magazine article, "I don't go to church a lot.")

At the 2008 Democratic National Convention, the party feigned a relaxation of its hardened pro-abortion stance, but it proved to be pure sophistry. As writer James Antle, III recounts, "Pro-life Democrats failed to nudge their party's position on abortion in an even marginally more pro-life direction – by rejecting partial-birth abortion, for instance – or to win approval of a 'tolerance clause' acknowledging the existence of abortion opponents within the Democratic Party. Instead, they got Democratic support for reducing 'the need for abortion' by increasing use of contraceptives and for wording to the effect that the party also 'strongly supports a woman's decision to have a child,'" as one liberal evangelical put it.[13]

Gosh, how magnanimous of them. The self-described anti-abortion Democrats bought it and congratulated themselves on their "progress," but Antle revealed it for what is really was: "crumbs tossed at pro-lifers from the Democratic platform committee's table."[14]

Having dispensed with this pesky abortion niggle, the Democratic Party could now get down to business as they reveled in the 2008 nomination of their new darling: the zealously pro-abortion Barack Obama.

For the ever more leftist party leadership, Obama had it all: charming, check; boyishly adorable, check; radically liberal, check; partly black, bonus. Born of a white American mother and a Kenyan father, his skin was sufficiently dark that most people would never wonder that one of his parents were white. Most would just assume, or choose to believe, that he was a black American from a black family and thereby represented black Americans. This strategic benefit wasn't lost on Democratic tacticians. He was the whole package. Sophisticated, charismatic, adaptable to any audience. Ivy League-educated at Columbia and Harvard, but in the blink of any eye capable of slinking into a down-home vernacular, dropping g's all over the place. Once rival Hillary Clinton was dispatched, no one, but no one, in the Democratic Party – especially anti-abortionists – would dare step in the path of this ascendant far-left socialist superstar and his giddy Democratic minions. All hope for any true moderation of the party's strident pro-abortion plank was lost with Obama as its head.

When Clinton finally did claw her way to the nomination eight years later, the official position of the Democratic Party platform was no less hostile to unborn children:

"We believe that every woman should have access to ... safe and legal abortion ... We will continue to stand up to Republican efforts to defund Planned Parenthood health centers ... We will appoint judges who ... will protect a woman's right to safe abortion ... We will continue to oppose – and seek to overturn – federal and state laws and policies that impede a woman's access to abortion, including by repealing the Hyde Amendment."[15]

With respect to Catholic teaching on abortion, the Democrats and Republicans could not have been farther apart in 2016. "A cursory look at the official political platforms of both parties will show a moral fault-line of differences existing between them," wrote Father Anthony J. Mastroeni, professor of theology at Christendom College.[16] Denver Archbishop Samuel

J. Aquila said the Democratic Platform "is aggressively pro-abortion, not only in funding matters, but in the appointment of only those judges who will support abortion and the repealing of the Helms Amendment, which prevents the U.S. from supporting abortion availability overseas. Conversely, the Republican party platform is supportive of the Hyde Amendment (which prohibits federal taxpayer money from being used for abortion) and just this year strengthened its support for life by calling for the defunding of Planned Parenthood, banning dismemberment abortion and opposing assisted suicide."[17]

In stark contrast to the Democrats, the 2016 Republican platform boldly called for a constitutional amendment to protect the unborn from abortion:

"The Constitution's guarantee that no one can 'be deprived of life, liberty or property' deliberately echoes the Declaration of Independence's proclamation that 'all' are 'endowed by their creator' with the inalienable right to life. Accordingly, we assert the sanctity of human life and affirm that the unborn child has a fundamental right to life which cannot be infringed. We support a human life amendment to the Constitution and legislation to make clear that the Fourteenth Amendment's protections apply to children before birth.

"We oppose the use of public funds to perform or promote abortion or to fund organizations, like Planned Parenthood, so long as they provide or refer for elective abortions or sell fetal body parts rather than provide healthcare. We urge all states and Congress to make it a crime to acquire, transfer, or sell fetal tissues from elective abortions for research, and we call on Congress to enact a ban on any sale of fetal body parts. In the meantime, we call on Congress to ban the practice of misleading women on so-called fetal harvesting consent forms, a fact revealed by a 2015 investigation. We will not fund or subsidize healthcare that includes abortion coverage.

"We support the appointment of judges who respect traditional family values and the sanctity of innocent human life. We oppose the non-consensual withholding or withdrawal of care or treatment, including food and water, from individuals with disabilities, newborns, the elderly, or the infirm, just as we oppose euthanasia and assisted suicide.

"We affirm our moral obligation to assist, rather than penalize, women who face an unplanned pregnancy. In order to encourage women who face an unplanned pregnancy to choose life, we support legislation that requires financial responsibility for the child be equally borne by both the mother and father upon conception until the child reaches adulthood. ...

"We thank and encourage providers of counseling, medical services, and adoption assistance for empowering women experiencing an unintended pregnancy to choose life. We support funding for ultrasounds and adoption assistance. We salute the many states that now protect women and girls through laws requiring informed consent, parental consent, waiting periods, and clinic regulation. We condemn the Supreme Court's activist decision in *Whole Woman's Health v. Hellerstedt* striking down commonsense Texas laws providing for basic health and safety standards in abortion clinics.

"We applaud the U.S. House of Representatives for leading the effort to add enforcement to the Born-Alive Infant Protection Act by passing the Born-Alive Abortion Survivors Protection Act, which imposes appropriate civil and criminal penalties on healthcare providers who fail to provide treatment and care to an infant who survives an abortion, including early induction delivery whether the death of the infant is intended. We strongly oppose infanticide. Over a dozen states have passed Pain-Capable Unborn Child Protection Acts prohibiting abortion after twenty weeks, the point at which current medical research shows that unborn babies can feel excruciating pain during abortions, and we call on Congress to enact the federal version ... We support state and federal efforts against the cruelest forms of abortion, especially dismemberment abortion procedures, in which unborn babies are literally torn apart limb from limb.

"We call on Congress to ban sex-selection abortions and abortions based on disabilities – discrimination in its most lethal form. We oppose embryonic stem cell research. We oppose federal funding of embryonic stem cell research. We support adult stem cell research ... We oppose federal funding for harvesting embryos and call for a ban on human cloning. ...

"We are proud to be the party that protects human life and offers real solutions for women."[18]

It is not the particular intent of this book to denigrate the Democratic Party or to elevate the Republican Party. But the Democratic Party has so substantially separated itself from Catholic doctrine that this circumstance cannot be ignored. This is not your grandfather's, or perhaps even your father's, Democratic Party.

The difference between the two parties on the Church's central moral issue of the day – abortion – could not be more profound. One is solidly for it, the other is solidly against it. And the depth of the Democratic Party's pro-abortion sentiment – and antipathy for the teachings of the Roman Catholic Church – were startlingly on display in emails exchanged among party operatives that were published by Wikileaks in 2016. "There needs to be a Catholic Spring, in which Catholics themselves demand the end of a middle ages dictatorship and the beginning of a little democracy and respect for gender equality in the Catholic Church," wrote Sandy Newman, a liberal activist who clearly didn't know or want to accept that the Catholic Church is not a democracy and, in fact, has as its head a benevolent dictator in Jesus Christ, who doubles as Our Lord and Savior. Newman was addressing no less than John Podesta, who was Hillary Clinton's campaign chairman. Podesta, a liberal Catholic who obviously strays from orthodox Catholic teaching, welcomed the idea.[19] "We created Catholics in Alliance for the Common Good to organize for a moment like this," he assured Newman, while cautioning that the moment for the liberal entity had not yet arrived.[20]

In a separate report from Wikileaks published on Oct. 10, 2016, Democratic activists were shown mocking the beliefs of Catholics. "It's an amazing bastardization of the faith," wrote John Halpin, of the left-wing Center for American Progress, in a 2011 email to Podesta and Jennifer Palmieri, who later became Clinton campaign's communications director. "They must be attracted to the systematic thought and severely backwards gender relations and must be totally unaware of Christian democracy."[21]

Systematic thought. Backwards gender relations. Christian democracy. It's as if they were earnestly trying to convince themselves that God had changed His eternal truths somewhere along the line and had adapted His to theirs. They had created their own reality, namely that the Catholic Church is something that it isn't, indeed that the Church's very doctrine, at radical variance from their "reality," was a "bastardization of the faith." They were elevating their own brand of Catholicity above that of the Church, itself.

As would be expected, the Wikileaks revelations ignited a counterblast of charges accusing the Democrats of unadulterated anti-Catholicism. Joseph Cella, founder of the National Catholic Prayer Breakfast, said the emails illustrate "the open anti-Catholic bigotry of (Clinton's) senior advisers, who attack the deeply held beliefs and theology of Catholics."[22] Bill Donohue, president of the Catholic League for Religious and Civil Rights, said Clinton had no choice but to "cut all ties" with Podesta. "The man is hell bent on creating mutiny in the Catholic Church and therefore must be fired," he said.[23] Political strategist Angela Flood concluded that the leaked emails revealed "an attempt to undermine the faith."[24] Father Peter Stravinskas wondered in an Oct. 16 homily, "how can we ignore the latest revelations about (Clinton's) staff mocking Catholic morality and even seeking to incite the laity to rebel against their bishops' teaching?"[25] Congressman Mike Kelly of Pennsylvania exhorted Catholics and others to "call on your bishops, call on your faith-based leaders" to condemn the remarks.[26] And *The Wall Street Journal* observed, "It's no secret that progressive elites despise religion, but it's still striking to see their contempt expressed so bluntly as in the leaked email chains that include Clinton campaign chairman John Podesta."[27]

And why such contempt? After all, to win elections, national political parties typically attempt to tamp down fighting within the ranks. That's the idea of "big tent" politics.

Well, yes, the Democrats want a big tent, but they simply don't want one that includes anti-abortion members. And because Catholics, who comprise a quarter of the American electorate, are by Church law bound to be anti-abortion, they would have to be converted from the magisterial teachings to a new kind of "American" Catholicism. Party leaders like Podesta thus began plotting an insidious takeover of the American Catholic Church, inventing nouveau terminology like "Christian democracy" and pejoratives like "backward gender relations" and "bastardization of the faith." They hoped, and surely still do, to redefine Catholicism in America, to democratize it, to further infiltrate its leadership and thereby estrange American Catholics from authentic, salvific Church teaching, especially on abortion. So massive is the Catholic vote, and so bellicose is the Democratic Party in promoting abortion, that it is worth such a formidable and unprincipled undertaking.

This only further establishes that it is not hyperbolic to label the Democratic Party, as Ponnuru did, the "party of death," nor is it invalid to label the Republican Party the "party of life." Their respective official declarations, and their expressed underlying sentiments, prove it. It is therefore nonsensical for a Catholic, or anyone for that matter, who places the life issue at the apex of moral imperatives – as Holy Mother Church, and therefore God, says we must – to be a member of the Democratic Party. Further, if a Catholic believes that promoting the availability of abortion can be a mortal sin – an assertion professed by bishops and other clerics cited in this book – then why would he associate himself with an unmitigated party of death? By mere dint of membership, he supports his party's agenda, which explicitly calls for promoting the wide availability of abortion, the issue that supersedes all others for the Catholic voter. George Marlin cites historian Kenneth Wald's postulation that Catholic defections from the Democratic Party are highest among those "most deeply involved in Parish life."[28] In other words, the more they understand the authentic teachings of the Church, the more seriously they understand their Catholic duty in the civic realm and its discordance with the Democratic Party.

The Rev. Kevin Bezner contends that dissident Catholics are variously self-deceptive, lack self-awareness, lack an interior life based on scripture and tradition, fail to know the truth of the faith, have poor or no Christian formation, or maybe even have "a cynical and outright desire to teach lies."

"Such a state of mind," Bezner wrote on Sept. 15, 2016 in *The Christian Review*, "is a particular disease in the Democratic Party, which has given us a long list of politicians who claim to be Catholic and yet promote and mouth positions on topics such as abortion and same-sex marriage that undermine Catholic teaching – and at the same time undermine our nation's morality and law. Two of the most prominent recent examples of such pseudo-Catholics are Joe Biden and Nancy Pelosi. Others are Mario Cuomo, Andrew Cuomo, and Patrick Kennedy."[29]

Few, if any, bishops have called these manifestly dissident politicians "pseudo-Catholics," but the bishops and other churchmen quoted herein have, in the past few years, called for a halt to the Kennedy Capitulation. And they have done so for one reason and one reason only: to save souls, including their own. They are fully aware that they will have to answer to God for the stewardship of their flocks. If they do not correctly teach and lead the Faithful under their care, then their own salvation is at stake.

Can a Catholic, in good conscience, ever vote for a Democrat? Of course. Despite the party's full-throated pro-abortion crusade, a Democrat who happens to be the most anti-abortion candidate* in a particular race is most certainly worthy of a Catholic's vote. (Indeed, he would be the candidate for whom a Catholic *should* vote. That there would be at least a few anti-abortion candidates in the Democratic Party, and some pro-choice candidates in the Republican Party, is to be expected. These are large populations. But, today, the two parties, themselves, have polar-opposite identities. As evidenced by their respective policy documents, i.e., their official platforms, one party is anti-abortion, and the other is pro-abortion (or "pro-choice" – same thing).

6

The Untaught Catholic Voter

I n 2004, Bishop George Thomas of Helena, Montana noted that "pollsters tout figures demonstrating that Catholic attitudes towards abortion on demand are scarcely different from the remainder of society."[1] It is difficult to imagine that anything has changed, more than 15 years on, and the numbers bear that out. A 2019 Pew Research Center survey showed that 61% of Americans, and 56% of Catholics, believe that abortion should be legal in all or most cases.[2]

So palpable is this seeming paradox that it caught the attention of a prominent non-Catholic syndicated columnist who chided Catholics for their acedia prior to the 2016 election. Catholics, wrote a discomfited Michael Gerson, tend to vote "almost exactly like their suburban neighbors," despite having an authoritarian structure and doctrine to which all members are required to conform.[3] Of course, as a Protestant, Gerson's standing to criticize another faith's voting behavior would be called into question by liberals who are perfectly satisfied with Catholics' widespread infidelity to the ironclad tenets of their faith. After all, those scoffers would surely observe, Protestants like Gerson don't even possess a consistent creed upon which to cast their votes. After acknowledging Jesus Christ as lord and savior, their beliefs are all over the map. Clearly, to the extent that they take into account their Christian faith at all, Episcopalians and members of the United Church of Christ would generally think and act far differently in the voting booth than their Baptist or Disciples of Christ brethren, though all of them are Protestant.

Notwithstanding, in evident admiration for the cohesion of Catholic dogma, separated from its implementation on society, Gerson calls out rank-and-file Catholics for not distinguishing themselves when they vote. "There is something vaguely disturbing," he wrote, "about the precise symmetry of any religious group with other voters of their same class and background. One would hope that an ancient, demanding faith would leave some distinctive mark."

In response, Catholic writer Russell Shaw provided context: "The erasure of such distinctive marks is of course part of the homogenizing effect of the process of cultural assimilation to which American Catholics, like the members of other religious and ethnic groups, have been subjected in the last two centuries. Among other things, this assimilation has involved – and goes on involving today – a steady, increasingly visible diminishment of religious identity."[4]

True enough, but merely equating the assimilation of Catholics to that of other religious and ethnic groups gives undeserved cover to the Church, both the hierarchy and the members. All Christians are called to oppose the secular culture, and Catholics must consider themselves even more duty-bound to do so, as it's a tenet of the faith. The Catechism is clear on this duty: "The disciple of Christ must not only keep the faith and live on it, but also profess it, confidently bear witness to it, and spread it."[5] Shaw is not incorrect, but he would surely agree that to ascribe Catholics' dereliction simply to the "homogenizing effect of the process of cultural assimilation" would be the shallowest of conclusions and would relieve them of institutional and personal culpability.

Cultural assimilation is more the result than a cause. The reasons that Catholics have become culturally assimilated are three-fold: 1) many and probably most are simply unaware that they have the twin personal duties to know authentic Church teachings and to impose them on secular society; 2) many have knowingly adopted moral positions that contradict non-negotiable Church teachings; and 3) some believe that they must uphold a longstanding family political heritage. "We are Democrats in this family. This is who we've always been, so this is who we must remain."

The evidence is abundant that most lay Catholics are largely ignorant about what the Church teaches concerning their Christian duty to impose their faith on the culture, politically and otherwise. In fact, they are poorly informed about their faith, period. Oh, they think they know it, but they don't, because of decades of faulty (one could argue, horrendous) religious formation. It therefore stands to reason that they cannot evangelize to others if they, themselves don't know what authentic Catholic faith teaches. Indeed, "evangelization of the American Catholics in the pew is probably the most difficult task of all," says Father Dwight Longenecker, the well-known American convert from Anglicanism. "They don't know what they don't know." It's that bad. They simply don't know what true Catholic doctrine is. Some of this is their own fault, some of it isn't. Church doctrine hasn't changed, but the teachers, and what they've been teaching, have. "For three generations now (lay Catholics) have been given watered down milk and been told it was wine," Longenecker says. "They actually think that Catholic-lite is what it's all about, and are astounded to think that there are some of us who think that they have actually been fed a version of Christianity that is scarcely Christianity at all."[6]

"Catholic-lite" has become so pervasive that Catholics are comfortable rationalizing even the most extreme political choices. In 2004, with the election approaching, Sioux Falls Bishop Robert Carlson recognized that this thinking had risen to the level of scandal. "Within the past few weeks at least two people proclaiming membership in the Catholic Church wrote letters to the editor to daily newspapers presenting flawed thinking on the Catholic teaching of abortion and their particular political beliefs," he said in a public statement. "As their bishop, I have no choice but to respond to their public action. ... The letters to the editor and statements I have received in a few private letters are clear examples of the erosion in Catholic formation for the last two generations.

"Today, nominal Catholics are often soft on abortion and badly misinformed about this and other aspects of the faith including the Eucharist and the proper formation of one's conscience. They fail to grasp the difference between the common good and excessive individual rights."[7]

Prior to the presidential election four years later, Bishop Robert Hermann, administrator of the Archdiocese of St. Louis, was provoked to respond similarly. "When I speak to some so-called good Catholics, I am shocked that they are quite ready to vote for a pro-abortion candidate under almost any circumstance," he wrote. "I find this hard to understand. We have heard the word 'abortion' so often that perhaps we no longer associate procured abortion with the killing of children, yet that is what it is."[8]

Despite their misapprehensions about Church teaching, these people think themselves "good Catholics." Many of them simply don't, even though they most certainly should, know any better. Appallingly, they comprise most American Catholics today – badly catechized, never theologically corrected, and likely to use the same voting criteria as their non-Catholic neighbors. After all, who is objecting? Not their pastors and not their fellow Catholics, as reflected in the aforementioned Pew data. They perfunctorily accept what the American Catholic Church has failed to challenge: that there is a wall between church and state that means their political decisions must not and cannot be influenced by religion – that God and state are separate, and *equal,* sovereigns, each reigning over distinct dominions. This describes the perception of that vast group occupying the pews today, and a subset of them isn't even paying attention to what's happening outside the church walls. They couldn't possibly practice their faith in an effective way, because they aren't aware of the societal issues to which they should apply it, or even their duty to do so.

Archbishop Samuel Aquila recounts a dinner at which the conversation turned to Obamacare's mandate that contraceptives, sterilizations and some abortifacients be covered through employers' health plans. "Most surprising to me was that all at the table were practicing Catholics who are involved in their faith," Aquila wrote in a subsequent pastoral letter, "and a couple of them had neither heard of the difficulty the Obama Administration ... created for the Little Sisters of the Poor, nor the litigation that has occurred trying to force them to violate their consciences. Catholic voters must make themselves aware of where the parties stand on these essential issues."[9]

Now, none of this is to say that there does not exist a segment of well-instructed Catholics who, by means other than the Church's flawed pedagogic norms of the past half-century, do understand authentic Catholic doctrine and do practice its evangelical application. They are not ignorant, inactive or uninformed. Unfortunately, there is another segment of Catholics, at the other end of the spectrum, who are just as convicted in actively opposing Church teaching, who choose certain precepts and reject others, often to comport with a personal political agenda. They are liberals who subjugate their Catholicism to secular politics. They adopt the groundless "seamless garment" doctrine (which holds that all moral issues are of equal weight) that has been conclusively rejected by the U.S. Conference of Catholic Bishops and the *Catechism of the Catholic Church*, itself. Thereby, they are not only dissidents, but heretics. To casually assert that they have become "assimilated" into the external Godless culture would be incorrect. They have not fallen into it by accident. Instead, they have helped to build it, and their malformed Catholicity draws unknowing faithful away from authentic teaching.

Especially if they are famous.

Bishop Robert Vasa of Baker, Oregon joined many other bishops, including the USCCB, itself, in calling out Catholic Congresswoman Nancy Pelosi after her outrageous 2008 assertion that the church's position on abortion is unsettled. Pelosi had cherry-picked fifth century speculation by St. Augustine that "there cannot yet be said to be alive soul in a body that lacks sensation" until at least 40 days after conception. The Church has long-since staunchly rejected Augustine's conjecture, while explaining that it had been based on the defective science of the day. Even Augustine used the term "yet," clearly suggesting that the scientific understanding was incomplete.

Vasa was quick to take umbrage with Pelosi's bluster. "It is highly disingenuous, deceptive and intellectually dishonest to take this ecclesial sound bite from 1,500 years ago and treat it as if it is the last definitive word on the subject," Vasa wrote to his flock shortly after Pelosi's remarks.

"This is particularly true since Augustine himself 'vigorously condemned the practice of induced abortion' despite the unavailability of accurate scientific information. ... Augustine also called the use of means to avoid the birth of a child 'evil work.' It would appear that the public official conveniently missed that part and thus does not allow Saint Augustine to form any part of her understanding of the evil of either abortion or contraception, while boasting that this is precisely what she has done. ...

"If I were to think a bit more critically, I would be inclined to conclude that the public official accepts the views of the Church which agree with her view and rejects those views which do not. In other words, she is not formed by either Augustine or the Catholic Church on any of these social or moral issues, but simply happens to agree on some points. This then would have nothing to do with any true conviction about the goodness, beauty or truth of the teachings of the Catholic Church, but rather pure political expediency."[10]

Pelosi, employing the modus operandi of celebrity Catholic dissidents, threw the fiction out there, absorbed the blowback by the bishops, and marched ahead with effective impunity. It was her word against the bishops, and Catholics could believe who they chose to believe. This technique has worked for dissident Catholic politicians and continues to work today, all because the prelates don't go far enough. They don't personally counsel the perpetrators and let it be known publicly that they've done so. They don't deny them Holy Communion. And they don't excommunicate them. The politician wins by drawing a public stalemate with the Church, the Bride of Christ, and the bishops abet scandal by their public weakness.

It happens over and over.

One of the most recent and notorious of these heretical Pied Pipers was 2016 vice presidential candidate Tim Kaine, who unabashedly and simultaneously touted his pro-choice and Catholic credentials, possibly because he believed it was permissible to do so, but certainly because it was politically expedient to do so. Hillary Clinton would not have chosen him if he hadn't been willing to make this self-compromise. Softening up the Catholic vote – using Kaine to convince Catholics that they could, in good conscience, vote for her – was critical to winning the White House. Had Kaine, or some Catholic like him, not been on the ticket, the Democrats' share of the Catholic vote would likely have been significantly smaller.

But irrespective of any sincerely held beliefs by Kaine, it was a ruse, nonetheless, because the notion that faithful Catholics can be pro-choice is an objective fallacy. It is simply a contradiction. Father Kevin Bezner, in September 2016, flatly labeled pro-choice politicians as "pseudo-Catholics": "Kaine, like so many other ill-formed and uninformed Catholics … has failed to put on Christ," Bezner said. "He is, however, the perfect product of Jesuit formation. He may think himself Catholic and may present himself as Catholic, but he is nothing more than the preacher of a false Gospel, a wolf in sheep's clothing. Be assured that any vote for Hillary Clinton, and so for Tim Kaine, is … a vote against the Catholic Church and Christianity. And it is a vote against Jesus Christ and God's law."[11]

And so, among the wayward Catholics, we have the poorly-instructed and the consciously dissenting. Then we have the third group, "family-tradition" Catholic voters, who aren't so much assimilated into today's culture as they are captured by the sacrosanct party preference of their forebears. They vote Democratic because their family always has, and who's going to question the morality of Grandma and the good sense of Grandpa? And so today they see no conflict between voting Democratic and Church teaching, because Nancy Pelosi and Tim Kaine and countless other Catholic officeholders assured them that it is okay.

Like many Catholics of his day, my own father was a Democrat who revered Jack Kennedy, had no hint of his heretical shenanigans, and held a rigorous skepticism about Republicans. But Dad, nor probably JFK, would have embraced what the Democratic Party has become more than a half-century later. It's been widely professed that today's increasingly radical, socialism-infested version "is not your father's Democratic Party," and that's literally true in my case.

My dad, whose family at one point during the Great Depression was living off his small-town paper route, was eternally grateful to Franklin Roosevelt and his New Deal policies. It's understandable that Dad, and many guys like him, went to great lengths to earn money by any ethical means possible, such as driving an older woman from Kansas to Arizona one winter, even missing Christmas at home to do so. So scarred was he by the hardships of the Depression that he became obsessed with making as much money as he could. He never wanted to experience those hardscrabble times again. This left him little time to pay attention to politics. But when he did allow himself to do so, it was always measured against FDR.

By 1960, television had been in our home for a while, and the presidential campaigns took place in our living room. The handsome, witty – and Democrat – Jack Kennedy positively wowed my dad. And he utterly despised Richard Nixon, owing more, probably, to perception than substance. He bought the "Tricky Dick" epithet wholesale. And Richard Nixon wasn't the Democrat.

And although Dad kept his voting record confidential, I know he voted for Kennedy against Nixon in 1960 and probably Hubert Humphrey against Nixon in 1968. But, remarkably, in 1972, I think he might have voted for Nixon, though he never admitted it. By then, information about presidential candidates was easier to hear, even if it was passively heard. And there was enough coming through the TV about the leftist policies of Democrat George McGovern to repel my dad. He would have had to grit his teeth to pull the lever for either candidate.

But not every "family tradition" Catholic Democrat made that discern-ment in 1972, and they still don't do so today. Father Anthony Mastroeni, writing in *Latin Mass* magazine in 2016, had harsh words for Catholics who hadn't seriously examined the change in moral values of political parties. "A word to those who persist year after year, mindless of seismic shifts that have taken place in political parties, voting the very same way their ancestors did: you do them no honor! If these same ancestors, though now dead and perhaps in heaven, now knowing what they knew not then, could make their words take flight, they would say something similar to what Saint Paul told those Christians of Galatia, grown deaf and muted to the truth and stuck in pagan thinking, "O you stupid Galatians! Have you gone mad?" [Gal. 3:1].[12]

Yes, the shifts have been seismic, but just as glacial. That the great Catholic unwashed have in such large measure acquiesced to such mortally sinful practices as contraception, abortion and homosexual "marriage" is not a shift that could have happened in short order. The metamorphosis of the lay faithful was decades-long. And it was insidious. The instigators, from within the church and without, needed many years to effectively distort the pliable young minds that would constitute today's clerical and lay Catholic leadership. But the revolution is now complete, as proven by the manifest heresy at the highest levels of the church and throughout. Even within the past decade or two, there has been a measure, however slight, of authentic Catholic doctrine volitionally transmitted to the culture. Popes St. John Paul II and Benedict XVI professed the church's beliefs on the non-negotiable moral issues of the day. But almost immediately after the election of Pope Francis in 2013, that trace of Catholic influence rapidly became almost imperceptible. As I heard one traditional priest pronounce in a January 2019 Sunday sermon, "Catholic culture is now dead. It simply doesn't exist anymore."

(It should be added here that the priest was actually giving hopeful reassurance to his parishioners on that day, recounting how Jesus reproved his fearful disciples after calming the storm. "Why are you so afraid? Do you still have no faith?")

How did Catholic culture die? In America, it began with the bishops, who did not protect it, and it is they who still reign over its demise. How can it be otherwise? Yes, there are 70 million other Catholics in the United States, many of whom have participated in the heretical mischief – and more, owing to "obedience" – who have acquiesced to it. But this is nothing that the bishops could not have prevented, at least prior to the recent confusion and strong arming of the Francis papacy (one example being the Vatican's extraordinary cancellation in November 2018 of the U.S. bishops' scheduled vote on sex abuse reform measures). But at any time before Francis, the American bishops would have enjoyed full authority to contain and correct the ever-increasing doctrinal and liturgical errors in American Catholic churches. They failed. Some, as we now understand from the sex abuse crisis, actively fomented the circumstances that led to the failure. Others were merely neglectful, looking the other way and rolling with the declining mores of the times.

There were pockets, but only pockets, of vigorous and principled resistance along the way. The nomination of pro-choice Catholic Sen. John Kerry as the 2004 Democratic presidential nominee prompted several bishops to declare that they'd had enough. Bishop Emeritus Rene Henry Gracida of Corpus Christi took issue with the USCCB's (intentionally?) pusillanimous presidential questionnaire, especially because of its "seamless garment" approach to the issues facing the American public. "While certainly there could be and should be a 'Catholic' position on most, if not all, of the issues covered by the questionnaire, from the perspective of the Church's teaching some issues far outweigh others in importance," Gracida said in a written statement. "For instance, there is no moral equivalence between the issue of abortion-on-demand and farm subsidies. The questionnaire should have been much shorter and should have been limited to questions on those issues on which there is a clear unequivocal teaching of the Church, e.g., abortion, cloning, assisted suicide, embryonic stem-cell research and marriage.

"There is no clear unequivocal position of the Church on such issues as the minimum wage, immigration, farm subsidies, etc. The inclusion of (such) questions in the questionnaire can only result in confusion in the minds of Catholic voters who do not understand that there is no moral equivalence between these two groups of issues."

So disturbed was Bishop Gracida that he suggested that the questionnaire simply be ignored. "I can only hope that both presidential candidates will refuse to reply to the questionnaire, or, if they do reply, that the leadership of the United States Conference of Catholic Bishops will recognize the danger to Catholic voters and will publish those replies with a clear teaching on the greater importance (of issues of intrinsic evil) that have far greater moral implications for the nation."[13]

And while there were a few individual bishops who spoke with equivalent clarity during the 2004 campaign, Dr. Robert Royal of the Faith and Reason Institute observed that "there remained a reluctance among the bishops as a body – and especially among laymen at the Bishops conference – to take the final step and require any politician running for office, and Kerry most notably among them, either to support church teaching on line-in-the-sand issues like abortion or stop calling themselves Catholic." Royal then questioned whether it would have mattered, anyway. "Fears that criticism of, and perhaps even ecclesiastical penalties for, such politicians would create a backlash ignores the fact that the bishops had already thrown away much of their influence through neglect."[14]

The same point was succinctly made by Catholic writer Maggie Gallagher, who said that if the bishops took no action against Catholics who "dissent from the Church's core teachings on things like abortion ... it is hard to see how the next generation of Catholics can avoid concluding the Church is just not serious."[15]

Today, though, with Catholic culture arguably dead, an increasing number of prelates (and priests) have become so alarmed that they are publicly making known their deep concerns. Among them are those cited herein who have explicitly rejected the "seamless garment," and who have boldly stated that how Catholics vote can have eternal consequences for their souls. They heroically face an entrenched church bureaucracy hell-bent on perverting the teachings of the holy Catholic Church, knowing still that Jesus remains with us in the boat.

7

A "Fallen Away" Opportunity

There is wide consensus that 25 percent of the American population is Catholic and that, therefore, 25 percent of the American voting public is Catholic. But these figures are misleading, not necessarily because the survey respondents lied, but because their self-identification, as a whole, doesn't signal what might be expected. According to a Gallup report released in April 2018, only 39 percent of American Catholics consistently attend Sunday Mass.[1] This would mean that, pursuant to Church doctrine, nearly two-thirds of American Catholics are in an ongoing state of mortal sin.

Further, if one can reason that a self-identified "Catholic" who doesn't practice his faith on Sunday should also not be expected to practice it on any other day, including election day, then his participation is meaningless in assessing the extent to which authentic Catholic values are represented in the voting booth. What this means is that just 39 percent of the purported 25 percent of Americans who say they're Catholic are likely to be reflecting on their faith at all when they vote. Therefore, for purposes of measuring the proportion of voters who exert Catholic values on elections, we can say that it is about 10 percent (39 percent of 25 percent) of the total voting public – *at most,* because there are surely some Catholics within that 10 percent who show up to vote but who do not bring along their Catholic values. They either believe that they shouldn't, due to a misunderstanding of the church/state-separation claptrap, or they don't know that church teaching affirmatively directs them to do so. Democratic pollster Stanley Greenberg concurred with the 10 percent figure, noting that they are "those most committed to and identified with the church and most likely to bring their Catholic identity into politics."

Catholics "who don't attend Mass regularly are more likely to vote liberal, and church-going Catholics are more apt to vote conservative," observes Patti Maguire Armstrong.[2] For example, while Barack Obama carried the overall Catholic vote in 2012, he won only 42 percent of Catholics who attend Mass weekly, with 57 percent voting for Mitt Romney, a non-Christian (he's a Mormon). These figures comport with believers of all religions, noted Catherine Harmon, managing editor of *Catholic World Report.* "Those who attend services weekly went 59 percent to 39 percent for Romney, and those who said they attend 'occasionally' went 55-43 for Obama."

Thus, to bandy about the notion that "the Catholic vote" in America is 25 percent of the electorate is meaningless. It says nothing. One might as well add to that figure the number of people who have left the Catholic Church and joined Protestant, Jewish and all of the other available faiths, because "Catholics" who do not practice their Catholicism are, by their acts, not voting representatives of Catholicism. Non-Catholics, obviously, do not intentionally vote according to Catholic values, and neither do non-practicing Catholics. For purposes of voting their faith, these two groups of lax Catholics and ex-Catholics are the same.

This is both a shame and an opportunity. Catholics are required by doctrine to vote and to vote according to Church teaching on the most important matters of the faith, i.e., in today's culture, the "non-negotiables" of abortion, human cloning, homosexual marriage, embryonic stem-cell research, euthanasia and religious freedom. That they don't is more than regrettable, because they are also required to learn these truths. Ignorance is no excuse, and their salvation hangs in the balance. But while Catholic precepts are currently represented by a maximum of 10 percent of American voters, the potential exists, ideally, for that percentage to more than double.

If 25 percent of voters call themselves Catholic, is it too optimistic to persuade, say, another 10 percent to vote consistent with Catholic values? Perhaps it is, but we must put no limits on evangelization, which means the goal, however daunting, must always be 25 percent – the entire American Catholic population.

Such an evangelistic effect would not be limited to the Catholic ranks. Born-again and fundamentalist Protestants share the Catholic positions on the non-negotiables. Public opinion researcher Steven Wagner recounted that Ralph Reed, as executive director of the Christian Coalition, knew that Catholics are critical to electing morally-fit candidates. "Reed's vision was of a Catholic and Christian conservative political collaboration, and this vision led him to invest substantially in the founding of an organization to do for Catholics what the Christian Coalition had done for evangelical conservatives," Wagner said.

Reed, Wagner said, observed "that a candidate for president espousing a socially conservative agenda can win every born-again, evangelical, and fundamentalist vote there is, but without the support of Catholics, that candidate is going nowhere."[4] Thus, if the true Catholic vote could be maximized, Reed's vision could be realized.

But for Catholics, that does not necessarily equate to mere adherence to a political ideology. Although Reed, the Christian Coalition and other such evangelical groups are clearly tagged as "conservative," Catholic orthodoxy carries no political label. Indeed, the term "conservative" appears nowhere in the definition of "orthodox," which is "conforming to what is generally or traditionally accepted as right or true; established and approved." (*New Oxford American Dictionary*) That Catholic doctrine comports with conservative Protestant political movements is coincidental, owing to Christian precepts and natural law. But, doctrinally, there cannot be a deliberate "Catholic conservative movement"; there can only be Catholic orthodoxy. This is true in doctrine, and it is true in practice, as Wagner observed about "active Catholics," i.e., the aforementioned "Catholic 10 percent":

"• *They are distinctively patriotic.* American exceptionalism – the idea the

America is a country with a historic mission and unique global importance – is deeply felt.

"• *Surprisingly, they are not necessarily pro-military*, despite the fact that many have had first-hand experience in the military.

"• *Active Catholics are not anti-government.* They have favorable opinions of the institutions of government, and they do not favor indiscriminate budget-cutting.

"• *Active Catholics are not in favor of unbridled free markets*, even though many consider themselves conservatives. Catholics tend to be concerned with the outcome of policies; they are not economically laissez-faire, because they are interested less in the process than in the results and are not reluctant to try to manage the economy for socially beneficial results.

"• *Active Catholics are tolerant* and do not savor political villains.

"• *Active Catholics are concerned about the plight of the poor*, yet overwhelmingly support recent welfare reforms.

"• *Active Catholics are opposed to job quotas* and other elements of affirmative action that offend the American ideal of equality.

"• *Active Catholics accept the existence of an absolute standard of morality.* This is, perhaps, the most profound yet subtle of all their characteristics, leading to a certain moral confidence, less confusion about the difference between pluralism and tolerance, and greater resistance to the claim of a moral right to do wrong, a central tenet of contemporary liberalism.

"Catholics are often accused of being big government liberals. As we have seen, active Catholics are not liberals, but they do resist anti-government rhetoric. This, coupled with their support for economic intervention, raises the question, 'in what sense are active Catholics conservatives?'"[5]

The answer is that they are *not* Catholic conservatives; they are Catholics who are faithful to Catholic doctrine. And while most active (orthodox) Catholics are not politically liberal, they might be conservatives only to the extent that that political ideology is in accord with their religious faith. In most respects, it is. Being strictly faithful to doctrine is the definition of orthodoxy – and conservatives, politically, religiously, or in any other sense, are by definition "strict constructionists." Therefore, their adherence to orthodoxy naturally tends to coincide with political conservativism.

8

America's Mythical "Law": Separation of Church and State

Perhaps no linguistic device has been more deceptively and effectively used to influence American public policy than the phrase, "separation of church and state." So inculcated into society is this false doctrine that it is universally accepted as a foundational law, a constitutional pillar believed to be embodied in the establishment clause of the First Amendment.

It is no such thing. The First Amendment says this and no more: "Congress shall make no law respecting an establishment of religion, or prohibiting the free exercise thereof; or abridging the freedom of speech, or of the press; or the right of the people peaceably to assemble, and to petition the Government for a redress of grievances."[1] By no reasonable stretch of the imagination does this first in the Bill of Rights direct that the respective affairs of government and religion shall not share ideals or overtly influence the affairs of the other. At variance with their modern, liberal and agenda-driven counterparts, originalist constitutional scholars ascribe to the text its plain meaning: religious bodies shall have the right to conduct their affairs without interference or abridgment of their beliefs by government. The words, "separation of church and state," or even any remotely comparable idiom, are simply not contained or implied in the First Amendment.

But, as has been shown, for nearly 140 years the United States Supreme Court has been whimsically redefining this phrase coined in 1802 by Thomas Jefferson, gratuitously imputing to it an altogether novel meaning: that Jefferson's "wall of separation between Church and State," though only a personal belief expressed in a private letter, was tantamount to a royal decree utterly protecting government from religion, though not religion from government, and that, moreover, it was somehow worthy of enshrinement into the Constitution by arbitrary judicial fiat.

Though popularly glommed onto the First Amendment, the justices effectively created a new amendment, so inventive was their reasoning, and if it is to be enforced as such, one might reckon that it ought to be codified as "Amendment I(a)," if only because it became an outgrowth, however aberrant, of Amendment I. But so as to preserve the pure meaning of Amendment I, it would better be tacked on at the end, as Amendment 28.

Professor Daniel L. Dreisbach contrasts Jefferson's letter with language of the First Amendment, writing in 2006 that "Jefferson's trope emphasizes *separation* between church and state, unlike the First Amendment, which speaks in terms of the non-establishment and free exercise of religion." In other words, Jefferson was not referring to the principles of the First Amendment at all in his letter to the Danbury Baptist Association. Dreisbach says the "'high and impregnable' wall central to the past 50 years of church-state jurisprudence is not Jefferson's wall; rather, it is a wall that Black – Justice Hugo Black – erected in 1947 in *Everson v. Board of Education*," in which Black wrote that using taxpayer funds to bus children to religious schools did not breach the "wall of separation" between church and state. [2]

Objection to Black's creative term, "high and impregnable" was swift, even among members of the high court. As Dreisbach recounts, several justices subsequently renounced the decision. "A rule of law should not be drawn from a figure of speech," said Justice Stanley Reed just a year later. Justice Potter Stewart later opined that the court's duty to resolve constitutional matters "is not responsibly aided by the uncritical invocation of metaphors like the 'wall of separation,' a phrase nowhere to be found in the Constitution." And Justice William Rehnquist offered that the "wall of separation" is "based on bad history, a metaphor which has proved useless as a guide to judging. It should be frankly and explicitly abandoned."[3]

Within a year, the U.S. bishops joined in, issuing a strong rebuttal to Justice Black's construal of Jefferson's wall. In their pastoral letter, "The Christian in Action," the bishops called Black's new interpretation of separation of church and state an "utter distortion of American history and law" and a "shibboleth of doctrinaire secularism."[4]

But their protestations could not plug the dike. Black's codification of this new concept devastated the peaceful coexistence that had produced reciprocal benefits for both religion and government in America. The bishops of 1948 could not have imagined the resulting secularism that would dominate America 70 years later, a state of affairs that has alarmed today's leaders of all religious denominations, including Catholic churchmen.

In 2008, Bishop Samuel J. Aquila, of Fargo, North Dakota, wrote in his diocesan newspaper that "the mission of the Church and the task of the State are distinct, but they are never completely separate. The constitutional distinction between Church and State is found in the non-establishment of a state religion. However, this is not the denial of the entry of God or moral convictions into the public square.

"The misinterpretation of the separation of Church and State as the denial of the entry of God or moral convictions into the public square reveals the reality that the religion predominately lived today is that of secular atheism, the denial of God, whether directly through the works of [outspoken atheist] Richard Dawkins and modern academia, or more subtly through practical atheism, living day-to-day life as if God didn't exist. Some Catholics in the separation of their faith from decisions in the political order abandon God and embrace secular atheism. Secular atheism goes hand in hand with secular humanism, namely, the idea that man alone can order society and the common life of the human race and that God has no part in this order. Secular humanism can never flourish, because the moment society abandons God's law it also abandons humanity. Abandoning the truth is directly opposed both to our ideals as Christians and to the founding principles of our country as seen in the Declaration of Independence which acknowledges the 'laws of nature's God' and 'the Creator.'"⁵

Bishop Thomas Olmsted, of Phoenix, cited "false notions about the separation of Church and state ... based on false understandings of the First Amendment to the U.S. Constitution, which in fact protects the practice of religion from coercion by the state, rather than limiting the religious voice." He said people of faith have become fearful of espousing their beliefs beyond the church walls. "If we let our faith impact on the way we practice a profession, engage the culture, or become involved in political struggles, then we are accused of imposing our faith on others," he said. "These voices have become increasingly strident in the United States over the past 50 years; and they can intimidate believers, making them afraid or uneasy to let their faith influence their involvement in the public square."⁶

Archbishop Charles J. Chaput, of Philadelphia, in 2012 endorsed an active role for Catholic clerics in the public realm, particularly in politics: "The 'separation of Church and state' can never mean that religious believers should be silent about legislative issues, the appointment of judges or public policy. It's not the job of the Church to sponsor political candidates. But it's *very much* the job of the Church to guide Catholics to think and act in accord with their faith."⁷

That contention was echoed by Father Anthony J. Mastroeni in his 2016 article titled, "Voting Your Catholic Conscience." "While the 'business' of religion is the saving of souls," he wrote, "this in itself necessarily includes matters of morality. And since there are no morality-free-zones in the business of legislation or politics, religion has a right to make its voice heard. The act of voting represents a judgment of conscience."⁸

The First Amendment's "free exercise" clause overrides the widespread misinterpretation of the church and state relationship, commonly ascribed to the "establishment" clause. The free exercise clause gives religion license to speak out loudly and often, and to do so in any venue it pleases. It "was not intended to protect the state from the church," Mastroeni notes, "but rather to protect the church from the state; to allow every religion to express its views freely and publicly. It was meant to include, not exclude, the voice of religion (in) the public square."⁹

Cardinal James Francis Stafford sees more than judicial mischief at work. He blames Jefferson, himself. "He introduced a latent and powerful virus which would eventually be used to diminish and then to wound mortally a theology of discourse in the public arena," he told a Catholic University of America audience in 2008. "It has led to the increasingly secularized states of the American union and their active hostility towards the Catholic Church. Some of these governments are threatening Roman Catholic adoption agencies because of their refusal to select same-sex couples as potential adoptive parents. They are forcing Catholic hospitals to accept medical procedures which are contrary to the dignity of the human person. They are insisting on hiring practices which will destroy the Catholic identity of health and social services under Catholic Church auspices. They have not refrained from coercing the individual conscience. Here the federal and state governments are enshrining the primacy of secular laws over against religious principles. These decisions are the legal and moral progeny of Jefferson's insistence on debarring personal faith from the public forum."[10]

Some Catholic commentators identify a broad, clandestine machination that they believe to have capitalized upon Jefferson's thesis: Freemasonry, of which Jefferson may have been a member. Could the cultural permeation of the "wall of separation" fiction have resulted, in part, from Freemasonry's power during the mid-twentieth century? In his 1994 book, *Behind the Lodge Door,* Paul A. Fisher opines that the preponderance of Masons holding seats on the Supreme Court from 1941 to 1971 may have contributed to the court's "determination to move the nation away from an emphasis on Judeo-Christian values in public life."[11]

Father Justin Nolan, of the Priestly Fraternity of St. Peter, concurs, and is likewise reluctant to cast Jefferson as a misquoted innocent in the "wall of separation" confusion. "Although I don't think Jefferson would have approved of modern judicial activism, I'm not so sure he wouldn't agree wholeheartedly with the idea of the purely secular state," Father Nolan told this author. "Although there is debate about whether he was or wasn't a Freemason, he certainly was a child of his rationalist times, a Deist, and not a believer in the Christian God. His famous 'Jefferson Bible' shows his repudiation of traditional Christianity and espouses an overtly Deist/rationalist belief system."

The "wall of separation" forces have been largely successful in cleansing government of religion, i.e., perverting the establishment clause. They have largely succeeded in disallowing prayer at public meetings and school athletic events, removed crosses and crucifixes from public buildings, supplanted "Christmas" with "holiday" or "winter" when referring to December civic activities. This has been relatively easy, partly because the "separation of church and state" mentality naturally accommodated a compatible sentiment: nonpartisanship. No Christian holiday – the thinking goes – especially a Christian holy day, should even be *acknowledged* by government in a nation that is inhabited by other religions. Such acknowledgment, in their view, would somehow be "establishment."

But "wall of separation" advocates have met greater resistance in re-characterizing and thereby diminishing the "free exercise" clause. What success they have had is largely the Church's own fault, the Church having struck a bargain to keep political talk out of its sermons – indeed, off campus altogether – in return for government lucre, i.e., direct parochial school and other subsidies, and most insidious of all: tax exemption. After enactment of the 1954 Johnson Amendment, which prohibited churches from endorsing or opposing specific political candidates, the American Catholic Church agreed to talk about anything except politics within the church walls and thereby has long since become a willing financial hostage of government.

Yet, despite this case of Stockholm syndrome, the Church in recent years has shown signs of rebellion. In 2006, Pope Benedict XVI said that while the Church should not engage in political battles, it "must not remain on the sidelines in the fight for justice."[12] In the United States, some prelates have ramped up their fight to proclaim Church teachings in the public square. After their decades-long concession regarding the establishment clause, American bishops have more actively been defending their right to free speech, even as that principle, itself, has come under broad attack in the secularization of the culture. In contrast to their earlier willingness to be muzzled in the pulpit, many bishops have been standing fast against this astonishing second constitutional threat and have been stirred to issue extraordinary, and corrective, counter-statements as the threat has grown.

In 1994, Archbishop Eusebius J. Beltran, of Oklahoma City, asserted the duty, not just the right, of the Church to speak out. "There are some who complain whenever the Church, or a bishop or a priest, addresses the societal issues of our day," he said. "However, as American citizens and members of local communities and states, it is our duty to participate fully in the process of government. It is therefore both an obligation and a right for the Church to speak out and give us direction."[13]

In 2004, Archbishop William E. Lori, of Bridgeport, Connecticut, illustrated the absurdity of liberals' redefinition of religious liberty. The First Amendment, he wrote, "in no way prohibits the Church from speaking out on issues and from helping her members understand how the positions of political parties and candidates stack up against the Church's social teaching. If the First Amendment prohibited such activity, then there would be no real religious freedom in the United States. After all, religious freedom is not merely the freedom to believe what one wishes to believe in the privacy of one's mind and home; you can do that in even the most oppressive gulag!"[14]

In 2007, when the aforementioned group of Democratic Catholic congressmen railed against Pope Benedict after he conceptually approved of sanctions against public officials who give scandal, Bishop Arthur J. Serratelli, of Paterson, New Jersey, was blunt in citing their hypocrisy. "Ultimately, the statement of the 18 politicians who publicly blasted the Holy Father is simply a refusal to allow the Pope freedom of speech and the Church freedom of religion," he said. "Now how American is that?"[15]

In 2008, Bishop Joseph A. Galante, of Camden, New Jersey, reminded his diocese that the First Amendment's free exercise clause is a limit on government, not on religion. The Constitution, he said, "requires that government be neutral toward religion, not that religion be kept from the public square. Our convictions regarding human life and dignity do not lose their right to be heard because they may happen to come from people of religious belief. As such, the Church has a responsibility to participate in the political process and to give voice to its core convictions in the public square."[16]

In a letter read in all diocesan parishes in 2016, Bishop William Murphy, of Rockville Centre, New York, stated that the Church has both "the God-given and constitutional right to proclaim religious truths in the public square."[17]

And the American bishops, as a body, have regularly confronted the free-speech threat head on. "Some question whether it is appropriate for the Church to play a role in political life," they wrote in their quadrennial, election-year document, *Forming Consciences for Faithful Citizenship.* "However, the obligation to teach the moral truths that should shape our lives, including our public lives, is central to the mission given to the Church by Jesus Christ. Moreover, the United States Constitution protects the right of individual believers and religious bodies to participate and speak out without government interference, favoritism, or discrimination. Civil law should fully recognize and protect the right of the Church and other institutions in civil society to participate in cultural, political, and economic life without being forced to abandon or ignore their central moral convictions. Our nation's tradition of pluralism is enhanced, not threatened, when religious groups and people of faith bring their convictions and concerns into public life.[18] ... The Church's obligation to participate in shaping the moral character of society is a requirement of our faith."[19]

And because "the Church" means all the baptized, that obligation is therefore integral to an individual's personal identity as a Catholic. He is not allowed, under Church law, to merely subsist in society, but rather must spread his Catholic belief throughout it. It is his Catholic duty. It is his Catholic identity. "Can a black man dissociate himself from his race when considering the positions of a party or candidate?" posited Father Peter M.J. Stravinskas in an October 2016 sermon at the Church of the Holy Innocents in New York City. "Can a Jewish woman put aside her Jewishness? In fact, would anyone even dare suggesting such a possibility? No, these aspects of one's person are integral to one's identity — and so is one's faith."[20]

The various artifices – especially those of church tax exemption and the spurious "separation of church and state" fallacy – employed to muzzle

Catholics and other orthodox Christians from the marketplace
debate are pure sophistry, a protracted exercise in illegitimate p
Priests can quite legally talk politics from the pulpit; they simp
advocate for or against an identifiable candidate, in accordance w
anti-religion Johnson Amendment, without risking the Church's tax-e
status. But they can legally talk about the issues of the day, even c
an election season, and tell their parishioners to vote for candidates
best advocate for the teachings of the Catholic Church. They can
tell their flocks how they should vote on ballot issues. But despite t
ecclesiastical duty to help the laity spread their Catholic identity in soc
most priests won't do these things, for a whole host of unacceptable reasc
that generally include ignorance of the law and cowardice.

The Johnson Amendment and the pervasive "church and state" lie hav
so intimidated and deceived America's priests that they simply refuse t
talk about politics at all. Like other Americans, they have been bamboozled,
propagandized into believing that any discussion about the issues of the day
is simply verboten. And even if they become aware that they may, in fact, talk
about or engage in anything and everything political, short of endorsing or
opposing an identifiable candidate, they mostly demur. They simply don't
want to deal with the inevitable outcry from parishioners who are either
misinformed about the law or the usually small number who object to the
priest's authentic Catholic teaching. Both groups will reflexively scream,
"separation of church and state"!

To which I respond, "Yes, indeed, do not establish a state religion, and
keep that state away from our right to fully, freely practice our religion in
our civic and political activities as citizens of the United States!"

And the chanceries are not blameless for the priests' reluctance. Even
those priests who exhibit a desire to provide authentic Catholic teaching in
the political sphere can be shut down by their bishops.

In a personal case in 2006, my pastor was initially quite enthused by my
request of him to allow a candidate forum to be held in the parish hall. A
week later he told me with regret, "The diocesan lawyer says no." But there
was absolutely no legal basis for that decision. To this priest's credit, he

curiously did not choose to seek the lawyer's advice when I then asked him to allow me and my little band of anti-abortion zealots to place leaflets on cars in the parking lot during all of the Sunday Masses just before election day. I guess he figured he'd sought enough legal guidance. His response to me? He walked away, threw up his hands and said, "If I don't see it, there's nothing I can do about it." God bless him.

But by the next election season, this pastor had been transferred, and his successor pounced on us in the parking lot. So steeped was he in legal ignorance that he hid in the nearby school and watched for us through the second-floor classroom windows. When he spotted us, all 300 pounds of him frantically lumbered onto the parking lot and ordered us to stop the leafleting. We refused, so he said he would make an announcement at the following Mass to ignore the leaflets on the cars. "Go ahead, Father, but you're advocating against the lives of unborn babies." That must have gotten to him – he made no such announcement from the altar. So God bless him, too.

(Although not the case in that instance, many hardline liberal Catholic pastors simply don't want orthodoxy promulgated anywhere on parish grounds. They run onto the parking lots, too, but it has nothing to do with parishioners violating the tax code.)

Today's parish priests operate under a fraudulent cloud of legal and social intimidation, and the Catholic faith and American society at large suffer for it. As recounted above, many bishops are beginning to confront the lie, but they must now educate their priests on what they are allowed to say. It's a simple instruction: priests can say anything, as long as it's doctrinally correct, and as long as they don't say specifically for whom to vote. Pretty simple. Further, legally talking politics would embolden the laity to properly spread the Church's authentic teachings in the world. Unfortunately, this idea has been effectively banned by the Church's acquiescence to yet another, and the inanest, of liberal ultimata: "Don't impose your beliefs on me!"

In the face of this stark upbraiding, Catholics politely, and shamefully, demure, as if they've been properly reminded not to be uppity. But such acquiescence to secular society is a dereliction of their Catholic duty, says

Archbishop Chaput. "Claiming that 'we don't want to impose our beliefs on society' is not merely politically convenient," he wrote in 2004, "it is morally incoherent and irresponsible."[21]

So ridiculous is this newly-contrived American "standard" that it betrays the very pluralism from which our codified laws derive. The Constitution, Chaput said, "does not, nor was it ever intended to, prohibit people or communities of faith from playing an active role in public life. Exiling religion from civic debate separates government from morality and citizens from their consciences."[22]

The dishonest, contemporary "imposition" touchstone directly conflicts with the supposed American bedrock of freedom of religion, the very foundation of the colonies' quest for independence from King George III. "Religious freedom means the liberty to bring one's beliefs and values into the public debate, to challenge the views of candidates for office, and to try to shape a society more worthy of the human person," wrote Archbishop Lori. "To do all that is not to impose a sectarian view on others but rather to advance the truth about the human person known to reason (natural law) but clarified by faith."[23]

After all, added Chaput, "People who support permissive abortion laws have no qualms about imposing their views on society."[24]

It is time for Catholics to come out from the shadows, said San Antonio's archbishop, José H. Gomez, a month before the 2008 election. "We live in a society that would like to privatize religion, to take it out of the public square," he said. "Privatizing religion would be, for all people of faith, an unholy compromise. We who profess to believe in God cannot allow him to be banished from the public square."[25]

Our forefathers, far from regarding religion as a foreign threat, understood that it must be a critical moral pillar for the new nation, said Bishop Aquila in his 2007 Legislative Mass sermon. Virtually all of them non-Catholics, they still knew that the dignity of the human person is bestowed by God and that the nation's citizens must uphold that truth at all costs. "To deny or remove God from political discourse," Aquila said, "only opens the door to the destruction of the human person and to violence such as war, genocide, murder, abortion, and euthanasia as so evidenced throughout the last century and at the beginning of this new century."[26]

And one-fifth into the new century, that door has been flung open, pouring out those consequences like never before.

9

Yes, I Am Trying to Impose My Beliefs on You

B oy, did JFK give Catholic politicians an out.

"I believe in an America ... where no religious body seeks to impose its will directly or indirectly upon the general populace or the public acts of its officials."

In one sentence, Kennedy set a new standard for heterodox Catholic office-holders, one that allowed them to become even more so. It would become a standard set in stone, because: 1) it was uttered by an established political megastar running for the most powerful office in the world, and 2) he would go on to win that office. Kennedy's tragic death, and the silly Camelot imagery that followed, only served to romanticize this modern heresy. If the larger-than-life John F. Kennedy said it, we can – we *must* – honor our fallen hero's great wisdom.

That lofty sentiment made it even easier for subsequent Catholic pols to rationalize separating their Catholic duty from their worldly ambition – and in some cases to pursue the preexisting non-Catholic morality that they held anyway. The Kennedy Capitulation was the political gambit that paid off big for generations of liberal Catholic office-seekers.

Of course, it was a colossal deceit, a vile mass seduction of American Catholics, and one that the Church thoroughly failed to adequately address or has ever come close to remedying. Indeed, church leaders made little sustained effort to correct Kennedy's self-serving false honorableness, i.e., that no political leader should ever deign to impose his moral beliefs on his own citizenry. It was a trope that dovetailed conveniently with Justice Blackman's notorious interpretation of separation of church and state and the generalized perverse understanding of the First Amendment that followed. Kennedy was effectively extending Blackman's mangled exegesis of Jefferson onto the governance of public discourse. Indeed, he was "imposing" a new code of conduct that enjoyed the recent sanction of a Supreme Court justice – and the U.S. Tax Code, thanks to Senator Lyndon Johnson and his infamous "Johnson Amendment" of 1954.

For Kennedy and his liberal Catholic progeny, the Faustian bargain of exchanging religious obedience for political expediency has, to this day, survived in deference to the genteelness of not "imposing" one's views on others. So abhorrent is the prospect of doing so that it would appear to be not just unseemly, but surely illegal. Under today's emerging Orwellian speech codes, doesn't imposing one's moral beliefs on others violate some campaign-finance law, or a "hate" law or, well, something?

No, of course it doesn't. Moreover, authentic Catholic doctrine, of which so many of today's "faithful" are woefully and alarmingly ignorant, itself proclaims that Catholics have every right to advocate their beliefs to others, including attempting to codify such beliefs into law. In fact, not only does the Church encourage its members to spread Catholic teaching far and wide (even in today's oppressively anti-Christian America), it obligates them to do so. *In other words, the Church actually imposes a duty upon Catholics to, in turn, impose Church teaching upon society.* How is this so? The American bishops answer by declaring this duty in blunt terms: "The Church's obligation to participate in shaping the moral character of society is a requirement of our faith," they said in *Forming Consciences for Faithful Citizenship.* By "the Church," of course, the bishops meant the Church's members, individually and as a body.

The Second Vatican Council also taught this precept, declaring that it is the task of the Catholic laity "to impress the divine law on the affairs

72

of the earthly city."[1] Was this meant to respond to and counter the errors of the Kennedy Capitulation, declared by JFK just five years before the commencement of the council? Probably not, as the deleterious effects of the Kennedy doctrine were yet to be widely felt by the mid-1960s. But in retrospect, the timing was rather ironic. Decades later, however, the full breadth of the "I will not impose" sophism was realized and had become alarming to many Catholic prelates, such as Bishop Joseph A. Galante.

"If we are true to our faith, we cannot retreat or hide behind the formula, 'I am personally for this or against this, but I will not impose my view on others,'" said Galante before the election of 2008. "This argument is as lacking in courage and integrity as it is specious. Surely, our responsibility as Catholics who are citizens is to act on our belief, to bring our belief into the public square, (and) charitably to give voice to the core principles that guide us."[2]

The introduction of the emotionally-charged term, "imposing beliefs" or "imposing morality" as a political accusation is a contemporary red herring. It's a weaponized paralogism, an illogical linguistic device that, by its mere utterance, is employed to preempt an opponent's arguments by invalidating his very right to introduce them.

And Catholics fall for it. They somehow, through intimidation or poor civics instruction, believe that they are bound to keep their religion at home or in their church buildings – anywhere but in the public square, their city hall, the statehouse or the U.S. capitol. Catholic citizens usually comply and recede, ignorant of their rights and responsibility. But liberal Catholic officeholders use the "imposing morality" trope as a weapon. Many of them commandeer this false belief and employ it as a political stratagem. And we let them get away with it.

Of the hollow phrase, "I'm personally opposed to but don't want to impose," Bishop Thomas Tobin asks if we "would let any politician get away with the same pathetic cop-out on other issues: 'I'm personally opposed to ... racial discrimination, sexual abuse, prostitution, drug abuse, polygamy, incest ... but don't want to impose my beliefs on others?'"

He goes on to liken such politicians to Pontius Pilate "who personally found no guilt in Jesus, but for fear of the crowd, washed his hands of the whole affair and handed Jesus over to be crucified. I can just hear Pilate saying, 'You know, I'm personally opposed to crucifixion, but I don't want to impose my belief on others.'"[3]

One of the most ardent clerics to propound on the subject is Archbishop Chaput, who verily condemns the companion proscriptions concerning Catholics "imposing their beliefs" and "separation of church and state."

"These are two of the emptiest slogans in current American politics, intended to discourage serious debate," he said. "No one in mainstream American politics wants a theocracy. Nor does anyone doubt the importance of morality in public life. Therefore, we should recognize these slogans for what they are: frequently dishonest and ultimately dangerous sound bites." The plain-speaking archbishop shredded the veil of deception that has smothered authentic Catholic citizenship for 60 years. "Lawmaking inevitably involves some group imposing its beliefs on the rest of us," he said. "That's the nature of the democratic process. If we say that we 'ought' to do something, we are making a moral judgment. When our legislators turn that judgment into law, somebody's ought becomes a 'must' for the whole of society. This is not inherently dangerous; it's how pluralism works.

"Democracy depends on people of conviction expressing their views, confidently and without embarrassment. This give-and-take is an American tradition, and religious believers play a vital role in it. We don't serve our country – in fact we weaken it intellectually – if we downplay our principles or fail to speak forcefully out of some misguided sense of good manners.[4]

"Claiming that 'we don't want to impose our beliefs on society is not merely politically convenient; it is morally incoherent and irresponsible ... [W]henever you hear that tired old argument that Catholics shouldn't "impose their views" on society, it's time to hit the bamboozle alarm — because that argument is almost always advanced by people who have every intention of imposing *their own* views on society."[5]

Chaput also showed how New York Gov. Mario Cuomo, in a famous 1984 speech, used the "impose" pretext to publicly renew the cover given to pro-choice Catholics by the Kennedy Capitulation 25 years earlier. "Cuomo's speech is a *tour de force* of articulate misdirection," Chaput said. "It refuses to acknowledge the teaching and formative power of the law. It implicitly equates unequal types of issues. It misuses the 'seamless garment' metaphor. It effectively blames Catholics themselves for the abortion problem. It selectively misreads history.

"In the end, Cuomo argued that 'approval or rejection of legal restrictions on abortion should not be the exclusive litmus test of Catholic loyalty.' With those words, he wrote the alibi for every pro-choice Catholic who has held public office since. ... In brief, it's OK to be Catholic in public service as long as you're willing to jettison what's inconveniently 'Catholic.'

"That's not a compromise. That's a deal with the devil, and it has a balloon payment no nation, no public servant and no voter can afford."[6]

Hence, Catholics absolutely should impose their beliefs on their fellow citizens. It's their duty. It's called evangelization. It's called defending Holy Mother Church, the bride of Christ. It's called leading our fellow man to truth. It's called saving souls, and God Almighty will surely judge us by it. We are Catholics before we're American citizens, Chaput said, "because we know that God has a demand on us prior to any government demand on us. And this has been the story of the martyrs through the centuries."

The bishops of Pennsylvania called for just such assertive, individual action in a pre-election day, October 1984 statement, and summarily dismissed the "imposition" canard. "The right to life is at the heart of all morality and the foundation of all just civil law," they wrote. "To assist this right no more legislates one religious viewpoint than do laws against child abuse, racial discrimination or murder. Therefore, Catholics must not be intimidated by claims that their position in defense of human life is an imposition of their morality on others."[7]

Indeed, one of their number, Bishop Edward Cullen of Allentown, Pennsylvania, went on to address the question of who, in truth, is imposing their beliefs on whom. "[W]e cannot agree at all with those who say that legislation that acts to preserve the life of the unborn is nothing but the imposition of 'our morality' or 'our religious point of view' on others," he said. "The fact is quite the opposite.

"To make legal the killing of the unborn is to impose on the most innocent and helpless of all an individual point of view, an individual morality (if one can call it that), which treats particular human beings as of no value. It is a point of view that condemns them to oblivion, with no say in the matter, with no chance even to make their existence felt."[8]

Even the "seamless garment" Pope Francis, who has de-emphasized abortion as an especial priority of the church, stresses the obligation of Catholics to participate in public policy generally. In his 2013 exhortation, *Evangelii Guadium*, Francis quotes his far more orthodox predecessor, Pope Benedict XVI, who said in *Deus Caritas Est* that the church (including individual Catholics) "cannot and must not remain on the sidelines in the fight for justice."[9]

So there it is. We must profess our Catholic faith in the public square, at the risk of ridicule, threats and even martyrdom. We have every right to do so, and we are commanded by God to perform that duty.

10

For Better or Worse, the Bishops Are
Still in Charge

I n the line of succession from the apostles, we have today's Catholic bishops. Despite the current tumult among them, the Catechism of the Catholic Church makes clear their authority:

• "Just as the office which the Lord confided to Peter alone, as first of the apostles, destined to be transmitted to his successors, is a permanent one, so also endures the office, which the apostles received, of shepherding the Church, a charge destined to be exercised without interruption by the sacred order of bishops." Hence the Church teaches that "the bishops have by divine institution taken the place of the apostles as pastors of the Church, in such wise that whoever listens to them is listening to Christ and whoever despises them despises Christ and him who sent Christ."[1]

• Bishops are "heralds of faith, who draw new disciples to Christ; they are authentic teachers" of the apostolic faith "endowed with the authority of Christ." [2]

• "The mission of the Magisterium is linked to the definitive nature of the covenant established by God with his people in Christ. It is this Magisterium's task to preserve God's people from deviations and defections and to guarantee them the objective possibility of professing the true faith without error. Thus, the pastoral duty of the Magisterium is aimed at seeing to it that the People of God abides in the truth that liberates. To fulfill this service, Christ endowed the Church's shepherds with the charism of infallibility in matters of faith and morals."[3]

• "Divine assistance is also given to the successors of the apostles, teaching in communion with the successor of Peter, and, in a particular way, to the bishop of Rome, pastor of the whole Church, when, without arriving at an infallible definition and without pronouncing in a 'definitive manner,' they propose in the exercise of the ordinary Magisterium a teaching that leads to better understanding of Revelation in matters of faith and morals. To this ordinary teaching the faithful 'are to adhere to it with religious assent' which, though distinct from the assent of faith, is nonetheless an extension of it."[4]

• "The power which they exercise personally in the name of Christ, is proper, ordinary, and immediate, although its exercise is ultimately controlled by the supreme authority of the Church. But the bishops should not be thought of as vicars of the Pope. His ordinary and immediate authority over the whole Church does not annul, but on the contrary confirms and defends that of the bishops."[5]

• "Episcopal consecration confers, together with the office of sanctifying, also the offices of teaching and ruling. ... In fact ... by the imposition of hands and through the words of the consecration, the grace of the Holy Spirit is given, and a sacred character is impressed in such wise that bishops, in an eminent and visible manner, take the place of Christ himself, teacher, shepherd, and priest, and act as his representative (*in Eius persona agant*)." "By virtue, therefore, of the Holy Spirit who has been given to them, bishops have been constituted true and authentic teachers of the faith. ..."[6]

So there it is. Catholic bishops are the authoritative teachers of Christianity. Still, while they speak as one voice in formal pastoral documents, they hardly do so otherwise amidst the contemporary events in the church and in the world. Some bishops are faithful to authentic Catholicism, i.e., orthodoxy, and others are liberal, i.e., products of warped formation for more than a half century. But they are, after all, human and sinners like the rest of us. The original disciples, themselves, all but one assuredly long since in Heaven, were tarnished in life: They showed insufficient faith during the storm at sea. They abandoned Jesus when the soldiers came to arrest Him. Thomas didn't trust Jesus at his word.

Just as there have been flawed popes – e.g., Steven VI, John XII, Benedict IX, Boniface VIII, Urban VI, Leo X, Clement VII – we naturally have had, and do have, some flawed bishops. It is necessary, therefore, for the faithful to discern which ones are to be followed. When bishops disagree among themselves, which ones are right?

In all matters, the correct answer is not which bishop is right, but rather the extent to which any one of them is comporting with Catholic doctrine. Catholics cannot follow the instruction or example of any prelate who clearly opposes the tenets of the faith. But on matters of prudential judgment – such as how best to conduct foreign policy, help the poor, or defend the nation – adherence to Catholic doctrine can vary. Bishops, and the faithful, are free to have opposing views on these issues. On matters that are non-negotiable, however, there can be no such variance. Again, these issues, in contemporary America, are identified by doctrinal Catholic theologians as: human cloning, homosexual marriage, embryonic stem-cell research, euthanasia, abortion and religious freedom. To be opposed to all of these activities is the sole Catholic position. And as the bishops cited herein declare, to take any other position can endanger a person's salvation.

In toxic quarters of the church today, there appear to be a few bishops who are soft on even these non-negotiable precepts, particularly on homosexual "marriage." To be clear, there is no evidence that any American bishop has explicitly endorsed homosexual marriage. But there has been disturbing evidence that homosexuality is not uncommon among Catholic clergy, which has led to manifest toleration of same-sex couples as members of some parishes. As just one example, in January 2019 a parish priest in Minneapolis allowed a same-sex, civilly married, couple – holding "their child" who was conceived by in vitro fertilization and carried to term via surrogacy – to address the congregation about their life style prior to Mass. They even joked that, like their son, Jesus had two dads. The congregation at St. Joan of Arc Catholic Community laughed and applauded. To his credit, the archbishop of St. Paul and Minneapolis publicly objected to the presentation and readily met with the pastor for correction.[7] But that such abominable activities could occur within dioceses at all speaks to the lack of liturgical training of priests and lack of preventive discipline exercised by some of today's bishops.

And there are some rogue Catholic clergymen who have, to some extent, gone their own way on the other non-negotiables as well. But while this subverts the authority of the bishops' office on matters of faith and morals, it does not obviate it. In a pastoral letter, Bishop Thomas Wenski of Orlando set out the bishops' intrinsic jurisdiction:

"Bishops as teachers of the faith have no special competencies in the world of business or politics – and in those worlds we have no regulatory or legal powers. We don't want such power – nor should we. But precisely as teachers of the Catholic faith we do have competence to tell businessmen or politicians or anyone else for that matter what is required to be a Catholic. It is totally within our competence to say that one cannot be complicit in the injustice of denying the right to life of an unborn child or an invalid elder and still consider oneself a good Catholic. It is totally within our competence to urge our Catholic people to participate in the political life of our nation with coherence and honesty. It is within our competence and our responsibilities as pastors to advocate for laws that protect the rights of all human beings from the first moment of conception till natural death."[8]

In 2008, Milwaukee Archbishop Timothy Dolan also made clear the authority of the bishops by defending two of his fellow prelates after they had chastised U.S. Senator Joe Biden and Representative Nancy Pelosi, both Catholics, for misstating Catholic policy on abortion. Dolan affirmed "that bishops are the authentic teachers of the faith. So, when prominent Catholics publicly misrepresent timeless Church doctrine – as Biden and Pelosi regrettably did … a bishop has the duty to clarify. Cardinal Justin Rigali and Bishop William E. Lori were thus hardly acting as politicians, 'telling people how to vote,' but as teachers."[9]

In 2004, Bishop John M. Smith of Trenton also asserted his episcopal authority in taking to task New Jersey Catholic Governor Jim McGreevey, who had routinely opposed the teachings of the church on life issues. "When he refers to himself as a devout Catholic and supports legislation and programs that are contrary to the teaching of the Holy father and the bishops, he is not a devout Catholic," the bishop said. "He cannot compromise what it means to be a Catholic." And then Smith made clear who's in charge of the Catholic Church in the state capital. "I speak, as your bishop, for the devout Catholics of the Diocese of Trenton," he said. "Jim McGreevey does not."[10]

In Kansas, Archbishop Joseph Naumann went further with a public officeholder in 2008, taking the rare episcopal step of ordering Governor Kathleen Sebelius to not present herself for Holy Communion because of her support for abortion. (This power, of course, was accorded to Cardinal Dolan as archbishop of New York City, but he declined to impose the same penalty on Governor Andrew Cuomo for signing legislation in 2019 that permitted abortion at any time during a pregnancy.)

As demonstrated by the more courageous of their number, the bishops are in charge of the teachings and policies of the Catholic Church within their dioceses, even though application and enforcement is excessively uneven. Some bishops stray from solid doctrine, and its public application, especially those who have been appointed in the era of Pope Francis. But the authority of the office, first invested in Christ's apostles, remains immutable.

11

The Bishops Fiddle While Rome's Church Burns

Although the bishops are still in charge, it's easy to understand why so many Catholics do not comply with the Church's mandate that they vote for the candidate (or electable candidate) who least approves of abortion. After all, it's not as if word has gotten around. The teaching of this teaching has been so dreadfully poor as to be virtually nonexistent, probably because some "seamless garment" bishops don't subscribe to the teaching. When bishops do issue pastoral letters relating to this common – and potentially mortal – sin, they do so infrequently. And parish priests are loath to preach this truth, because the immediate blowback from the back pew would apparently be too much for one man to endure. It's easier to preach about being nice to your neighbor and, you know, seeing Jesus in everyone.

But by failing to proclaim this most urgent reality, they have opened the door to an epidemic of heretical behavior within the Church that demands equal and opposite response. Such was the case in September of 2016, when the long-established group with the fraudulent and dissembling name, "Catholics for Choice," evoked the righteous condemnation of a local archbishop after running a full-page newspaper ad asserting that "Public funding for abortion is a Catholic social justice value." Archbishop Gustavo

Garcia-Siller of San Antonio not only performed his duty in publicly correcting the apostate contention, but also suitably mocked the dissidents for their ham-fisted proselytizing. "It is our hope that one day Catholics for Choice will take the time to acquaint themselves with basic Catholic teachings and acknowledge the truth of the Catholic faith," he responded. "For more than 2,000 years, the Church has steadfastly proclaimed that respect for all human life at every stage is foundational to the Catholic faith. ... Direct abortion, or the intentional killing of a human being living in the womb, is always seriously immoral because as persons the right-to-life is the most basic and fundamental right we possess."[1] Bravo, Archbishop Garcia-Siller.

A fellow Texas prelate was spurred to publicly support his cross-state colleague. In a piece titled, "The Absurdity of Catholics for Choice," Bishop Joseph E. Strickland of Tyler, Texas said that the group "attempted to mislead the public by claiming that they are a legitimate voice of the Catholic Church. ... The teaching of the Catholic Church regarding the sanctity of life in the womb is ancient and clear. Certainly not every Catholic embraces this truth as fully as I would hope. But it is truly absurd and diabolical for a group which embraces the pro-choice, pro-death agenda, and denies life to countless human beings simply because they haven't yet been born, to attempt to co-opt the term Catholic."[2] Bravo, Bishop Strickland.

Two years before the San Antonio ad, Catholics for Choice had launched a similar disinformation effort in Colorado that caused the bishops there to also act to publicly reassure the faithful that the Church, of course, remained firmly opposed to abortion. Catholics for Choice, which has long been denounced by the USCCB as a non-Catholic entity and "an arm of the abortion lobby,"[3] has been waging war on the Church since its founding in 1973 (it was founded as Catholics for a Free Choice). The Canadian Conference of Catholic Bishops and the Archdiocese of Mexico have joined in declaring the group as anti-Catholic.

One bishop who set an especially laudable example for other prelates to follow – though few, if any, have – was Bishop Fabian Bruskewitz of Lincoln, Nebraska, who in 1996 issued an interdict forbidding Catholics in his diocese, under penalty of automatic excommunication, from membership in Catholics for Choice and a handful of other heterodox organizations. He drew a line in the sand. Had other bishops over recent decades acted with the same courage – and charity for the souls in their care – the true teaching of the Church on abortion would today not be so staggeringly murky for so many American Catholics. The teaching, in truth, is anything but murky. But widespread reticence by bishops and priests to fervently preach it exposes the faithful to louder, more frequent and fallacious propaganda. "Who am I to believe when I am bombarded by pro-abortion disinformation, but my bishop and priest don't just as frequently respond?"

An unopposed lie gains acceptance by its repetition. Indeed, this was the guiding principle of Nazi propaganda minister Joseph Goebbels, who reputedly said, "If you tell a lie big enough and keep repeating it, people will eventually come to believe it." Catholic clerics have not told the lie, but they have been largely remiss in adequately countering it. It is their sole duty to lead souls to Heaven, and they absolutely do not do that by failing to make the No. 1 moral crisis of our time their highest pastoral priority. They therefore should be constantly teaching and guiding their flocks on the ongoing calamity of abortion. If abortion is truly the moral equivalent of mass murder or the Nazi gas chambers (the magnitude of either actually being less than that of abortion), then how can bishops and priests not be giving it an outsize amount of attention? The least they can do, in, say, half of their sermons, is to make sure that the souls under their care are reminded that there is only one acceptable Catholic teaching about abortion: that it is a mortal sin to abet it, even by failing to vote for the candidate who most opposes it.

But because they don't, bishops and priests allow groups like Catholics for Choice to carry on effectively unchallenged, and the Catholic laity eventually come to believe that the non-Catholic beliefs of such groups are somehow in sufficient harmony with Church doctrine. The ensuing confusion provides a wide field for rebellious oddballs, even within religious orders, like the occasional "social-justice" nun who decides that the bishops don't know what they're talking about and that only she and her adrenalized followers can bring remedy to the oppressively paternalistic Church and this wretched, overpopulated world. Take rogue Franciscan Sister Michelle Nemmers. A couple of years before she died in 2006, her local ordinary was compelled to slap her down for contending that in some circumstances abortion is acceptable. Archbishop Jerome Hanus would have none of it. "When Sister Michelle declares that there are times when it is permissible to have an abortion, she is wrong," the Iowa prelate said in no uncertain terms. "Even when she says, 'It should be the extreme last choice,' she is wrong. It is never morally permissible to procure or to support or to cooperate in an abortion. Sister Michelle seems to want to present herself as a teacher of Catholic thought. As the Catholic archbishop of Dubuque, it is my responsibility to assert that she is not a qualified teacher of Catholic thought. What she has said is erroneous. No Catholic who desires to be in communion with the Catholic Church should accept or follow her words."[4]

Another nun, Sister Simone Campbell, had long crossed the U.S. bishops before one of them took her to task in October 2008. A prominent "social-justice" zealot who the Democratic Party has co-opted to burnish its "Catholic" bona fides, Campbell incurred public castigation from Bishop Alexander Sample, of the Diocese of Marquette, Michigan, after she was quoted by the Catholic News Service (of all places) as saying that presidential candidate Barack Obama was the better anti-abortion candidate (compared to Republican John McCain) because the health-care programs he favored would supposedly cause more poor women to carry their children to term. This, she strained to argue, was in keeping with how the U.S. bishops defined the moral responsibility of Catholics.

"As one of those bishops," Sample responded, "I beg to differ."[5]

Campbell, who earned a law degree after deciding it wasn't enough to simply be a nun and whose smart businesswoman attire makes her unrecognizable as one, is the longtime executive director of NETWORK, a left-wing, social-justice lobbying group. She again defied the bishops by supporting Obamacare, which, though, did earn her a big hug from President Obama when it passed – and a speaking slot at the 2012 Democratic National Convention. No doubt, she's a nun who can hobnob with the bigwigs. But her high-profile, anti-Catholic activism put her squarely in the crosshairs of Pope Benedict XVI when he initiated his investigation of widespread dissent among American nuns. Quite likely, Benedict's attention was especially triggered when Campbell infamously declared, "I don't think it's a good policy to outlaw abortion," advancing the dubious notion that her fondness for preventative social programs is somehow incompatible with criminalizing the murder of children.[6] She apparently believes that we can't have both.

Bishop Sample again took her to task. "What Sister did not say is that as recently as February 2008, Senator Obama was credited by Planned Parenthood of the Chicago area as having a '100 percent pro-choice voting record in both the U.S. Senate and the Illinois Senate.' His commitment to ensuring that abortion rights in this country continue is well documented." And, of course, Obama proved Sample altogether correct after he assumed the presidency, governing as an abortion zealot. Sample also chided CNS and its writer, Dennis Sadowski, for allowing the piece to misrepresent the bishops' teachings, especially reprehensible for a reputedly Catholic news service.[7] Bravo, Bishop (now Archbishop of Portland, Oregon) Sample.

The proliferation of "Catholic" anti-Catholic groups is rampant, and responsibility for that lies at the bishops' feet. Most do not elevate the abortion issue sufficiently. Nor do they coerce their priests to do so. Dissidents will always emerge in human societies, but in the Catholic Church they simply cannot be allowed to sow serious error among the faithful. But while countless Catholic politicians sanctimoniously ventilate their "personally-opposed, but…" mumbo jumbo, the bishops wring their hands and then sit on them, almost never using them to publicly slap the scandalmongers silly. They thereby enable the very scandal they are charged with correcting, i.e., *effectively* correcting, by taking definitive, demonstrable disciplinary action. The mild, sporadic, here-and-there rebuke by a bishop doesn't get the job done. They need to start acting like men. They need to be Jesus in the temple. They need to start using their ultimate teaching tool, that of imposing very public discipline, such as denying Holy Communion and even imposing excommunication, as the *Catechism* instructs that they should do. Indeed, excommunication is prescribed in Canon 1398 for procurement of an abortion, in Canon 1329 for cooperation in an abortion, and in Canon 1364 on the ground of heresy.

Of course, making the case isn't a slam dunk, which in one sense is unfortunate and, in another, fortunate. It's a quandary that confirms canon lawyer Cardinal Raymond Burke's observation that "The first thing I would tell a student of canon law is, canon law is not for the faint of heart."[8] But the remedy is available, nonetheless.

Burke's view is evident in the question of excommunication based on heresy. In January 2019, canon lawyer Edward Condon, for example, wrote that Andrew Cuomo should be excommunicated on the ground of heresy as a "straightforward application" of canon law. Condon argued that this sanction is feasible in light of the New York governor's "consistent and vocal support for" New York's abhorrent legislation that allows for abortion until birth, Cuomo's "unique role in enacting it and his flouting of the clear and public admonitions of two bishops." Critical to Condon's conclusion is his argument that the Church's teaching on abortion is tantamount to a *credenda* teaching, i.e., an article of faith. "Indeed, the Congregation for the Doctrine of the Faith has made it clear that included in those teachings 'to be believed with divine and Catholic faith' is 'the doctrine on the grave immorality of direct and voluntary killing of an innocent human being,'" Condon said.[9]

But canon lawyer Edward N. Peters, no ally of the dissidents, responded otherwise, asserting that most Catholic politicians who defy the Church and its teaching on abortion are not, per se, guilty of heresy and therefore cannot be excommunicated for it. Canon 751 defines heresy as "the obstinate denial or obstinate doubt after reception of baptism of some truth which is to be believed by divine and Catholic faith." In the case of Cuomo, who many Catholics have demanded be excommunicated, Peters argues that the governor's behavior does not, canonically, rise to the level of excommunication and especially not *latae sententiae,* i.e., automatic, excommunication. While scandalous and despicable, Cuomo's words and actions do not appear sufficient "to prove his *doubt or denial of an object of belief,"* Peters contends.[10] In other words, he is saying that Cuomo and his ilk can be dissidents from Church teaching, but still admit that those teachings are valid and correct. Of course, this is what we all, as sinners, do.

Even so, Peters leaves the door open a crack for excommunication of the likes of Cuomo. He is quite sympathetic to the frustration of the many Catholics who pine for the clarity that would be evinced by severely disciplining Catholic public figures who so appallingly misrepresent and arrogantly defy the faith. And he doesn't rule out excommunication altogether. "In my view, the only reason not to excommunicate Cuomo is that no canon law seems to authorize an excommunication against him on the facts as they stand today," Peters wrote. But while dismissing heresy as a ground for such a penalty, Peters readily endorses graduated disciplinary measures for wayward public figures, beginning with, say, denial of communion. "Cuomo could be prosecuted, right now, for violating Canon 1369 (using public shows or speeches to seriously damage good morals), and a 'just penalty' (probably not excommunication at first, but that's just my view) could be imposed," Peters said. "If Cuomo spurned that sanction, it could be augmented, up to and including excommunication. Under canon law as it stands, the best approach for bishops facing these foul acts by Catholic politicos seems to be, besides invoking Canon 915, the preemptive issuance of a particular penal precept enforced by canonical sanctions including, at least by way of augmentation, excommunication. To my knowledge none has been tried in these cases, but nothing else seems to be working."[11]

A program consisting of such escalating penalties may not have been tried, but bishops such as Garcia-Siller, Hanus, Sample, and especially Bruskewitz, who have taken concrete action to correct or penalize scandalous Catholics, are to be commended for having exercised their responsibility with such force and clarity. Of course, the overarching question is why should they have had to do so at all? In an institution that is founded upon the most authentic, enduring and rigid moral precepts – because they were bestowed by God – how can such antithetical voices even arise? Why are they allowed to so freely persist? What gives such dissidents the self-possession to so audaciously crusade against the Church that Christ, Himself, established, to which He gave sole teaching authority, and which He said is to be obeyed? After all, to strive against the Catholic Church is to strive against God.

The answer to these questions is simple: *Catholic churchmen allow it.* And not for any good reason, but for bad, reprehensible, irresponsible reasons. They just fail to perform a major portion of the job which God has entrusted to them.

If we lived in a time of predominantly Christian values, or even when the Church, alone, was generally united in its acceptance of Catholic teaching, there would not be a crisis such as the present one to address. But we don't live in such a time, and so the bishops must summon the courage to lead and to set down markers for the faithful. It is the charitable thing to do. Call it "tough love." After all, the ultimate purpose of any ecclesiastical penalty is to bring wayward sheep back to the faith. It is very much within the bishops' grasp to do it, and they must do it. They are the only ones who can do it. And if they do, they can change world, because the influence of the Catholic Church is massive, pervasive. But if they don't, nothing will change, except that the damage to the Church will worsen.

It is up to each bishop to act, and it is a mere matter of each one's willingness to say yes – as Jesus did and as Mary did, even knowing the dire personal sacrifices that awaited them. Our bishops must find the courage to say yes to the challenge of jointly and universally preaching the truth and accepting all of the hardships that will surely ensue. They were not ordained for an easy life. They were ordained for an heroic life. It is the life that they should fervently desire and live.

12

"I'm Personally Opposed to Abortion, And Any Law Against It"

Virtually all pro-choice Catholic politicians say that they personally oppose abortion but that they don't want to "impose their moral beliefs" on others. Well, why the hell not? Isn't that why they run for office in the first place? They're perfectly willing to impose their moral beliefs in every other way. They impose their moral beliefs in matters of national defense, the federal budget, social services, aid to the poor and all kinds of other societal issues. Therefore, their self-effacing proclamation that they don't want to impose their beliefs is a lie. In fact, it's two lies. Imposing their moral beliefs on society is precisely what they *are* doing, and if they were truly personally opposed to abortion they would be opposing it in their *public* acts as well.

If a Catholic politician says he is personally opposed to abortion "because that's what my church teaches," the follow-up question should be, "Do you agree with the Church's teaching, as expressed in the *Catechism of the Catholic Church*, that every human being has the 'right to life and physical integrity from the moment of conception?'"[1] In other words, is it a human being or not? If his answer is yes, then he is a self-admitted hypocrite who is mortal-sinfully abetting murder. If his answer is no, then he disagrees with his church's teaching and has no reason to be personally opposed to abortion. Therefore, said the 18 bishops of Pennsylvania just prior to the election in 1984, "To be 'personally opposed' to such an evil as the killing of the unborn and yet to support it as a legal option for society is the most unreasonable and hollow claim of all."[2] Fifteen years later, another Pennsylvania bishop, Donald Trautman, of Erie, made the same point in a speech on the anniversary date of *Roe v. Wade:* "Elected officials cannot simultaneously commit themselves to human rights while eliminating the weakest among us. No one can collude in the killing of innocent life."[3]

The "personally opposed, but don't want to impose" line is pure artifice. Most generously, it may be rationalization to the point of self-deception, but it is artifice nonetheless, because it constitutes disobedience to the Catholic Church and therefore disobedience to God, Himself. The politician is contriving an excuse to contravene God's law on a non-negotiable matter. He "is either fooling himself or trying to fool you," wrote Father Stephen F. Torraco, Ph. D, in *A Brief Catechism for Catholic Voters.* "Outside of the rare case in which a hostage is forced against his will to perform evil actions with his captors, a person who carries out an evil action – such as voting for abortion – performs an immoral act, and his statement of personal opposition to the moral evil of abortion is either self-delusion or a lie."[4]

Such a politician, who claims to be Catholic, cannot have it both ways. "This split between the faith which many profess and their daily lives deserves to be counted among the more serious errors of our age," said the fathers of the Vatican II council.[5] "He cannot have a public and a private face," wrote Cheyenne, Wyoming Bishop David Ricken. "He cannot believe as a private citizen that abortion is the massive evil that the Catholic Church teaches that it is and declare it to be 'good' for his country and for his fellow citizens. He also cannot declare himself to be morally neutral in his public persona."[6] Even John Kennedy, Ricken noted, who opened wide the door for what Phoenix Bishop Thomas Olmstead called the "ludicrous" personally-opposed standard,[7] "had the honesty to say that if he ever saw a conflict between his faith and his duties as president, he would resign."[8] Today, Kennedy's political progeny make no such pledge.

So nonplussed are some bishops by the utter irrationality of the "personally opposed" ploy that Bishop Arthur Joseph Seratelli of Peterson, N.J. was driven to ask, "Has logic been banished from our land? How can someone personally hold that abortion is murder and yet say, 'because my constituency wants it, I will support abortion'? How can anyone logically say my religion does not affect my decisions on these issues of life?"[9] They cannot, of course, but, Your Eminence, who demands that politicians be logical? Who demands that they subordinate themselves to the authority of the Catholic Church, to which they claim membership? Indeed, who demands that they even recognize that the absolute authority of the Catholic Church as to its non-negotiable teaching on abortion is binding upon every Catholic? In twenty-first century America, few dare to be so bold. Sufficient public and clerical pressure is absent, and so the politicians have free reign to cunningly propound their apostasy.

"The Second Vatican Council was abundantly clear on this matter," noted Bishop Michael Sheridan, of Colorado Springs, in a 2004 pastoral letter. "Nor, on the contrary, are they any less wide of the mark who think that religion consists in acts of worship alone and in the discharge of certain moral obligations, and who imagine they can plunge themselves into earthly affairs in such a way as to imply that these are altogether divorced from the religious life. *This split between the faith which many profess and their daily lives deserves to be counted among the more serious errors of our age.* Long since, the Prophets of the Old Testament fought vehemently against this scandal and even more so did Jesus Christ Himself in the New Testament threaten it with grave punishments. Therefore, let there be no false opposition between professional and social activities on the one part, and religious life on the other.'"[10]

Archbishop Henry J. Mansell, of Hartford, further bores into the inherent contradiction of the "personally opposed, but" reasoning. "Why are they personally opposed to abortion? If they are opposed because abortion is the taking of an innocent human life, then the stakes are raised considerably. If they really believe that, they have the responsibility to take steps to protect, support and promote that human life."[11] Bishop Thomas Tobin, of Providence, Rhode Island, asked the same question of "personally opposed, but" Catholic presidential candidate Rudy Giuliani in a public RSVP to a campaign fundraiser in 2007. "Hey, Rudy," the bishop responded, "you say that you believe abortion is morally wrong. Why do you say that, Rudy? Why do you believe that abortion is wrong? Is abortion the killing of an innocent child? Is it an offense against human dignity? Is it a cruel and violent act? Does it harm the woman who has the abortion? And if your answer to any of these questions is yes, Rudy, why would you permit people to ... kill an innocent child, offend human dignity, commit a cruel and violent act or do harm to the mother? This is in the name of choice? Huh?"

Tobin blistered Giuliani for his "defection from the Catholic faith on this moral issue." "Rudy's preposterous position is compounded by the fact that he professes to be a Catholic," Tobin wrote. "As Catholics, we are called, indeed required, to be pro-life, to cherish and protect human life as a precious gift of God from the moment of conception until the time of natural death. As a leader, as a public official, Rudy Giuliani has a special obligation in that regard."

Is the weakest person on earth guiltless for failing to help stop a murder or suicide, if he somehow has the power to do so? Of course not. If anyone, individually or as part of a group, has the power to stop a murder, how can they not act to do so? Holding public office does not provide a sanctuary from that moral obligation. Indeed, far from exempting oneself from this responsibility for fear of "imposing their belief on others," an officeholder has an even greater duty to act. "As a leader, as a public official, Rudy Giuliani has a special obligation in that regard," Tobin said. [12]

"Personally opposed, but" is a position that "is as lacking in courage and integrity as it is specious," said Bishop Joseph A. Galante in 2008.[13] The purveyors of the trope are "asking us to believe that his or her position is just as valid as the position of the Catholic Church," added Bishop Lawrence E. Brandt of Greensburg, Pennsylvania, in a 2004 pastoral letter. "This must be viewed as intellectual sleight of hand! This is also demeaning to the intelligence of any informed Catholic." In fact, he said, when such public officials renew their baptismal vows each Easter, they would appear to be – far from recommitting to their Catholic faith – actually "bearing false witness to the Catholic faith." Anyone who takes such a stance thereby becomes "intellectually condescending to every Catholic by making himself or herself the sole judge of what 'Catholic' means."[14]

The bishops' case is especially effective by way of analogy. "It would be inconceivable today that someone would say that they were personally opposed to slavery but thought that slaveholders should have the choice," observed Bishop F. Joseph Gossman of Raleigh, North Carolina. Wasn't that a principal rationale for, and lesson of, the Civil War? Moreover, "few would accept the logic of the argument that driving under the influence of alcohol is wrong but that each driver should be allowed the choice to drive in that condition," Gossman said.[15]

Even the late political commentator Charles Krauthammer, who was a supporter of abortion legalization, employed the slavery parallel to dispose of a Catholic vice presidential candidate's duplicity in 2004. "When Geraldine Ferraro … says she's 'personally opposed' to abortion," Krauthammer wrote, "she means this: 'I wouldn't have one myself and I wouldn't want my children to have one, but I won't go around telling people whether to have one or not.' Unfortunately, Ferraro is confusing belief with practice. If the person says, 'I refuse to own slaves, but I won't go around telling others what to do,' it is correct to say that he does not practice slavery, but can one really say he is opposed to it?"[16]

No, of course, and even if Ferraro had truly believed in the validity of her position, she had no rightful prerogative to invent her own Catholic theology. "Some say that Catholics who conscientiously disagree with the Church's teaching on the sanctity of life may, in good conscience, support legal abortion or abortion funding," wrote Bishop John J. Myers of Peoria, Illinois. "This position misunderstands the nature of conscience and the role of 'authoritative teaching' in Christian life."[17]

To the "personally opposed, but" absurdity list can we not add sexual abuse, drug abuse, prostitution, incest or any other societal ill? Bishop Tobin, who labeled the phrase a "pathetic cop-out,"[18] cited a conspicuous historical parallel. "When I hear someone explaining this position, I think of the sad figure of Pontius Pilate in the Gospels, who personally found no guilt in Jesus, but for fear of the crowd, washed his hands of the whole affair and handed Jesus over to be crucified," Tobin said. "I can just hear Pilate saying, 'You know, I'm personally opposed to crucifixion, but I don't want to impose my belief on others.'"[19]

Like Ferraro, another Catholic vice presidential candidate, Tim Kaine, also likely fell victim to self-delusion (here granting him the benefit of substantial doubt) in 2016, elevating personal rights above the teaching of Almighty God. He averred that he is "a traditional Catholic" and "personally opposed to abortion," consistent with his belief "that matters about reproduction and intimacy and relationships and contraception are in the personal realm. They're moral decisions for individuals to make for themselves." Then, for a fleeting moment, he morphed into a raging libertarian. "And the last thing we need is government intruding into those personal decisions. So I've taken a position which is quite common among Catholics."[20] Well, sadly, the last part contains some truth. But Catholic apologist Trent Horn had a field day exploding Kaine's well-worn casuistry.

"First, saying you're a traditional Catholic because you personally oppose abortion only puts you to the right of a handful of radicals who love abortion and think it should be some kind of sacrament," Horn said. "Most people, including Catholics (as Kaine himself admits) *personally* oppose abortion. What makes someone a traditional Catholic is if he *actively* opposes abortion, so a traditional Catholic politician would seek to outlaw the procedure."[21] Pope St. John Paul II explained this to Kaine and everyone else, in his encyclical, *The Gospel of Life:* ... "The legal toleration of abortion or of euthanasia can in no way claim to be based on respect for the conscience of others, precisely because society has the right and the duty to protect itself against the abuses which can occur in the name of conscience and under the pretext of freedom."[22]

The "personally opposed, but" refuseniks have latched onto a spiritually catastrophic sophism. Whether by self-delusion or sheer malice, the hypocrisy has consequences, warns Bishop Myers: "The fallacy of this kind of 'personal' opposition should be apparent to anyone who considers the reasons for opposing abortion. One who acts to permit the unjust killing of

95

the unborn is ordinarily formally complicit in it. ... No officeholder would support legislation protecting everyone else's life, but permitting his or her own life to be taken at the will of another. Any politician who wills that the unborn be excluded from the protection of the law therefore commits a grave injustice."[23]

When a Catholic ecclesiastic uses the term "grave" he means "mortally sinful." Now, why he doesn't go ahead and say "mortally sinful" is apparently out of a perceived abundance of self-effacement, I suppose, but it is, to be sure, an overabundance; he does the hearer no favor by holding back. Amid today's cacophony, such moderation is overwhelmed and rendered fruitless. For decades, priests, bishops and popes have been telling pro-abortion politicians to correct their ways, but has there been any significant effect? No, because there has been a paucity of ensuing discipline imposed for noncompliance. And so, like recalcitrant children, wayward Catholic politicians gleefully persist in their defiance of Church authority, surely to their own spiritual detriment, and subjecting the faithful to scandal.

Finally, Bishop Tobin contemplates the ultimate disposition of their own souls: "How these intelligent men and women will someday stand before the judgment seat of God and explain why they legitimized the death of countless innocent children in the sin of abortion is beyond me. ('But God, really, I was personally opposed to it, but I just couldn't do anything about it.')"[24] Of course, with due credit to Tobin and the other bishops who have publicly, if sparingly, objected, will many bishops, themselves, have to answer for their wholly ineffective collective response to this disgraceful public scandal? After all, the bishops authored *Living the Gospel of Life: A Challenge to American Catholics*. Should the bishops not be maximally, constantly aggressive in reprimanding errant Catholic politicians? Should they not heed their own words for the salvation of their flocks? And for the salvation of their own souls?

13

Joe & Nancy Wrestle With God Almighty

T he matter for which Cardinal Rigali and Bishop Lori jointly
admonished Senator Biden and Congresswoman Pelosi was the
companion assertions the politicians made to give cover to pro-
abortion Catholic politicians during the 2008 elections. Biden tried to float
the spurious notion that "my church has wrestled with this (moral issue)
for 2,000 years" and that the Church therefore allows a great deal of room
for debate on the subject.[1] Pelosi asserted that the Church's position on
abortion is unsettled, even mendaciously harking to St. Augustine for a
long-since discredited strand of evidence.[2]

Augustine had questioned whether "ensoulment" occurs before 40 days
in the womb, as sensation did not seem to occur until then – according
to the understanding of fifth century science. But Augustine condemned
abortion nonetheless, because even early scientific misunderstanding did
not supersede the known immorality of the act.

"While in canon law these theories led to a distinction in penalties between
very early and later abortions," Rigali and Lori wrote, "the Church's moral
teaching never justified or permitted abortion at any stage of development.

"These mistaken biological theories became obsolete over 150 years ago
when scientists discovered that a new human individual comes into being
from the union of sperm and egg at fertilization. In keeping with this
modern understanding, the Church teaches that from the time of conception

(fertilization), each member of the human species must be given the full respect due to a human person, beginning with respect for the fundamental right to life."[3]

Bishop W. Francis Maloolly of Wilmington, Delaware also saw a duty to weigh in. "Some ancient and medieval theologians did see a difference between early abortions and ones that occurred later in term," he wrote, "because with the limited medical knowledge of the time they did not know then what we scientifically know now: that a fetus is a living human being from conception. Nevertheless, they universally condemned all abortions."[4]

"The Christian tradition from the earliest days reveals a firm antiabortion attitude," wrote Father John Connery, S.J. in his 1977 book, *Abortion: The Development of the Roman Catholic Perspective.* "The condemnation of abortion did not depend on and was not limited in any way by theories regarding the time of fetal animation. Even during the many centuries when Church penal and penitential practice was based on the theory of delayed animation, the condemnation of abortion was never affected by it. Whatever one would want to hold about the time of animation, or when the fetus became a human being in the strict sense of the term, abortion from the time of conception was considered wrong, and the time of animation was never looked on as a moral dividing line between permissible and impermissible abortion."[5]

As self-identified Catholics, Biden and Pelosi surely have had access to the *Catechism of the Catholic Church,* which informs that "Since the first century the Church has affirmed the moral evil of every procured abortion. This teaching has not changed and remains unchangeable. Direct abortion, that is to say, abortion willed either as an end or a means, is gravely contrary to the moral law."[6]

Since the first century, Joe and Nancy. Deep research is not required. It's right there in the Church's instruction manual and plentifully elsewhere.

Still, on NBC's "Meet the Press," Pelosi brazenly rolled out her invention that the Church's teaching that life begins at conception is only "about 50 years old" and therefore "shouldn't have an impact on the woman's right to choose."[7] Apart from her self-delusion or blatant lying, what would the age of a particular doctrine, "about 50 years" in Pelosi's fallacious telling, have to do with whether it's condemnable? Well, nothing. She was just trying to slip one by us. That's what paralogists do. And even if she were correct, an official Church doctrine would be no less valid merely because it was only 50 years old.

Who knows where Pelosi dreamed up her "50 years" fiction? Perhaps she was referring to the early 1960s Second Vatican Council, which pronounced abortion an "abominable crime" and said that "life must be protected from the moment of conception."

But that was merely a restatement of the Church's unbroken precept. "The practice of abortion has been condemned by Christian teaching since the earliest days of the Church," wrote Bishop John Myers. "Over the centuries, the magisterium has never deviated from its clear and firm teaching that the direct killing of innocent human beings, whether born or unborn, is always gravely wrong. ... The Church's condemnation of abortion predates by centuries developments in the sciences of embryology and genetics which place the humanity of the unborn child beyond question."[8]

As to Pelosi's third-rate prevarication – and Biden's first-rate fabrication that "the Church leaves a great deal of room for debate on the subject" – the prelatic reaction was swift and certain. "This is simply incorrect," said Maloolly. "The teaching of the Church is clear and not open to debate. Abortion is a grave sin because it is the wrongful taking of an innocent human life."[9]

Of Pelosi's canard, Bishop Robert Vasa minced no words. "It is highly disingenuous, deceptive and intellectually dishonest to take this ecclesial sound bite from 1,500 years ago and treat it as if it is the last definitive word on the subject," he said. "This is particularly true since Augustine himself" vigorously opposed abortion, "despite the unavailability of accurate scientific information." Vasa all but accused Pelosi, whose spokesman cited her "long proud record of working with the Catholic Church on many issues," of outright deceit, suggesting that that record may "have nothing to do with any true conviction about the goodness, beauty or truth of the teachings of the Catholic Church but rather pure political expediency."[10]

Cardinal Edward Egan, among the many prelates who took Biden and Pelosi to task for spouting apostasy, issued a rebuke that was especially stinging. "Anyone who dares to defend that they (the unborn) may be legitimately killed because another human being 'chooses' to do so or for any other equally ridiculous reason should not be providing leadership in a civilized democracy worthy of the name," he wrote in an open letter.[11]

At about the same time in the pre-election weeks of 2008, Archbishop Chaput laid into prominent Catholic legal scholar Douglas Kmiec for misrepresenting the tenets of the church in Kmiec's endorsement of Barack Obama. Chaput said it is "wrong and often dishonest ... to neutralize the witness of bishops and the pro-life movement by offering a 'Catholic' alternative to the Church's priority on sanctity of life issues."[12] Of course, that's precisely what Biden and Pelosi were doing, too.

What drives Catholic politicians to spread such shameless heresy probably deduces to pride and ambition. But what makes it particularly scandalous is the pure and patently obvious falsity of it. The Catholic Church has always condemned abortion. Always means *since the beginning.* The earliest book of Christian instruction, the *Didache* (or *The Teaching of the Twelve Apostles),* "admonishes: 'Thou shalt not procure an abortion, nor commit infanticide,'" said Baltimore Archbishop Edwin O'Brien in response to Biden and Pelosi. "This solemn teaching has never been in doubt since those earliest days."[13] Bishop Maloolly, too, said that the ancient *Didache* "explicitly condemns abortion without exceptions. It tells us there is a 'way of life' and a 'way of death' and abortion is a part of the way of death. This has been the consistent teaching of the Church ever since." So timeless is this maxim, Maloolly notes, that the Church actually "received the tradition of opposing abortion from Judaism. In the Greco-Roman world, early Christians were identifiable by their rejection of the common practices of abortion and infanticide."[14]

That would mean that Biden's church, far from wrestling with the abortion issue for 2,000 years, has never wrestled with it at all. It was rejected from the beginning, not "about 50 years" ago. It is the Joes and Nancys who are wrestling. Their opponent is the Catholic Church and thereby Almighty

God, Himself.

Pelosi has been the preeminent pro-abortion Catholic on the American scene in recent times, and it would not be unreasonable to surmise that her scandalous example, as with any sin, could be diabolically influenced. As a self-professed "devout Catholic," what other rational answer would there be? "With her support of same-sex marriage, abortion, and so on, it is clear that Pelosi despises all things Catholic," wrote Judie Brown, president and co-founder of the American Life League, a Catholic grassroots organization. "Yet she continues to make public statements that she is a 'devout Catholic.' It makes no sense at all."[15] Catholic writer Deacon Keith Fournier concluded that Pelosi's motives are deliberate, conscious and evil: "She is intentionally and publicly leading others into error."[16]

How so? Brown provides the answer: "When average Catholics see the (Tim) Kaines and Bidens and Pelosis of our nation doing and saying things that defy the Lord and His Church's teachings, those Catholics are either confused or convinced that the very idea of sin itself is debatable." It's music to the ears of Satan: "Sin itself is debatable." That this contemptible falsehood is floated at all is "a tragedy that cannot be ignored," Brown contends. "It is the cause of an avoidable Catholic crisis. With the passing of each day, the disgrace increases and the nation's Catholics sink ever deeper into the abyss of ignorance, at best, deliberate acceptance of evil, at worst. And who is to blame? The silence of those who should never be silent is the answer. This avoidable Catholic crisis waits for heroic Catholic shepherds to step up and crush it. Where are they?" Brown provides the answer to that question as well. Priests and bishops, she says, "have avoided truth for the sake of their personal comfort, their political judgments, or their pride."[17]

Indeed, the bishops have rarely disciplined individual politicians and instead have mostly lobbed general rebukes in their direction. In fact, theologian Thomas D. Williams, Ph. D, noted how "unusual" it was that, during the 2016 campaign, numerous U.S. bishops criticized Kaine's claims of being a faithful Catholic, given his dissent from the Church's essential moral teachings on abortion, same sex marriage, homosexual adoptions and the ordination of women as priests. "All of these positions are clearly contrary to well-established Catholic teachings," wrote Bishop Thomas J. Tobin in a Facebook post.[18] Of Kaine and then Vice President Biden, Archbishop Charles J. Chaput said that these two "prominent Catholics both seem to publicly ignore or invent the content of their Catholic faith as they go along." They are fooling themselves, Chaput added, "and, even more importantly, misleading others."[19]

There have been exceptions. Bishop Blase Cupich of Rapid City in 2002 took on Senator Tom Daschle for encouraging financial contributions to help the National Abortion and Reproductive Rights Action League elect pro-abortion candidates. A statement from Cupich was read at all Sunday masses in his diocese: "It is clear that the senator has ... aligned himself with the strident position of NARAL. ... The senator regrettably has crossed the line, and I cannot let it go unanswered."[20]

Albany, New York Bishop Edward Scharfenberger was just as direct in publicly "reminding" Congressman Paul Tonko, Albany Mayor Kathy Sheehan and state Assemblywoman Patricia Fahy, all Catholics, that their speeches at a rally to continue public funding for Planned Parenthood required correction, "both for the well-being of the individuals' souls and to avoid scandal among the Catholic faithful. ... I am entrusted with the solemn duty of reminding them of the unambiguous teaching of our faith on the matter of abortion, informing them that it is inappropriate and confusing to the faithful to hold yourself out publicly as a Catholic while also promoting abortion, and challenging them to embrace the Gospel of Life and to renounce their public support for Planned Parenthood."[21]

To the cover story that the rally focused only on Planned Parenthood's non-controversial activities, like pregnancy testing, Scharfenberger deftly exploded the ruse. It is like "saying that a man who beats his wife sometimes gives her flowers," the bishop said.[22] The reaction from the targeted politicians was predictable, given the rarity of such ecclesiastical admonishment. Fahy sounded positively hurt. "I was a little taken aback by the comments and the tone," she told the *Albany Times Union*.[23] Well, no kidding. The heretofore never-disciplined would, of course, be taken aback when finally corrected by an authority.

Sheehan's reaction was utterly petulant and employed one of Planned Parenthood's refined tactics: obfuscation. Comparing Planned Parenthood to an abusive husband is "profoundly flawed and deeply offensive," she huffed.[24] She knew well the pro-abortion Catholic politician drill – deliberately mischaracterize the criticism and then feign indignation. How dare you (would she be respectful enough to add, "Your Excellency?") compare this fine organization to a vile, despicable, abominable wife-beater! But her disingenuousness was transparent. Far from comparing a wife-beater to Planned Parenthood, per se, the good bishop was, contrary to Sheehan's misdirection, and self-delusion, comparing a wife-beater to an abortionist, which is what Planned Parenthood is, irrespective of other services it provides. Indeed, Sheehan may not have used the terms "abortion" or "pro-choice" that day, but neither did she, in her Catholic duty, publicly denounce Planned Parenthood for its primary role as an abortion business.

In another case, Congressman Patrick J. Kennedy stated that Bishop Tobin instructed him to not receive Holy Communion because of his pro-abortion stance. Tobin acknowledged that he had written a letter to Kennedy in 2007, though he never intended that the matter to be publicized. "At the same time," Tobin said, "I will absolutely respond publicly and strongly whenever he attacks the Catholic Church, misrepresents the teachings of the Church, or issues inaccurate statements about my pastoral ministry."[25]

In 2008, Archbishop Joseph Naumann of Kansas City in Kansas forbade pro-abortion Governor Kathleen Sebelius from receiving Holy Communion. That prohibition followed her to Washington, D.C. when she became Barack Obama's secretary of health and human services. Then-Archbishop Raymond Burke, prefect of the Apostolic Signatura, extended that proscription to the entire United States, saying, "After pastoral admonition, she obstinately persists in serious sin."[26]

And on October 27, 2019, presidential candidate Biden was denied Holy Communion by a Florence, South Carolina priest, Father Robert Morey, who was following the Charleston Diocese's policy to withhold the Eucharist from politicians who support legal protection for abortion.[27]

But such targeted opprobrium is rare. Instead, bishops usually just issue a broad statement that paraphrases the Catechism. It typically goes like the one, issued in 2004, that governs the Charleston Diocese: "Catholics in political life have the responsibility to exemplify in their public service (the) teaching of the Church (on abortion), and to work for the protection of all innocent life," wrote Archbishop John F. Donoghue of Atlanta, Bishop Peter J. Jugis of Charlotte, North Carolina, and Bishop Robert J. Baker of Charleston. "There can be no contradiction between the values bestowed by Baptism and the Catholic Faith, and the public expression of those values. Catholic public officials who consistently support abortion on demand are cooperating with evil in a public manner. By supporting pro-abortion legislation they participate in manifest grave sin, a condition which excludes them from admission to Holy Communion as long as they persist in the pro-abortion stance."[28]

Well and good, but with all due respect, your excellencies, yada yada yada. Because you and your brother bishops rarely name names, the politicians don't reform themselves, and the people have stopped listening. Your words hardly rise to the level of empty threats.

Some scattered disciplinary actions, though, have been taken by a very few prelates. Pelosi's bishop, for example, publicly corrected her on multiple occasions, Fournier reports, "but really, that is so far from being good enough that it hardly matters."

And the USCCB, as a body, has long weighed in, but only with predictably tepid and overarching pastoral statements:

• "We urge those Catholic officials who choose to depart from Church teaching on the inviolability of human life in their public life to consider the consequences for their own spiritual well being, as well as the scandal they risk by leading others into serious sin. We call on them to reflect the grave contradiction of assuming public roles and presenting themselves as credible Catholics when their actions on fundamental issues of human life are not in agreement with Church teaching. No public official, especially one claiming to be a faithful and serious Catholic, can responsibly advocate for or actively support direct attacks on innocent human life ... No appeal to policy, procedure, majority will or pluralism ever excuses a public official from defending life to the greatest extent possible."[29]

• "No political leader can evade accountability for his or her exercise of power. Those who justify their inaction on the grounds that abortion is the law of the land need to recognize that there is a higher law, the law of God. No human law can validly contradict the commandment: 'Thou shalt not kill.'"[30]

• "Those who formulate law therefore have an obligation in conscience to work toward correcting morally defective laws, lest they be guilty of cooperating in evil and in sinning against the common good."[31]

• "Let no Catholic office-holder hide behind a record of doing good for the poor and marginalized in society, but then vote in favor of abortion, partial birth abortion, or euthanasia. The failure to protect and defend life in its most vulnerable stages renders suspect any claims to the 'rightness of position' in helping the poor."[32]

Such mere restatements of Church teaching, instead of direct reprimand of named politicians, have also been the approach of every modern pope. Most notable is the 1995 encyclical of Pope St. John Paul II, *The Gospel of Life*, which, observed Bishop Lawrence E. Brandt of Greensburg, Pennsylvania, "reaffirmed the constant teaching of the Church and reiterated that those who are directly involved in lawmaking bodies have a grave and clear obligation to oppose any law that attacks human life. For these individuals, it is impossible to promote such a law or to vote for it."[33] Brandt noted that the Vatican Congregation for the Doctrine of the Faith further instructed "that voting for legislation that permits or enables abortion is gravely wrong. It furthermore reaffirms that any attack on human life, which is based on abortion (e.g. fetal stem cell research), is likewise gravely wrong. If abortion is an intrinsically grave evil action, then legislative support is then cooperation in a grave moral evil."[34]

Pope Benedict XVI never equivocated in setting out Church teaching on abortion, as exemplified by his approbation of Mexican bishops in 2007 for admonishing politicians to not support abortion.[35]

Even the mercurial and regularly confusing Pope Francis has had his moments of orthodox teaching about abortion politicians, although his denigration of the Church, just six months into his papacy, for becoming "obsessed" with abortion, eclipsed a contrary and forthright message he had sent just two weeks into his papacy. (Of course, this is an example of why he is so confusing.) In a letter to the bishops of Argentina, he said that pro-abortion politicians should not be eligible for Communion, pursuant to the *Aparecida Document,* which was issued by the Fifth Conference of the Bishops of Latin America and the Caribbean in 2007. "These are the guidelines we need for this time in history," Francis wrote.[36] It was a momentary cause for rejoicing, and relief, for anti-abortion Catholic groups, particularly because as it came on the heels of the papacy of doctrinal stalwart Benedict XVI.

On the most important moral issue for Catholics, Francis would, it seemed at that time, carry on the legacy of his predecessor. "We are renewed in our joy over the election of Pope Francis," said Judie Brown, of the American Life League, in a letter to all U.S. Catholic bishops. "One of the reasons for our happiness is the Holy Father's reiteration of Catholic teaching as enunciated in Canon 915."[37] That canon provides that those "who have been excommunicated or interdicted after the imposition or declaration of the penalty and others obstinately persevering in manifest grave sin are not to be admitted to holy communion."[38] Brown reminded the bishops that "the United States has her share of Catholics in public life who persist in their support of abortion while, at the same time, receiving Christ in the sacrament of Holy Eucharist. We write to ask you, in view of this recent news report, to act on Pope Francis' call and deny the sacrament of Christ's real presence – body, blood, soul, and divinity – to every pro-abortion Catholic in public life who has not repented of his support for the heinous crime of abortion."[39]

But, of course, Francis subsequently lessened his anti-abortion fervor, and hopes that he would activate the bishops faded away. And much of the Catholic faithful still asks, "Where are they?"

Most bishops would bemusedly respond, "We've been right here all along." But where? Ensconced within the walls of the chanceries?

That's apparently where seven of them were when a substantive anti-abortion bill, one outlawing partial-birth abortion, finally was debated and finally passed by both houses of Congress in 1996, only to be vetoed by Democrat Bill Clinton. The House overrode that veto, and with just seven more votes the Senate would have done the same, allowing the measure to become law. But a group of eight Catholic senators foiled the override effort. Daschle of South Dakota, Dodd of Connecticut, Harkin of Iowa, Mikulski of Maryland, Moseley-Braun of Illinois, Murray of Washington, and Kennedy and Kerry of Massachusetts – all Catholics and all Democrats – voted to sustain Clinton's veto.[40] Where were their bishops? Why were they not personally and publicly vigorously upbraiding those Catholic senators? Do bishops not understand that their own salvation is also at risk when they insufficiently chastise a public official who is in their pastoral care?

It would necessitate Republicans taking control of the White House and both houses of Congress to pass the ban, even on such an obviously gruesome and inhumane method of abortion. Finally, in 2003, with GOP majorities in both houses, President George W. Bush signed into law a ban on partial-birth abortion.[41]

That it takes such a fortuitous aligning of the stars for a significant anti-abortion bill to become law has been the singular overriding frustration for anti-abortion activists, particularly those who are rank-and-file Catholics. Again they ask, "Where are the bishops? If only the Church would assert its moral authority."

But in recent decades the American bishops have essentially been absent. Oh, they've periodically decried the unfaithfulness of dissident Catholic politicians in general terms, but that has done nothing to sway the politicians' voting records. It's gone on so long that the bishops surely believe that any further effort to *charitably* correct these wandering sheep will continue to be ineffective. But despite this failure, most bishops are loathe to take the next step. They refuse to use their ultimate hammer. And that leads to suspicion.

Why have the bishops not imposed ecclesiastical penalties on Catholic public officials who flout Church teaching on abortion? It's not as if that teaching is subject to prudential judgment, one on which good Catholics can legitimately disagree. And it's not as if the indirect, general pronouncement approach, as opposed to a disciplinary, punitive approach, hasn't been given a chance. It's been spectacularly failing for a half century. Within a year of the 1973 *Roe v. Wade* decision, the Vatican was moved to clarify Church teaching:

"It must in any case be clearly understood that whatever may be laid down by civil law in this matter, man can never obey a law which is in itself immoral, and such is the case of a law which would admit in principle the liceity of abortion. Nor can he take part in a propaganda campaign in favor of such a law, or vote for it."[42]

American Catholics quoted the declaration to pro-abortion Catholic politicians, but they were unpersuaded. In 1995, Pope John Paul II resurrected the words of the 1974 document, proclaiming that, as to any law permitting abortion, it is "never licit to obey it, or to take part in a propaganda campaign in favor of such a law or to vote for it."[43] But American Catholic officeholders remained unmoved. The pontiff's words were dismissed by the politicians as hackneyed platitudes from a far-off land. "In America," they surely told themselves, "we have always been refugees from European authority, and doubly so as enlightened liberal Catholics – and we wouldn't want to be accused of taking orders from the pope. JFK said so!"

The bishops continued their broad, general denouncements of such behavior, but would rarely go any further. Philip Lawler notes the confusion of anti-abortion Catholics about their bishops over the years: "In frustration, pro-life Catholics questioned why their bishops did not take action to discipline the wayward politicians. The Code of Canon Law stipulates that anyone actively involved in an abortion – the woman who procures it, the doctor who performs it, the man who pays for it – is subject to the penalty of excommunication. ... If this penalty is invoked for involvement in one abortion, conservative Catholics wondered aloud, how could it not apply to those lawmakers who, by their votes, allowed tens of thousands of abortions?"[44]

Implicitly noting the failure of the American bishops to discipline Catholic politicians who were giving such public scandal (one might ask if the bishops were doing the same by their inaction), the fiercely anti-abortion Knights of

Columbus made a stab at reigning in their pro-choice members who held political office. But this time it was Rome that directly threw a wrench in the works. The Knights' request to exclude such politicians from membership was shut down by the Vatican Secretary of State in stunning fashion: "Don't you dare make a move without the approval of Church authorities," came the crystal-clear and exceedingly perplexing retort from Cardinal Agostino Casaroli.[45]

Is it therefore any wonder that American Catholics feel perfectly free to vote as they wish? For decades, "Church authorities" have seemed to be talking out of both sides of their mouths. Broad condemnations of pro-abortion politicians have been routinely issued, only to be followed by, at most, prelatic neglect. Indeed, far from mere nonintervention, bishops have seemed to deliberately avoid calling out perpetrators of scandal. For example, they permit dissident Catholic officeholders to receive Holy Communion, as if they were perfectly in good standing. The bishops have thus largely become regarded as not only derelict, but perhaps even cowardly – or worse yet, complicit. "The only logical conclusion by someone standing aloof from the argument," Lawler writes, "was that the bishops had accepted the Hyannisport argument: that under some circumstances, a vote for abortion – a vote in flagrant defiance of Church teaching – could be justified."[46]

Well, why not? After all, your excellencies, it's only a matter of life and death.

Amidst this now entrenched, permissive atmosphere in the Church marched the Obama Administration in 2008, with no Catholic solidarity blocking its barefaced plan to "fundamentally transform America." Included in the transformation, of course, was the brazen liberalization of the nation's abortion laws, at both the federal and state levels. The Democratic Party dutifully followed Obama's lead, officially embracing a right to abortion as an official plank and imposing a candidate purity test hard upon.

It has gone on long enough. Bishops, especially amid the raging crises within the Church, are derelict to merely sit back and issue the occasional pastoral letter on right and wrong. They must now leave their thrones and lead the charge on the battlefield.

The truly estimable David L. Ricken, Bishop of Green Bay, who has been among the least tentative in proclaiming Church teaching on abortion, inadvertently showcased the problem in a 2008 article. "Some politicians holding political office," he wrote, "have tried to say that the Catholic Church has not spoken clearly about abortion or against abortion and its moral gravity. And yet, the Catholic Church's official teaching could not have been clearer about this for centuries."[47] Yes, your excellency, the teaching has been clear, but the Church has quite obviously not spoken enough about it. There should be no heretical Catholic politicians, but they are rampant. And their scandal is allowed to mislead the faithful because they go undisciplined. Even the most preeminent of the Church's teachings must be repeated incessantly, especially the most important teachings of God. Sure, we read the bishops' periodic public statements, such as those that emerge every January in conjunction with the *Roe v. Wade* anniversary, but there has been no concerted, demonstrable campaign to consistently teach the faithful that they cannot, with any nuance, lay claim to the Catholic faith if they are not unreservedly against abortion and willing to always actively oppose it.

In the case of a public official, due to innate public scandal, the ecclesial action should follow that of Archbishop Naumann – private counseling and then very public and real discipline. The faithful in Kansas were taught a great and lasting lesson when the archbishop disciplined the state's governor: A Catholic cannot be allowed to receive Holy Communion in defiance of Church law, because to mock the Catholic Church is to mock God. (This is the same heroic archbishop who kicked the Girl Scouts out of archdiocesan parishes because of its ties to Planned Parenthood.[48]) It is the duty of bishops, as successors of the apostles, to protect and enforce the law of God. It is this sort of public action that truly teaches the faith, as opposed to mere essays that are read once during the Sunday sermon and forgotten before the Consecration.

As prominent writer and speaker Father Roger J. Landry observes, the Church's decades-long strategy of simply sweet-talking pro-choice Catholic politicians has been a failure. "Let us take an honest look at the numbers," Landry wrote. "When we survey the long list of pro-choice Catholic politicians from both parties ... is it possible to say that the strategy has worked with any of them? Over the last three and a half decades, can we point to even one success story?

"Another way to assess the results of the education-alone strategy is to measure the direction that pro-choice Catholic politicians have moved over the years. Even if they haven't experienced a total conversion, have they moved closer toward limiting abortions or toward making abortions easier to access? The facts show that the vast majority of personally opposed, publicly pro-choice Catholic legislators have become far less personally opposed and far more publicly in favor over the duration of the strategy.

"In the initial years after *Roe versus Wade*, publicly pro-choice Catholic legislators generally whispered their support for abortion. They displayed a palpable sense of shame, letting their abortion position out just enough so that it wouldn't cost them the votes of abortion supporters. That discomfort began to dissipate after Governor Mario Cuomo's 1984 pro-choice defense at Notre Dame. We've now come to a situation when pro-choice Catholic legislators vigorously curry the favor of Planned Parenthood, NARAL Pro-Choice America and Emily's List; scores of Catholics in Congress have the chutzpah to co-sponsor the Freedom of Choice Act, which would eliminate almost every abortion restriction ever passed at the federal or state level; and 16 out of 25 Catholic Senators vote against conscience protections to prevent their fellow Catholics in the medical field from being forced to participate in abortions and sterilizations."[49]

Father Landry calls for a radically new approach, one that is based on the instruction of Jesus, Himself. It is a process that would get the message across to the politicians and the Catholic constituencies that, however wrongly, are misled by their example. It is a measured approach, but one that has a final step that would be conclusive and thereby effective: Excommunication.

"Jesus spoke of a different way in the Gospel (Mt 18:15-18)," Landry said. "It involves not merely general educational statements that we hope offenders will apply to themselves in conscience, but the type of one-on-

one instruction traditionally called fraternal correction. If that fails, and fails repeatedly, Jesus enjoined us to regard the offender as someone who no longer belongs to the community, who is no longer a member in good standing. This may seem harsh, but we should remember that Jesus always seeks nothing but the best for his Church and for individual sinners, even obstinate sinners. Implied in Jesus' strategy is that education involves not just information, but formation, and that you can't form disciples without discipline. This is a lesson that, after four decades of the undeniable failure of another approach, we need to consider anew."[50]

This is now a full-blown crisis that calls for a sweeping, definitive and ongoing response. Occasional pastoral letters that are read one time and then ignored until the next one irregularly shows up have proven to be ineffective. The problem with most of today's "shepherds" is that they are very happy to lead their flocks. That's easy – just fleetingly remind everyone, once in a while, to pray and go to Mass. But the shepherds are loath to *rescue* the lost sheep. That's a hard task, and, astonishingly, most of them don't seem motivated or courageous enough to do it, probably because it exposes them to certain ridicule from enemies of the faith. But to actually do so would save souls by testifying to the Christian truth, the very purpose of the Catholic Church. And amid the ridicule, it would earn each bishop the allegiance – all for God – of faithful Catholics who would delightedly and gratefully respond to his invitation to "Rejoice with me, I have found my sheep that was lost." That is how a shepherd truly leads.

14

Catholic Doctrine According to Alfred

C atholics for Choice is just one of numerous dissident cabals that make it their business to travesty the teachings of the Church. In the summer of 2016 there emerged an apostate Catholic voter's guide from another dissimulating group, "Catholics in Alliance for the Common Good" (CACG), backed by billionaire-leftist-subversive George Soros.

"Just what we need," read a June 2016 blog post at Connecticut Catholic Corner, "another progressive voter guide for liberals to push their anti-Catholic agendas on stupid Catholics voting in this year's Presidential election."[1]

The heretical handbook was ever so cannily titled, "A Revolution in Tenderness: A 2016 Election Pope Francis Voter Guide." Not so remarkably, it enjoyed no imprimatur of Pope Francis at all, nor even his remote approbation, even though the phrase, "revolution in tenderness," was originated by Francis. But that sort of nicety doesn't matter to liberals. Rectitude is not their modus operandi. However, deception very much is, and the false appropriation of St. Peter's office is justified by them as a means to an end (which, of course, the Church condemns in its maxim that it is never acceptable to do wrong to achieve a perceived greater good). But again, the immorality of the means doesn't matter to the liberal institution. The end is the all. Liberalism, itself, not fealty to the Holy Catholic Church, is the god of liberals.

Other dissident Catholic groups helped to produce the so-called "Pope Francis Voter Guide," including: Pax Christi International, which has been accused of adopting the Palestinian narrative and working to delegitimize Israel; the Leadership Conference of Women Religious, which under Pope Benedict XVI was investigated by the Vatican for opposing core Catholic beliefs; and the Faith in Public Life Catholic Program, another Soros-subsidized organization that was founded with help from a pro-choice group, the Center for American Progress.

It wasn't the first time that CACG had published such a specious guide. The 2016 edition, "like the 2012 guide before it, stacks the deck in favor of pro-choice politicians who promise to protect the poor, the environment, and LGBT rights – but not the rights of the unborn or of the family," noted Anne Hendershott, Ph.D, in *Catholic World Report* shortly after the guide came out.[2] The 2012 edition, of course, obviously wasn't a "Pope Francis" guide (he was still a cardinal) – it was called a "Catholic" guide. The name change in 2016 was surely intended to co-opt the office of the pope and to stave off any criticism from Church fathers for improper use of the word "Catholic." The authors were willing to trade that criticism for separate flak for their unauthorized use of Pope Francis's name. (One doubts, though, given the content, that any objection from Francis would have been strenuous. This was, after all, truly *his* kind of voter's guide.) What emerged in full force in the 2016 version, Hendershott noted, was the certifiably left-wing agenda on such issues as gun control, climate change and the Black Lives Matter movement. There was little emphasis on abortion, religious liberty or the more critical non-negotiable issues upon which Catholics should actually be basing their votes, i.e., embryonic stem-cell research, euthanasia, homosexual marriage, human cloning and religious freedom.

Moreover, the guide coaches the reader with a series of loaded questions to ask of candidates: What is each candidate's proposal on "alternatives to abortion and euthanasia?" Not whether the candidate actually opposes abortion and euthanasia. How will each candidate ensure that all Americans have access to health care? Not whether the existing and oppressive, pro-choice "Obamacare" system opposes authentic Catholic doctrine.[3]

And why are the following two questions asked at all when they concern matters of prudential judgment, not core Catholic teaching? After all, if prudential judgment issues are left to each Catholic's own reckoning, why are these groups trying to "guide" us to vote only as they want us to vote? The reason, of course, is that this "Pope Francis" guide is not a "Catholic" guide at all. It's secular, leftist propaganda masquerading as a definitive volume of Catholic precepts.

– The guide absurdly veers off the rails in posing the question, *"What truth do we discover in Ferguson when we encounter the suffering there and our own blind spots are removed?"*[4] The supercilious authors have discovered a "truth" in the Ferguson matter, and now you have to identify it. There's no allowing that you may have found a different truth in the 2015 racial incident. If you did, then you're not seeing it as Pope Francis (purportedly) would, and therefore you're not seeing it as a good Catholic should. So why ask the question at all? Why not just say, "This is the conclusion you must draw in order to be a good Catholic?" The Pope Francis guide allows for only one truth, even though this is strictly a matter of prudential judgment, not intrinsic Catholic teaching. But the guide's truth is put forth as the only truth, because the pope's name is on the cover. And oh, by the way, were you aware that you have a "blind spot?"

– Here's another strictly prudential matter that the guide sets up as a Catholic litmus test: *What is the candidate's policy for addressing climate change?*[5] Not the threshold question of whether climate change actually exists, as many credible scientists, and any Catholic is allowed to, deny. But in the guide the existence of climate change is presented as an indisputable premise, not the open question that it is. Even if it weren't, the issue of climate change is not a core Catholic matter, but only a secondary one, at most, irrespective of the Earth-centric proclivity of the doctrinally enigmatic Pope Francis.

When the guide touches on religious liberty it swiftly diverts from the central issue, instead bemoaning that "the issue of religious liberty has often morphed into a partisan wedge."[6] Translation: This religious liberty thing is really getting in the way of our left-wing agenda on stuff like homosexual marriage, contraception and abortion. Is the Church's real concern about religious liberty that is that it is "a partisan wedge?" That's like saying that the real problem with genocide is that the victims and perpetrators conceptually disagree. The guide outrageously turns a blind eye to the genuine crisis: that religious liberty is under unprecedented attack in America by left-wing activists, legislators and judges. And it thereby deliberately goes further astray, farcically denigrating faithful Catholic groups like the Little Sisters of the Poor, who were constrained to sue over Obamacare's mandate that they provide contraception to employees in order to protect their overriding religious freedom rights. The guide promotes the altogether secular ethic that "no Catholic institution – or any institution – should use a false notion (a false notion?) of religious liberty to discriminate against anyone they employ or serve, particularly the LGBTQ community."[7]

And there it is. If there were any doubt about the true purpose of this "Catholic" guide, it is answered in that transparently anti-religious-freedom and anti-Catholic scolding. Make no mistake: The authors are contending, under the guise of Church doctrine, that a Catholic voter must not "discriminate" against the "LGBTQ community," which is to say explicitly – because, after all, this is a voter guide – that a Catholic should actually support *particularly* the LGBTQ political agenda. To not practice one's faith by *opposing* these damnable philosophies is to, ipso facto *support* them. The LBGTQ political agenda includes a multitude of monstrous sins, homosexual "marriage" being at the forefront. The guide thus concludes that the Church's teaching on the aberrant sexual fetishes of the "LGBTQ community" are in error. At minimum this is heresy, and because it renounces Church doctrine it is arrant apostasy.

How do these dissidents reconcile their rejection of true Catholic doctrine with their pledge of fidelity to it when they recite the Nicene Creed at Mass? Well, when they declare aloud that they "believe in one, holy, Catholic and apostolic Church" they are simply lying. They don't believe in it at all. They are avowed enemies of the Magisterium, and so enemies of the Catholic Church, itself, and thereby enemies of God.

Far from dogmatically Catholic, the "Pope Francis Voter Guide" directs members of the Holy Catholic Church to endorse the very opposite of dogma, i.e., a catalog of demonic life styles. Its twisted message is that it would actually be sinful to refuse to participate in such perversions by, for example, not baking the cake, not providing the flowers or not renting out the reception space for a homosexual "wedding." Instead of calling such participation what it truly would be – a sin of cooperating in evil – "The Pope Francis Voter Guide" would deem refusal a "sin of discrimination."

And surely, would it not then follow that it is sinful for a priest to refuse to perform the wedding? Or to refuse to say Mass at the ceremony? The guide brazenly rejects authentic Church teaching while stealthily supplanting it with another. The guide plainly avers that valid Church teaching constitutes a "false notion of religious liberty." Such a statement directly controverts the fundamental teaching of the Church and contemporary pronouncements by the bishops. And it so flouts longstanding American societal norms as to be insurgent at least and nonsensical at worst. So sacrosanct was the principle of religious liberty in civil society that our nation's founders codified it in the (very) first amendment to the United States Constitution. This counterfeit "Pope Francis Voter Guide" is not based on Catholic teaching at all. In truth, it is a transparently *anti-religion* political document produced by committed *adversaries* of religious liberty.

But it sure fooled a lot of priests, deacons and nuns. Or did it? Perhaps this leftist Catholic propaganda is precisely what many of them wholeheartedly believe:

– Deacon Terry Barber of Sacred Heart Catholic Church in Lacey, Washington, couldn't contain his enthusiasm. The "wonderfully titled" guide, he wrote in the parish bulletin, "strikes me as being so important. ... Tenderness and gentleness are qualities we'd like to feel from our candidates."[8] Never mind that they may "tenderly" and "gently" favor abortion or even infanticide.

– The Sisters of the Precious Blood directed its readers to the guide in its June 2016 online newsletter, the table of contents of which also included articles on "Peace, Justice, Care of Creation," "Labor Trafficking," "Racism," though nothing about abortion, euthanasia, homosexual "marriage," human cloning, embryonic stem-cell research or religious freedom. Oh, but their newsletter also contained a lovely article on gardening. And another one on the fun of hunting morel mushrooms. And an appeal to save paper, ink and the environment by not printing the newsletter on your home computer.[9]

– The Sisters of St. Francis of Philadelphia were positively giddy in promoting the Pope Francis guide in their newsletter. But they offered, reluctantly, a formality: "Our bishops, in *Faithful Citizenship,* encourage us to consider all issues."[10] There, got the officialdom out of the way – the bishops made us say that. Now we can get to the other voting guide that we really like! But the sisters' nod to the bishops' document is incomplete and misleading. The Bishops' *Faithful Citizenship* document absolutely does not "encourage us to consider all issues" *equally.* Instead, it clearly prioritizes the issues that Catholics must consider in the voting booth. "A Catholic cannot vote for a candidate who favors a policy promoting an intrinsically evil act, such as abortion, euthanasia, assisted suicide, deliberately subjecting workers or the poor to subhuman living conditions, redefining marriage in ways that violate its essential meaning, or racist behavior, if the voter's intent is to support that position. In such cases, a Catholic would be guilty of formal cooperation in grave evil."

Is everybody listening? YOU CAN'T VOTE FOR SUCH A CANDIDATE. To review: Those specific "intrinsically evil" matters cited by the bishops are abortion, euthanasia, assisted suicide, abuse of workers and the poor, homosexual marriage and racism. (Others they didn't cite in that document are religious liberty, human cloning and embryonic stem-cell research.) "At the same time," the bishops continue, "a voter should not use a candidate's opposition to an intrinsic evil to justify indifference or inattentiveness to other important moral issues involving human life and dignity."

Fair enough, but those "other important issues" are largely matters of prudential judgment, about which Catholics can indeed vary in their individual, virtuous and remedial approaches. But still, those issues remain inferior to the bishops' list of "intrinsically evil" – or non-negotiable – stances upon which Catholics must first base their vote. The Sisters of St.

Francis, who, by the way, add to the fraud by slipping in the phrase, "LGBTQ lives matter here" in their newsletter, deliberately neglect to delineate this very clear stratification of issues by the bishops.

These sisters typify the bogus "seamless garment" mindset by brazenly flouting *Faithful Citizenship's* explicit instruction that "all issues do not carry the same moral weight and ... the moral obligation to oppose policies promoting intrinsically evil acts has a special claim on our consciences and our actions."[11] So paramount is this maxim by the bishops that they repeat it, consciously preempting the dissidents' reflexive claim that the bishops are commanding Catholics to be single-issue, or five-issue, or six-issue voters. "As Catholics we are not single-issue voters," they write. "A candidate's position on a single issue is not sufficient to guarantee a voter's support. *Yet if a candidate's position on a single issue promotes an intrinsically evil act, such as legal abortion, redefining marriage in a way that denies its essential meaning, or racist behavior, a voter may legitimately disqualify a candidate from receiving support.*"[12] (Emphasis added.)

(Longtime Catholic political consultant Deal Hudson proffers a semantic approach to this question of single-issue voting, as set out in the last chapter of this book.)

To be extraordinarily generous, entities and individuals like the Sisters of St. Francis of Philadelphia, could simply be getting caught up in any given ventilation from the Holy See, even when it doesn't actually issue from the Holy See, as in the case of the "Pope Francis" guide. But more cynically, and far more likely, most of these people are all too eager to cherry-pick their voting philosophies and eagerly embrace "our kind of voting guide," defective as it is. The kind that assures that "LGBTQ lives matter here," which constitutes unequivocal approbation for that mortally-sinful life style. The question must be asked: Are these sisters trying to help people get to Heaven or assist them on the road to hell?

– On October 2, 2016, St. John's Parish at Creighton University published a list of "Faithful Citizenship Opportunities," a title that appeared to draw on the bishops' official document but actually undermined it by including only liberal priorities. The list of opportunities included "Catholic

Social Teaching and Local Issues," "Immigration: Fear, Fiction and Fact," "Racism," "Climate Change" and "The Death Penalty."[13] No mention of any opportunity, for example, to pray at the local abortuary, an opportunity that is especially efficacious when done with others. But there *was* an invitation to pick up a copy of the "Pope Francis Voter Guide" on Sunday morning. But would you expect a Jesuit college to put the Church's intrinsically-evil priorities ahead of secondary social-justice issues?

– Also on October 2, 2016, the pastor of Atlanta's St. Paul of the Cross Catholic Church highlighted the upcoming election by citing in the Sunday bulletin "two very practical guides." Father Jerome McKenna breezily took note of the bishops' official "Faithful Citizenship" guide, but then gushed about the quite unofficial Pope Francis guide and some of the issues covered, none of which met "Faithful Citizenship's" higher standard of "intrinsically evil" issues.[14] Well, McKenna does mention that the Pope Francis guide discusses religious freedom. But, as indicated above, on that topic the Francis guide is quick to finger-wag that no "false notion" of religious liberty should be used to elevate the authentic doctrine of the Catholic Church, particularly in the realm of condemnable sexual behavior. Apart from that vast arena of mortal sin, the Francis guide assures, we are called to freely testify to God's other, not-so-old-fashioned, admonitions.

The lengths to which the Left will go to silence advocates of Catholic orthodoxy know no bounds. In 2008, a George Soros-funded group called "Catholics United" (a title to which I would add, "Against the Doctrinal Teachings of the Holy Catholic Church") prodded the Internal Revenue Service to investigate William Donohue, president of the Catholic League for Religious and Civil Rights, for his published opposition to their apostate agenda. Donohue, bulldog that he is, did not cower, and the IRS ultimately found no reason to remove the Catholic League's tax-exempt status. But that the IRS's Exempt Organizations Division, which was then headed by notorious liberal operative Lois Lerner, was so willing to be co-opted for obvious political purposes was service enough for the purposes of Catholics United. The effects of harassment, in the guise of such police authority, are enormously punitive – emotionally, administratively and financially. The cost to Catholics United? A postage stamp. Accurately identifying it as an "obscene political game," Donohue said the practice "extends beyond the IRS. It extends to left-wing activists, funded by left-wing tycoons, all for the purpose of silencing conservatives."

Of course, these groups like Catholics United that fraudulently appropriate "Catholic" in their names claim non-partisanship while working feverishly to advance their leftist, heterodox policies. "Although the organization claims that its goal is to 'move beyond partisan and ideological divisions,'" said Anne Hendershott in her 2016 piece, "the leadership of CACG reflects the leadership of the Democratic Party and its allies in organized labor."[15] She noted that the board chairman of CACG at that time was Alfred Rotondaro, a senior fellow at the left-leaning Center for American Progress, who had written articles critical of the Church and its teachings. Hendershott noted that Rotandaro, who died in 2017, lambasted the bishops' opposition to Obamacare "because of what he interprets as the bishops' misplaced concerns about public funding for abortion."

Just like that, the 2000-year-old Catholic Church, the only church established by Jesus Christ, Himself, the one to which He gave sole teaching authority, is flippantly taken to task by, you know, Alfred. If ever there was a backbench theologian, Rotandaro filled the role. He further declared – again, as the chairman of this "Catholic" organization – that the Church has no right to bar women from ordination. "I have never seen any rational reason why a woman could not be a priest."[16] And to top off his rant, this faux Catholic leader unblushingly announced to the world that "Gay sex comes from God."[17]

Catholic doctrine according to Alfred.

That's how CACG and its ilk define moving "beyond partisan and ideological divisions." In other words, if you agree with them, you have seen the light and moved beyond those divisions. But if you don't, you're still stuck in your dark partisanship and ideology – that is, you're still faithful to authentic Church doctrine.

So disingenuous are these liberal charlatans that they can't conceal their scheme for long. Their fanaticism gets the best of them. In 2012, Catholics

United even took to sending letters to Catholic priests in Florida, informing them that Catholics United was monitoring "illegal political activities by Churches in the State."[18] Of course, Catholics United publicly claimed the high road, virtuously contending that its policing of partisan sermons and political activity was only to "help protect you and your parish community from losing your 501 c (3) tax-exempt status." It was a bald-faced lie. Priests don't know what they can and can't say regarding politics, so they almost always play it safe and say nothing, especially when they receive intimidating mailings from supposedly "Catholic" groups. That makes it so easy for the anti-Catholic imposters to achieve political victory. They claim legal expertise with a thinly-veiled threat, cloak it all in altruism and thereby dissuade priests from any political talk at all. But such priests are either ignorant, cowardly or lazy, because they have a lawful right and duty to allow political discussion on their grounds and within their church walls. Indeed, they absolutely must preach on the issues of the day, which they are legally allowed to do. Yes, there are legal limits, but Catholics United and its allies intentionally leave the impression that nothing about elections can be communicated in churches. And that is utterly incorrect.

For example, the distribution of political literature of any kind – even express advocacy for or against the election of an identified candidate – does not threaten a church's tax-exempt status if the church is not the distributor. And churches don't have to prohibit it by others. "The mere permission of distribution of campaign materials by others in the church parking lot is not regulated by the Internal Revenue Code," advise attorneys for Priests for Life. "The Code and its regulations are designed to limit only the activities and expenditures of nonprofit organizations.

"Distribution of campaign materials by others outdoors, in a public parking lot, is not an activity or expenditure of the church. ... There are many cases recognizing the free speech rights of individuals and protecting speech and petitioning, reasonably exercised, in public areas, even when the property is privately owned. ... In other words, churches not only may permit campaign statements to be distributed in their public parking lots, they cannot prohibit such distributions because the parking lots are open to the public."

The general fear by Church officials of losing tax-exempt status is therefore simply misplaced or, in the case of liberal, dissident priests, more about keeping authentic Catholic doctrine off their campuses. The latter are another matter entirely, but Father Frank Pavone, executive director of Priests for Life, is puzzled by the trepidation of the former. "This is still another flash point of fear fueled by an overanxious and underinformed legal counsel (retained by dioceses)," he writes in his 2012 book, *Abolishing Abortion: How You Can Play a Part in Ending the Greatest Evil of Our Day.* Not only is such activity permitted by the IRS code, but the agency is highly unlikely to take even a passing interest in it. "We have seen the unwillingness of the IRS to punish churches for their own activities and expenditures," Pavone writes. "How much less willing would they be to punish churches for someone else's activities and expenditures? If a church wants to stop this activity, its leaders have to find a different reason than tax law."

Even from the pulpit, political speech is regulated only to the extent that certain words are used in connection with identifiable candidates. Those "magic words," such as "vote for," "vote against," "elect" or "defeat" in reference to a specific candidate, constitute express advocacy, which non-profit entities cannot employ in their communications. But while a priest cannot say from the pulpit, "Vote for Joe Blow" or "Vote against Mary Jones" he can say, "Joe Blow is the most anti-abortion electable candidate in the race. Catholic teaching holds that it can be a mortal sin to not vote for the most anti-abortion candidate." Although it describes the candidate and Church teaching, it is not express advocacy, and it is entirely within the permissible strictures of U.S. Supreme Court precedent. But most priests are afraid to provide their parishioners with anything close to that kind of valuable voting information. It would be so helpful to parishioners if they would merely lay out the abortion stances of the candidates sometime prior to the election, which they are permitted to do.

As noted in the anecdote cited earlier, I and some friends a few years ago leafleted the parking lot of a large Catholic parish during all the Sunday Masses. We consulted the pastor prior to doing so, and he correctly and appropriately told us that if he didn't see it then he couldn't stop it. He was under no obligation to do anything about it anyway, but we appreciated his decision to bother himself with other matters. The leaflet, itself, very simply stated that Joe Blow, the incumbent state senator, had voted against a ban on partial-birth abortion and that his opponent, Mary Jones, had voted for a ban on partial-birth abortion. No endorsement, no magic words. No express advocacy. Perfectly legal. There was nothing particularly courageous about this pastor's considered inaction. It was simply what all Catholic pastors should do. Mary was a huge underdog in the race and was outspent five to one. But the leafleting of this single Catholic Church parking lot substantially contributed to replacing an entrenched pro-abortion incumbent with an anti-abortion challenger in one of the greatest upsets in the history of the state legislature. Thank you, Father, you handled it as all priests should.

But four years later, as previously recounted, this priest's successor tried to stop our efforts, presumably because he simply didn't understand our right to do so and the Church's legal immunity from any harm.

Such is the paradox of the Catholic priest who is either ignorant of election law or too craven to fight for Catholic convictions. Unless he, himself, is an outright heretic, he will eventually experience compunction for effectively assisting the pro-abortion forces by his silence. The personal conflict is stark, and it is ludicrously incoherent. Such a priest will be dogged by moral inconsistency until either he or his bishop restores order by beginning to dauntlessly preach the Church's truth.

While liberals were elated by the appearance of the pagan "Pope Francis Voter Guide," they were just as repelled by the U.S. bishops', i.e., the Catholic Church's, official guide, *Forming Consciences for Faithful Citizenship.* Writing in 2015, career Catholic dissident Michael Sean Winters labeled it a "trainwreck," mostly because of its doctrinally correct condemnation of homosexual "marriage." "At a time when racial tensions are their worst in my adult lifetime, the proposed text equates same-sex marriage with racism, calling them both intrinsic evils," bemoans Winters, "even though civil same-sex marriage is not, and cannot be, an intrinsic evil."[19]

Oh really? Why not? Sin is sin. And if both homosexual "marriage" and racism are both mortally sinful, what else are they if not intrinsically evil? But what Winters is really upset about is that homosexual "marriage" is categorized as being *just as evil* as racism and other intrinsically evil practices as abortion, euthanasia, human cloning and embryonic stem-cell research. To Winters's mind, the real consequence isn't mortal sin, itself (you know, that pesky eternal damnation thing), but rather the uncomfortable way that it will make some people feel in this life. "I can scarcely imagine a comparison better designed to alienate young Catholics," Winters huffs.[20] Well, it may indeed alienate some wayward young Catholics, but the bishops' guide, unlike the Pope Francis guide, is actually designed to do just the opposite. It is meant to attract Catholics, young and otherwise, to truth and thereby to God. While some dissidents may become or remain recalcitrant "so that they may live as they wish," to quote Mother Teresa, truth-seekers seek truth, and that can only be provided by the magisterium. Mr. Winters's silly lament about running off kids hardly stands up to promulgating authentic doctrine. After all, God doesn't need young Catholics. Young Catholics need God.

Winters moves on to reveal more of the liberal agenda, railing at the bishops for removing the words "or telling people how to vote" from a sentence that begins "The Church's leaders avoid endorsing or opposing particular candidates...." Winters wants to know why "or telling people how to vote" was dropped. "Do they want to be real clear that they are telling people that if they vote for a Democrat they are going to burn in hell?"[21] Well, maybe, Mr. Winters. But a less hysterical inference would allow that the only job of the bishops is to get people to Heaven, irrespective of a candidate's party membership. And not "telling people how to vote" would be a dereliction of their God-bestowed duty, endangering their own souls. To the contrary, Mr. Winters, the Church's leaders must indeed tell people how to vote, in ways such as these, for example:

• "As a Catholic, you must vote for candidates who support the Church's teaching on the non-negotiable matters of abortion, homosexual 'marriage,' human cloning, embryonic stem-cell research, euthanasia and religious liberty. All other moral issues are secondary to these."

• "If you don't vote for the most anti-abortion (or electable anti-abortion) candidate in any given election, you may jeopardize your eternal salvation."

• "Candidate Smith has a record of voting for abortion, and candidate Jones supports all anti-abortion legislation. You should make your decision based on this information."

These are all perfectly acceptable statements that can be made from the pulpit by any deacon, priest or bishop in any Catholic Church. Each one promotes the Church's doctrine without explicitly endorsing or opposing an identifiable candidate, in conformity with the U.S. Supreme Court's "magic words" test enunciated in *Buckley v. Valeo (1976)*. Of course, that a test is needed at all is an offshoot of sprawling campaign finance law that exists to keep church members from being influenced by their religious beliefs when they vote. It is a naked violation of free speech, and indeed we can thank a raging liberal, Lyndon Johnson, for codifying it into the culture with the so-called "Johnson Amendment" of 1954. Johnson's hammer was and remains the potential loss of tax-exempt status for churches. But the Supreme Court has long held that churches face no such peril if they do not explicitly endorse or oppose an identifiable candidate. This doesn't mean a priest cannot say the name of a candidate – he can describe any candidate's positions all day long. But he simply can't say something akin to "Vote for" or "Vote against" a particular candidate. (Incidentally, on ballot *issues*, the priest can say anything he wants.)

So, Mr. Winters, there's your answer.

Winters writes for the recusant *National Catholic Reporter*, a newspaper based in Kansas City, Mo., that was established in the 1960s to counter vestiges of orthodoxy after the Second Vatican Council. So virulently anti-magisterial is the *NCR* that it has been consistently denounced by Catholic churchmen, with two Kansas City bishops, exercising their prelatic right, demanding that "Catholic" be removed from its name.[22] But bumptiously citing its "independent news source" identity, the paper steadfastly has refused to comply. To do so the paper would be relinquishing the same tack deviously used by the publishers of "The Pope Francis Voters Guide":

deception, beginning with the title of the publication. Pope Francis had nothing to do with the publication of the guide bearing his name, and the ludicrously-titled *National Catholic Reporter,* far from reflecting the doctrine of the Catholic Church, in fact actively opposes it. Both publications purport to serve Catholicism, but both exist to undermine it and serve heterodox, liberal political activism. In the case of the *Reporter,* this is manifest in its raging opposition to the Church's teaching on homosexuality:

• In 2003, the *NCR* was nominated for an award from GLAAD, an acronym for "Gay & Lesbian Alliance Against Defamation" in the category of "Outstanding Magazine Overall Coverage."[23] GLAAD is now known by its acronym only, as bisexual, transgender and other depraved sexual constituencies have provided an irresistible opportunity to increase its ranks.

• The *NCR* was again lauded by GLAAD in advance of Pope Francis's 2014 visit to the United States. GLAAD produced a media guide for reporters that encouraged them to not only use commentators from its own organization, but also from the gay-friendly *NCR.*[24]

• Also in 2014, an *NCR* editorial engaged in profound religious bigotry by upbraiding the Roman Catholic Church for promulgating the beliefs of ... the Roman Catholic Church. Discarding the Church's precept that non-negotiable issues, such as homosexual "marriage," supersede matters of prudential judgment, such as immigration and poverty (as enunciated in the *Catechism of the Catholic Church*), the *NCR* whined that "It is mystifying, with so many social problems needing attention, to watch so much of the U.S. Catholic leadership obsessed with these sexual matters."[25] Actually, it's not mystifying at all. Being on the wrong side of "these sexual matters" can send a soul to hell. That's not true as to "social problems," the remedies for which are subject to each person's own prudential judgment.

• Further confirming its identity as a publication that supports homosexual (and, *de facto,* mortally sinful) behavior, the *NCR* impudently bestowed its 2015 "Persons of the Year" title on two Catholic men who are "married" to each other and are "parents" to two children.[26] (They were plaintiffs in the *Obergefell v. Hodges* Supreme Court case that declared homosexual "marriage" a constitutional right.) Even the anomalous Pope Francis, who so often appears to concur with Church liberals, is on record opposing same-sex parenting, although it was apparently a stressful concession. "It is painful to say this today," he said in June 2018. "People speak of varied families, of various kinds of family," but "the family [as] man and woman in the image of God is the only one."[27] But in yet another display of religious bigotry – all part of the liberal political scheme to undermine 2,000 years of Catholic doctrine – the *NCR* declared that its award showed that the Church is "past the time of 'love the sinner' [and 'hate the sin'] platitudes" and that "countless gay, lesbian and transgender Catholics" don't deserve "confused, uneven and often cruel" treatment by the Church.[28]

Well, the first part is wrong – what was mortally sinful before remains mortally sinful today, and always will. But the second part is actually true – no one deserves confused and cruel treatment, and that's why Holy Mother Church, in its charity, desperately tries to persuade practicing homosexuals to renounce their aberrant sexual behavior so that they may live with God in eternity. There is, of course, only one other eternal result, and *The National Catholic Reporter* seems to prefer it.

15

The Holey Seamless Garment

In short, there is no legitimate, intact, "seamless garment," as the term is popularly understood. It is a garment full of holes.

This modernist, false notion that has taken hold among liberal Catholics to justify voting behavior contrary to authentic Catholic doctrine is a corruption. It's fully a contemporary outgrowth of an ideology devised, innocuously enough, by noted pacifist Eileen Egan in 1971 to set out a "consistent ethic of life." It began with the commendable goal of opposing abortion, capital punishment, assisted suicide, euthanasia and unjust war. But the "seamless garment" allusion to Jesus's robe, that his executioners didn't tear apart, was the perfect imagery for Catholic liberals to hijack: "Jesus's garment of love includes everything," they gush, "as there are no seams separating one societal ill from another."

This, of course, is nonsense, and within a span of five years this novel, seamless approach had, itself, become a front-and-center controversy within the Catholic Church in America. Worried during the presidential campaign of 1976 that the executive committee of the National Conference of Catholic Bishops was leaving the impression that it favored the more conservative Gerald Ford over Democrat Jimmy Carter, the NCCB's administrative board one week later rushed out a superseding "Resolution of the Administrative Council" that essentially overrode the executive committee's emphasis on abortion and endorsed the seamless garment tack:

"Abortion and the need for a constitutional amendment to protect the unborn are among our concerns," read an obligatory preface to the resolution. But then followed the false equivalency to mollify the liberals. "So are the issues of unemployment, adequate educational opportunity for all, and equitable food policy both domestic and world wide, the right to a decent home and healthcare, human rights across the globe, intelligent arms limitation and many other social justice issues. ... the Catholic Bishops of the United States have often publicly stated and we here reaffirm – deep commitment to the sanctity, dignity, and quality of human life at all states of development, as well as to legislation and public policy which protects and promotes these values in all contemporary contexts."[1]

But truth would out. The U.S. bishops would soon modify, arguably to the point of reversal, this cavalier rewrite of eternal verities.

Even when Cardinal Joseph Bernardin of Chicago, with whom the "seamless garment" is mostly identified, began building upon the idea in 1983, his purpose was not to de-emphasize the intrinsically evil issues of abortion, euthanasia and other murderous acts. Rather, his thrust was to unify increasingly estranged conservative and liberal Catholics, by urging them to stand for moral principles *generally* on such matters as abortion, capital punishment, poverty, euthanasia and unjust war. For a time, Bernardin's effort at cohesion was successful. Prominent Catholics from both ends of the political spectrum signed on. But the Left saw it as another irresistible opening to muddle Church teaching by subverting this "consistent ethic" philosophy. It was certainly ripe for subversion, having been established without the explicit caveat that certain issues carry more weight than others. Thus, this initiative that called on all Catholics to support any and all Christian tenets was easily recharacterized as a rationale to define each of those tenets as morally equivalent. "This came as welcome news to the liberals," columnist Joseph Sobran understated, "since it turned 'life' into a checklist, in which abortion was one of many items, and not necessarily the most urgent. You could be 'pro-life,' according to the Bernardin standard, merely by supporting the welfare state."

But conservative Catholics smelled a rat, Sobran said. "They sensed that this new 'seamless garment' was really just a way of minimizing the special problem of abortion, at a time when more than a million abortions were being performed in America every year. Liberal Catholics, on the other hand, loved the idea. But somehow the imperative of consistency worked only one way. We never heard any of them say, 'Well, it's not enough for me to support the welfare state. If I'm really going to be pro-life, I must also fight to end legal abortion.'"

Cardinal Bernadin, himself, soon recognized that the Left had corrupted the "seamless garment" idea to advance its own political agenda. In 1988 he told the *National Catholic Register:* "I know that some people on the left, if I may use that term, have used the consistent ethic to give the impression that the abortion issue is not all that important any more, that you should be against abortion in a general way but that there are more important issues, so don't hold anyone's feet to the fire just on abortion. That is a misuse of the consistent ethic, and I deplore it."

Well and good. Cardinal Bernadin, the most prominent exponent of the original, doctrinally-correct seamless garment philosophy, thereby publicly stated that he deplored its bastardization. But that was apparently the extent of his lament, and it did nothing to stop the seamless garment's rampant adulteration. Indeed, adherents, such as Fordham University professor Charles Camosy, still pine for it to transform the Democrats' reputation as the "Party of Death" to the "Party of Life." By promoting the seamless garment deception to liberal Catholics who are loathe to vote for an anti-abortion Republican, "Democrats can make a home for these stranded voters," Camosy wrote in 2016. "Opening a big tent to pro-lifers would not only offer a hospitable climate for Democrats who value a 'whole life' ethic, which weaves together common Democratic concerns like care for the impoverished and elderly with an equal interest in the unborn; it would also put them in a good position to win the next generation."[2]

Camosy was buoyed, briefly, by a blog post by Father Dwight Longenecker, a well-known and outspoken South Carolina priest who is certainly no liberal. Harrumphing that conservative Catholics just don't understand the Church's social justice teachings, Camosy said that it was "so heartening" to see Longenecker seeming to make the same point, to wit:[3] "No economic system is perfect and no single economic system can be said to be 'Catholic,' but it would not be inconsistent for a Catholic to vote for a Democratic Socialist" like Bernie Sanders, Longenecker argued. "Indeed, the reason so many Catholics voted for the Democratic Party over the years was because they perceived the Democrats to be the party of the poor, the marginalized, the workers and the 'little guy.'"[4]

"So far so good," Camosy observes. "It is Catholic doctrine that wealth exists to be shared; private property is under a social mortgage for the common good; workers must be paid a living wage; health care is a human right, and we must be on the side of the poor first. For Catholics, these are non-negotiables."[5]

Well, no, these are not "non-negotiables" as that term is conventionally used, i.e., to denote ironclad criteria for Catholic voting. This is Camosy's attempt to co-opt, for the purpose of equating all issues, something said by a prominent right-of-center Catholic clergyman in Longenecker. While it is true that wealth should be shared, health care should be available to everyone, and the needs of the poor must be addressed, those issues are "non-negotiable" only in the sense that they are included in high-minded Church teaching. But they are not matters of "intrinsic evil," because the severity of and means of remedying those issues are left to each Catholic's "prudential judgment."

Camosy tries to muddle the meaning of "non-negotiable" in a way that his catalog of social justice issues can be considered to be as prominent as the true non-negotiables that countless Catholic leaders have identified as having more weight because of their acute threat to the culture: abortion, euthanasia, homosexual marriage, embryonic stem cell research, human cloning and religious freedom. Seamless-garment champions, as political liberals, will engage in any semantic sleight-of-hand to bring all Catholic voting criteria under their concocted cloak. That's how they seek to dilute true doctrine and thereby sanctify their liberal to-do list.

Having expressed his delight at Longenecker's supposed concession on Catholic social teaching, Camosy was, however, constrained to come clean about Longenecker's context. Longenecker's piece was titled, "Can a Catholic Vote for Bernie Sanders?," and Longenecker concluded that, yes, he could do so based on Sanders's viewpoints, as a self-described "Democratic Socialist," on the aforementioned prudential judgment social issues. But, as Camosy laments, Longenecker went on to say that because Sanders's abortion stance is a superseding, disqualifying factor, a Catholic could not, in fact, vote for him. "The Catholic Church's teaching is clear," Longenecker said, "To vote for a candidate who actively supports abortion is a serious sin."

That would seem to have definitively answered the question. But Camosy audaciously countered that "this is not Church teaching," citing the often misconstrued snippet from Joseph Cardinal Ratzinger, who in 2004, as prefect for the Congregation of the Faith, sent a memorandum to the American bishops that said, "When a Catholic does not share a candidate's stand in favor of abortion and/or euthanasia but votes for that candidate for other reasons, it is considered remote material cooperation, which can be permitted in the presence of proportionate reasons."[6] The orthodox Ratzinger surely didn't mean to blindside the American bishops with a bombshell, but he did seem to be giving the liberals a surprise, if unintended, gift that they could misuse – a broadly ambiguous excuse to vote for a pro-choice candidate.

The imprecision of Ratzinger's missive spurred a two-fold misunderstanding. One, it gave the impression that voting for a pro-choice candidate is more permissible than Ratzinger actually meant. That wrong impression was repeated in the USCCB's subsequent *Faithful Citizenship* document. But Bishop Robert F. Vasa was one of several bishops who clarified the teaching in the pages of their respective diocesan newspapers. "The document (*Faithful Citizenship*) does not say, for instance, that it is just fine to vote for a pro-abortion candidate as long as one votes for that candidate only because of his or her stand on other important social issues," he wrote. "Casting a vote, even for reasons other than the candidate's pro-abortion position, is still casting a vote for the preservation of 'a legal system which violates the basic right to life,'" (quoting *Faithful Citizenship*). No declared policies on other issues excuse a candidate's support for abortion, Vasa said. "Just as a vote for a genocidal maniac is a vote for genocide and a vote for the avowed torturer is a vote for torture … so a vote for a promoter of abortion, when there is another less evil alternative, is a vote for abortion."[7]

The second misunderstanding created by Ratzinger's inadequate instruction was the troublesome term, "proportionate reasons." Now *there's* a subjective turn of phrase. It seems to give license to just about any excuse to vote for a pro-choice candidate. The U.S. bishops had requested guidance from the Prefect of the Congregation for the Doctrine of the Faith (Ratzinger), but instead were saddled with a new problem: how to complete and add practicality to Ratzinger's troubling "proportionate reason" rationale. Here's how a few bishops did so:

• "I cannot conceive of a proportionate reason that could outweigh the deaths of nearly 50 million children killed by abortion," said Archbishop Elden F. Curtiss of Omaha.[8]

• "I do not know any proportionate reason that could outweigh more than 40 million unborn children killed by abortion and the many millions of women deeply wounded by the loss and regret abortion creates," said Archbishop Charles Chaput.[9] "Catholics who support pro-choice candidates … need a compelling proportionate reason to justify it. What is a 'proportionate' reason when it comes to the abortion issue? It's the kind of reason we will be able to explain, with a clean heart, to the victims of abortion when we meet them face to face in the next life – which we most certainly will. If we're confident that these victims will accept our motives as something more than an alibi, then we can proceed."[10]

• "[T]here are no 'truly grave moral' or 'proportionate' reasons, singularly or combined, that could outweigh the millions of innocent human lives that are directly killed by legal abortion each year," wrote Bishops Kevin Farrell of Dallas and Kevin Vann of Fort Worth in a joint statement.[11]

• "Could a Catholic in good conscience vote for a candidate who supports legalized abortion when there is a choice of another candidate who does not support abortion or any other intrinsically evil policy?" posited Archbishop Joseph F. Naumann of Kansas City in Kansas, and Bishop

Robert W. Finn, Bishop of Kansas City-St. Joseph, Missouri. "Could a voter's preference for the candidate's positions on the pursuit of peace, economic policies benefiting the poor, support for universal health care, a more just immigration policy, etc. overcome a candidate's support for legalized abortion? In such a case, the Catholic voter must ask and answer the question: What could possibly be a proportionate reason for the more than 45 million children killed by abortion in the past 35 years? Personally, we cannot conceive of such a proportionate reason."[12]

• "What evil could be so grave and widespread as to constitute a 'proportionate reason' to support candidates who would preserve and protect the abortion license and even extend it to publicly funded embryo-killing in our nation's labs? wrote Archbishop John J. Myers. "Certainly policies on welfare, national security, the war in Iraq, Social Security or taxes, taken singly or in any combination, do not provide a proportionate reason to vote for a pro-abortion candidate."[13]

• "[S]uch (proportionate) reasons would certainly need to be not only morally grave but also proportionately grave – that is, equally serious or even more serious than abortion," wrote Virginia Bishops Paul S. Loverde, of Arlington, and Francis X. DiLorenzo, of Richmond.[14]

As Archbishop Chaput so vividly explains, the unborn victims of abortion would surely confirm that any such "proportionate reasons" do not exist or are even conceivable in the United States today. "Frankly, it is hard to imagine," said Archbishop Myers. "No candidate advocating the removal of legal protection against killing for any vulnerable group of innocent people other than unborn children would have a chance of winning a major office in our country. Even those who support the death penalty for first-degree murderers are not advocating policies that result in more than a million killings annually."[15]

The editor in chief of *The Integrated Catholic Life,* Deacon Mike Bickerstaff, notes that abortion, infanticide and euthanasia are direct attacks against human life and that "the only proportionate reason that I can imagine would be other, greater direct attacks on the right to life of human persons. I don't see anything like that in the current landscape."[16]

Therefore, there is only one realistic situation in which a Catholic could vote for a pro-choice candidate: that is if there is no other candidate who is less pro-choice.

"The conditions under which an individual may be able to vote for a pro-abortion candidate would apply only if all the candidates are equally pro-abortion," said Bishop Vasa. "And then you begin to screen for the other issues and make a conscientious decision to vote for this pro-abortion candidate because his positions on these other issues are more in keeping with good Catholic values. It doesn't mean that you in any way support or endorse a pro-abortion position but you take a look in that context at the lesser of two evils."[17]

Added Archbishop William E. Lori, "[T]he Catholic voter may vote for a pro-abortion politician if both candidates are equally pro-abortion,"[18] assuming there are only two candidates in the race.

Archbishop John F. Donoghue of Atlanta delved deeper into this discernment. "[T]o vote for someone in order to limit a greater evil, that is, to restrict insofar as possible the evil that another candidate might do if elected, is to have a good purpose in voting," he said. "The voter's will has as its object this limitation of evil and not the evil which the imperfect politician might do in his less than perfect adherence to Catholic moral principles. Such cooperation is called material, and is permitted for a serious reason, such as preventing the election of a worse candidate."[19]

Bishops Farrell and Vann concurred: "If both candidates running for office support abortion or 'abortion rights,' a Catholic would be forced to then look at the other important issues and through their vote try to limit the evil done."[20]

But like all seamless garmenters, Camosy jumped all over Ratzinger's "proportionate reasons" caveat. He even tried his hand at identifying some proportionate reasons – which he should have avoided doing, because all of his examples fall squarely within the dominion of a voter's prudential judgment, irrespective of his best efforts to color them otherwise, e.g., protecting children after they are born, social injustices that push women toward abortion, helping the poor generally, and other quality-of-life circumstances. "In voting for Sanders on the basis of the above reasons ...," Camosy wrote, "a person is strongly affirming the need to protect prenatal children, while at the same time also giving due reverence to the other serious and non-negotiable values at stake in this election."[21]

"While at the same time." "Other serious and non-negotiable values." Camosy's was just another tortuous and ultimately futile attempt to make issues concerning quality of life tantamount to issues concerning the taking of life.

In his zeal, Camosy is glaringly shortsighted, or perhaps giving him too much credit, disingenuous, about the nature of Ratzinger's hypothetical. In 2012, blogger Deacon Mark Gallagher reasoned that the future Pope Benedict XVI included the "proportionate reason" principle "because the Church has over 2,000 years of experience with leaders of countries throughout the world and knows there have been crimes equal to or greater than the million legal abortions annually in America (Adolf Hitler being only one example)." Therefore, Gallagher noted, the proportionate reason principle does not apply to the United States, because "We do not have nor would our legislative, executive and judicial branches of government permit the killing annually of a million citizens through starvation or freezing. Nor do we have candidates advocating an unjust war that would involve a first-strike nuclear attack on millions of innocent persons."[22]

Employing another of the Left's maneuvers to legitimize its dissident stance, Camosy concludes by seeking to bring us all happily under the mantle of the seamless garment, judging that "these disagreements are an important sign of a healthy church, one that finds both parties to be foreign territory."[23] My goodness, no. Does the Left not accept any plain definition of right and wrong? Polar opposite views about Church teaching are most certainly not signs of a healthy church. A healthy church would not be tormented with stark division about what constitutes truth and therefore doctrine.

Camosy then invokes peace and harmony, having us all join hands in a kumbaya reverie: "Let us engage these debates in the spirit of family, united by having a common brother in Jesus, and let us all bring a healthy dose of skepticism for approaches that make idols out of secular political agendas." What he means, of course, is a healthy dose of skepticism for the Church's true teaching on authentic non-negotiable issues.

16

Clerics All Dolled Up in Their Seamless Garment

The deliberate deceptions of Camosy and his ilk have been decidedly successful. It is fact that Catholics in the pews don't know how to vote in accordance with Church teachings. "The reason is simple," writes Deal Hudson, publisher of *The Christian Review*. "Catholic voters are unaware of the distinction between the handful of issues that are 'settled' or 'non-negotiable,' and those that are not, meaning 'prudential judgments.' Most political issues are prudential, meaning the individual person applies a general principle to a specific situation. Issues of immigration, war, taxation, climate change, minimum wage, education, foreign policy, and internet policy are all prudential. Whereas, the *settled* matters, meaning settled in Church teaching, are five in number: abortion, euthanasia, embryonic stem cell research, cloning, and same-sex marriage, because they are intrinsic evils that can never be voted for or supported in any way by Catholics."[1] (Because of recent threats forged by homosexual and other leftist groups, some Catholic observers have added religious liberty as a sixth non-negotiable.)

Hudson's piece was written in July 2016, and the outcome of the presidential election four months later might suggest that rank-and-file Catholics were starting to understand their voting responsibilities. In fact, commentator Matt C. Abbott saw Donald Trump's victory among

Catholics (by a margin of 52% to 45% for Hillary Clinton[2]) as a sign of hope. "Thankfully," he wrote, "it appears that many Catholics – with the help of a dedicated pro-life movement – are finally beginning to see through that ugly 'seamless garment' embraced and promoted by a number of clergy and religious over the last 30 years."[3] I'm not so confident. Trump may have carried the Catholic vote, but there is little reason to think that abortion played any greater role in his election than it did in the two victories of the pro-abortion Barack Obama who won the Catholic vote twice. The "seamless garment" lives on today as an "acceptable" set of criteria upon which Catholics believe they may vote. And it stands as a corrupted version of the "consistent ethic of life" concept entirely because the institutional Church doesn't definitively and persistently condemn it. This, alone, allows it to survive and virulently flourish. If Catholic voters can be persuaded that abortion is of no greater import than, say, deliberately running a stoplight, then liberals can propound the fallacious seamless garment propaganda as if it's an authentic tenet of the Church. And when any bishops and priests choose to counter this notion at all (acknowledging here that some actually endorse it), they do so ineffectively.

Catholic apologist Tim Staples recounts his dismaying encounter with a priest who had clearly been seduced by seamless garment propaganda. To Staples's contention that Catholics can vote only for anti-abortion candidates, the priest responded, "Tim, I don't think this is as black and white as you say it is. What about the death penalty, war, immigration, health care, education, etc.?" Thus commenced a lunchtime lesson in Catholic doctrine. Staples schooled the priest on the Church's "just war doctrine," which holds that war can be justified in certain situations. (CCC 2309 and Ecclesiastes 3:8) Staples then reminded (we can only hope it was a reminder) that the death penalty has always been upheld as a legitimate and potentially just punishment in Scripture (Genesis 9:6) and in Catholic tradition, even if the need for it today is rare or practically nonexistent (CCC 2267). As to education and health care, Staples instructed the priest, the Church's teaching that they are "rights" does not mean that the Church believes they must be doled out for free. "Nor does it mean they have to be or even should be provided by the government," he said, adding that "the principle of subsidiarity and the Church's condemnation of socialism must (also) be taken into account." But so entrenched was the priest's unfamiliarity with Church teaching that his only response was, "You make a good point, Tim."[4]

You make a good point, Tim? What was being recited to this priest was ironclad, irrefutable Church teaching, and this priest could only deadpan, "You make a good point," as if it was information that the priest had the liberty to merely take under advisement. That this random cleric, who happened to be the pastor at a parish where Staples was giving a talk, was so obviously ill-informed, bespeaks the magnitude of clerical ignorance. And it is ignorance only where it isn't actually a liberal clerical agenda to knowingly and actively ignore Church teaching and promote the false seamless garment "doctrine."

But the problem isn't that most priests and bishops are activists who intentionally use the seamless garment to advance a liberal agenda. Indeed, the USCCB, as a body, has made clear that the "non-negotiable" issues must take precedence over "prudential judgment" issues when a Catholic enters the voting booth. And a multitude of bishops and priests have been forthright in issuing individual statements concurring with the USCCB's stance. No, the problem isn't one of doctrine; it's a problem of frequency. Quite simply, bishops and priests don't proclaim the Church's teaching on this subject often enough.

Oh, earnest, laudable efforts pop up – perhaps every four years, or so – usually as a presidential election approaches. Most of these formal "election statements" from the chanceries look like this one from the Diocese of Sioux Falls, South Dakota in August 2004: "There is a faulty thinking today that all life issues are equal or the same," wrote Bishop Robert J. Carlson to his flock. "Even some priests and religious and a few politicians try to promote this. The philosophical fallacy that underpins this argument is called relativism. It teaches that all things and issues are relative and up to the individual to decide which is of greater importance. Some elements in the media favor it as it 'squares' in their minds with the sense of strong individualism fostered by the culture. It goes hand-in-hand with the attitude, 'whatever I think or believe, whatever I value or want, whatever I feel or desire must be correct.' ... But the teaching of the Church, which corresponds with reality and the natural law, is that all life issues are not equal or the same."[5]

Well done, Bishop Carlson. Bold and unequivocal. And readily forgotten and dismissed. Such one-shot essays appear in the lightly-read diocesan newspaper and might even be recited at the Sunday Masses just prior to election day. But that's it. The parish priest doesn't build on it in a follow-up sermon. ("Too risky. The liberal parishioners would harass me all week long.") Any first-year advertising student knows that an idea is successful only if it is sufficiently repeated. But the bishop's quadrennial statement sits alone, bereft of the urgent moral compulsion necessary to compel corresponding voting behavior. And it therefore fails to crowd out the cacophony of voices that incessantly promote the winsome seamless garment. That some of those voices are those of renegade clerics cements the confusion of Catholic voters. "My bishop said this, but that bishop said that."

To be sure, adherents of the seamless garment argue that their novel "doctrine" is legitimized by the pronouncements of particular iconoclastic bishops who have taken it upon themselves to declare that virtually all issues upon which the Church takes a moral stand have equal importance. This is perhaps the greatest manifestation of relativism in today's culture, as we have prelates of the Catholic Church actively subverting the sole entity granted supreme moral teaching authority by God Almighty, Himself. This circumstance renders meaningless the inherent stratification of sin – that some sins are more serious than others. Can any Christian honestly believe that general policies on poverty and immigration carry the same moral urgency as policies on the beastly act of directly and deliberately killing a little girl or a little boy?

It is true that just as there has been seamless garment advocacy from some bishops, there have been countervailing statements from other bishops, like the aforementioned Bishop Carlson, who have unequivocally stated that the issues upon which Catholics must weigh their votes are not of the same moral weight. And, therefore, the Catholic voter is presented with a dilemma: Which group of prelates is correct? And does it matter?

Notwithstanding their attempts to turn the question into a debatable one, the "seamless garment" bishops are, quite simply, dissenters from Church doctrine, according to no less than their own governing body, the USCCB. The magisterial authority of the Roman Catholic Church allows for internal debate on issues of "prudential judgment," but it does not allow for dissent on irrefutable matters, from the faithful in the pews or the faithful on the altar. The Church is not a democracy. It is a benevolent oligarchy with internal police powers; it makes its own laws, requires that its members abide by them, and can impose penalties on them for not doing so. Beyond this life, penalties and rewards are left to the wisdom and providence of God.

In their definitive document, *Forming Consciences for Faithful Citizenship,* the U.S. bishops could not be clearer about the existence of a hierarchy of moral issues facing Catholics when they make voting choices. Nor could they be clearer about which issues take priority. They say, quite simply and without qualification, that "all issues do not carry the same moral weight":

"In making these (voting) decisions," the bishops state, "it is essential for Catholics to be guided by a well-formed conscience that recognizes that all issues do not carry the same moral weight and that the moral obligation to oppose intrinsically evil acts has a special claim on our consciences and our actions."[6]

The document goes on to say that the consistent ethic of life "does not treat all issues as morally equivalent nor does it reduce Catholic teaching to one or two issues."[7]

"Aha!" the seamless garmenters will say. "There it is. Catholic teaching on how to vote encompasses the whole teaching, not just abortion and euthanasia!"

Well, nice try. *Of course* a consistent ethic of life doesn't reduce Catholic teaching to one or two issues. But the overriding import of that sentence in the bishops' document is that *the "consistent ethic of life" doesn't treat "all issues as morally equivalent."* The bishops are therefore saying that the "consistent ethic of life" doesn't mean "seamless garment" at all. In fact, it means precisely the opposite: The bishops explicitly define the "consistent ethic of life" in a way that altogether invalidates the notion of it being a seamless anything. Indeed, there are very pronounced "seams," as the bishops further declare, without ambiguity, that the several issues involving "intrinsic evil," such as abortion and euthanasia, eclipse issues subject to a Catholic voter's prudential judgment: "This culture of life begins with the preeminent obligation to protect innocent life from direct attack and extends to defending life whenever it is threatened or diminished: …"[8] To be clear, that statement says that the preeminent obligation is to protect from direct attack innocent human life; it does not say that the preeminent obligation is to protect human dignity or quality of life.

Still, as plain as this verbiage is, liberal Catholics nonetheless aggressively parse and manipulate these words to fit their own narrative. The "culture of life," they say, includes caring for immigrants, the poor, the imprisoned and a whole host of societal unfortunates, an assertion that serves to blur the bishops' true meaning. Indeed, liberals do the same with every component of the bishops' plain statement. To these dissenters, any oppressed group of people constitutes "innocent life" who are under "direct attack" or are "threatened or diminished."

That, obviously, is not what the bishops mean by "life" or "innocent life."

But the bishops must have anticipated this ploy, because they immediately define what they truly mean by referencing their earlier pastoral letter of 1998, a continuation that the liberals deliberately disregard. The liberals ignore that the phrase, "threatened or diminished," in the bishops' statement doesn't end with a period, but with a colon, which means that they're not finished and that you're supposed to read what follows. And what follows in the next paragraph is their very specific meaning of "direct attacks on innocent life."

"All direct attacks on innocent human life, such as abortion and euthanasia, strike at the house's foundation."[9]

They don't say that "direct attacks on innocent human life" include other injustices regarding racism, poverty, hunger, employment, education, housing and health care. No, they very narrowly, very specifically, cite the two "murder issues," abortion and euthanasia, in defining what they mean by "all direct attacks on human life."

Therefore, the bishops make a clear distinction between issues of "human dignity" and issues of "human life." They say that issues of "human dignity" are certainly to be considered by the Catholic voter, but that those issues are structurally dependent upon, and necessarily subordinate to, "direct attacks on innocent human life, such as abortion and euthanasia," which are foundational issues.

Here's how they put it:

"Any politics of human dignity must seriously address issues of racism, poverty, hunger, employment, education, housing, and health care. ... If we understand the human person as the "temple of the Holy Spirit" – the living house of God – then these issues fall logically into place as the crossbeams and walls of that house. *All direct attacks on innocent human life, such as abortion and euthanasia, strike at the house's foundation.*"[10]

In this passage the bishops establish and delineate two categories of issues: Those pertaining to quality of life are issues of "human dignity," and do not include abortion and euthanasia which warrant their own category – "human life" – that does not include the lesser issues that fall into the aforementioned category of "human dignity."

The bishops' reasoning should be obvious. Conditions involving human dignity can be altered, improved. Lyndon Johnson's "War on Poverty," though burdened by a decidedly misguided strategy, demonstrated a will to address the plight of the poor. The same is true of man's contemporary initiatives to alleviate the problems of hunger, employment, education, housing and health care.

But the bishops separated and elevated euthanasia and abortion from issues of mere "human dignity." Man cannot alter or improve a person undergoing the "conditions" of euthanasia or abortion. Dead is dead. Euthanasia and abortion are conditions of, and threats to, "human life," not just "human dignity." "[T]here are many ways of being pro-life," said Cardinal Francis George, Archbishop of Chicago, "but none of them has the same priority as the question of abortion or euthanasia."[11]

17

The Seamless Garment Torn Apart

There is No "Seamless Garment" – For Catholics, Abortion is the Most Important Political Issue.

A s we have noted, the widespread acceptance of the "seamless garment" fiction among Catholics is due more to abysmal communication from the bishops than radical advocacy for the myth. To be sure, there are plenty of American priests and bishops who promote the heresy. Some of these are simply liberal dissidents, and others are, like the people in the pews, just wrongly informed. But that an officially discredited myth is still believed by a large segment of Catholics is not for lack of trying by Church clerics, many of whom, consistent with the teaching of the USCCB, have publicly renounced it. Here are their denunciations of the seamless garment: (The offices cited are those held at the time of the quotation.)

Bishop Samuel J. Aquila

Fargo, North Dakota

Abortion is the Gravest Attack.

"As faithful Catholics we acknowledge that the gravest attacks against the dignity of human life are those that destroy innocent human life as in abortion, euthanasia and genocide."[1]

The Right to Be Born is the First Among All Rights.

"Another misunderstanding among some Catholics is that abortion is just one issue among many issues. They will say 'I am not a one issue person.' ...

"Nevertheless, there are fundamental rights that no civil society may take away. The fundamental right to life is essential to all other rights (CCC 2273).

"Therefore the right to life, from the moment of conception until natural death, is the first among all rights and the first issue that must be taken into consideration, acted upon and protected."[2]

We Must Place the Right to Life First.

"We are created in the image and likeness of God. We must, as our forefathers did, place the God-given inalienable rights first, beginning with the right to life from the moment of conception until natural death."[3]

Bishop Raymond J. Boland and Bishop Robert W. Finn

Kansas City-St. Joseph

"Life is the most fundamental right."

"The perception, at times, that there are no perfect candidates makes it that much more important to evaluate the moral weight of some issues in comparison to others. First and foremost on any prioritized list of issues the Church has affirmed the protection of innocent human life. ..."

"As your pastors in this Diocese of Kansas City-St. Joseph, we stand united with the U.S. Bishops as they have written, in solidarity with the Pope's great encyclical on the Gospel of Life, that 'Catholic public officials are obliged to address each of these issues [racism, poverty, hunger, etc.] as they seek to build consistent policies which promote respect for the human person at all stages of life.' But it must be understood clearly: 'Being 'right' in such matters can never excuse a wrong choice regarding the attacks on innocent human life' ('Living the Gospel of Life,' USCCB. n. 22). Life is the most fundamental right. Without it there can be no liberty, no justice, no pursuit of happiness."[4]

Bishop Earl Boyea

Lansing, Michigan

Other Rights Are Meaningless if the Right to Exist is Denied.

"Respect for human dignity is the basis for the fundamental right to life. It is also the basis for all those things needed to live with dignity – for example, work, fair wages, food, shelter, education, health care, security and migration. But these other basic human needs lose all meaning and purpose if the fundamental right to life – the right to exist – is denied."[5]

Bishop Lawrence E. Brandt

Greensburg, Pennsylvania

Abortion Has Priority Among All Issues.

"Because abortion is about human life itself, it has priority of place among all the issues related to life."[6]

Archbishop Daniel M. Buechlein

Indianapolis

Among Issues, Protecting the Unborn is the "Premier Priority."

"On the forefront are issues pertaining to the dignity of human life. Among these, the premier priority is the protection of the unborn from the moment of conception."[7]

Bishop Raymond L. Burke

La Crosse, Wisconsin

Abortion is the Fundamental Issue.

"Some will say that the defense of innocent life is only one issue among many, that it is important but not fundamental. They are wrong. In the natural moral law, the good of life is the most fundamental good and the condition for the enjoyment of all other goods."[8]

Bishop Robert J. Carlson

Sioux Falls, South Dakota

Life, Itself, is Primary. It is "The Issue."

"[T]he teaching of the church, which corresponds with reality and the natural law, is that all life issues are not equal or the same. In fact, there is one which is primary, life itself. It is so basic and foundational that if it is not upheld, all other issues and rights are meaningless. Opposition to abortion binds every Catholic under pain of mortal sin and admits of no exceptions.

"Life is 'the issue,' because every other right is dependent upon it. Understand that this is not simply one bishop's opinion, but is the truth as revealed to us through the church founded by Christ."[9]

Archbishop Charles J. Chaput

Denver

Even the First Champion of the "Seamless Garment" Conceded That Some Moral Issues Carry More Weight Than Others.

"In offering his own thoughts on Catholic social teaching, the late Cardinal Joseph Bernardin warned against the misuse of his 'seamless garment' imagery to falsely invest different social issues with the same moral gravity. Many social issues are important. Many require our attention. But some issues have more weight than others. Deliberately killing innocent human life, or standing by and allowing it, dwarfs all other social issues. Trying to avoid this fact by calling the unborn child a lump of pre-human cells is simply a corrupt and corrupting form of verbal gymnastics."[10]

The Right to Live is Foundational to Social Justice.

"Catholics have an obligation to work for the common good and the dignity of every person. We see abortion as a matter of civil rights and human dignity, not simply as a matter of religious teaching. We are doubly unfaithful – both to our religious convictions and to our democratic responsibilities – if we fail to support the right to life of the unborn child. Our duties to social justice by no means end there. But they do always begin there, because the right to life is foundational."[11]

Some Issues Are Jugular. The Right to Life Comes First.

"Catholics have a duty to work tirelessly for human dignity at every stage of life, and to demand the same of their lawmakers. But some issues are jugular. Some issues take priority. Abortion, immigration law, international trade policy, the death penalty and housing for the poor are all vitally important issues. But no amount of calculating can make them equal in gravity.

"The right to life comes first. It precedes and undergirds every other social issue or group of issues. This is why Blessed John XXIII listed it as the first human right in his great encyclical on world peace, *Pacem in Terris*. And as the U.S. bishops stressed in their 1998 pastoral letter Living the Gospel of Life, the right to life is the foundation of every other right."[12]

A "Right" to Abortion Cannot Outweigh the Right to Life.

"[A] so-called 'right' to partial-birth abortion can *never* outweigh a child's right to life – and any 'right' to kill the innocent undermines every other right of the human person."[13]

The "Seamless Garment" Debases Christian Thought.

"[N]o equivalence can ever exist between the intentional killing involved in abortion, infanticide and euthanasia, on the one hand, and issues like homelessness, the death penalty and anti-poverty policy on the other. Again, all of these issues are important. But trying to reason or imply them into

151

having the same moral weight is a debasement of Christian thought." *(As archbishop of Philadelphia)*[14]

Bishop Edward P. Cullen

Allentown, Pennsylvania

Other Rights Don't Outweigh Killing the Innocent.

"It would be little more than the dreadfully selfish claim to take care of those whom we have decided are worth allowing to live in the first place, while we decide that others are not worth caring about, not even to the extent of allowing them to take their first breath.

"Many of the things about which we argue or disagree in terms of social programs may truly be varying points of view, each of which has something to recommend it, and upon which we may come to valuable compromise, even if we cannot come to full agreement. The far more basic issue of the sacredness of life itself cannot be satisfied by such a political compromise.

"Once again, the bishops capture this truth in some well-chosen words. 'For example, while no candidates or public officials support nuclear war, they may disagree about how to avoid it. On the right to life issue, however, the disagreement is not in strategies for protecting human life, but whether some lives should be protected at all. This fact changes the way in which a candidate's position should be evaluated.'"

"Here is the point at which we must be perceptive about what candidates claim and equally perceptive about the reality of the basic issues involved. We cannot ever afford to become blind to the basic issue of life, thinking it is enough for us to be concerned about the other issues and only those.

"The bishops go on: 'No commitment to promote other rights by a public official can outweigh a refusal to help end the legalized killing of the innocent.'"

Archbishop Elden F. Curtiss

Omaha, Nebraska

No Issue is More Important Than Abortion.

"In this election, like many before it, we are faced with a conflict of values in candidates. There are many serious issues at stake ... but none is more important than abortion."[16]

Abortion is a Greater Evil Than the Death Penalty.

"Catholic teaching does not weigh opposition to capital punishment the same way it weighs opposition to abortion.

"The thousands of innocent pre-born babies killed every year by abortion constitute a greater evil than the execution of a few convicted felons by the state, not only because of sheer number of deaths, but because of the gravity of the act itself.

"Therefore opposition to abortion must be a priority for Catholics who support the Church's teaching about the sacredness of all human life."[17]

Before All Other Rights is the Right to Be Born.

"We are surely not one-issue people, because we have to be concerned about the well-being of everyone in our society, and especially those who are hurting and in need. ... But the very first right we must protect, if all human rights are to be protected, is the right to life for the unborn."[18]

Bishop Thomas G. Doran

Rockford, Illinois

Saying "There are Other Issues" is Inane.

"Others say, 'There are other rights besides the right to life. There are other issues besides abortion.' These statements seem inane. What right can you exercise if you are dead? What issues do you have that would last beyond the grave?"[19]

Bishop Kevin Farrell

Dallas, and

Bishop Kevin Vann

Fort Worth

Let Us Be Clear – Not All Issues Have the Same Moral Equivalence.

"As Catholics we are faced with a number of issues that are of concern and should be addressed, such as immigration reform, healthcare, the economy and its solvency, care and concern for the poor, and the war on terror. As Catholics we must be concerned about these issues and work to see that just solutions are brought about. There are many possible solutions to these issues and there can be reasonable debate among Catholics on how to best approach and solve them. These are matters of 'prudential judgment.' *But let us be clear: issues of prudential judgment are not morally equivalent to issues involving intrinsic evils. No matter how right a given candidate is on any of these issues, it does not outweigh a candidate's unacceptable position in favor of an intrinsic evil such as abortion or the protection of 'abortion rights.'"[20]*

Bishop Ronald W. Gainer

Lexington, Kentucky

Abortion is the Paramount Issue of Our Time.

"Catholic moral teaching is not a hodge-podge of competing and equally valid opinions.

"Granted that there are many and complex issues that are in our hearts and on our minds as we go to the polls ... For that matter, Catholics and all people of good will can arrive at different opinions and various solutions for such issues as the delivery of health care, the revitalization of the economy, the use of military force, taxation policies, and the many other issues that face voters in the upcoming election.

"However, we must be aware that not all political issues carry the same moral weight and that there is a serious moral obligation on all of us to oppose in conscience and in action those issues that are intrinsically evil. We are not free to choose whether or not we shall oppose those things which in and of themselves are always and everywhere morally evil.

"From this, it is clear that the defense of the sacredness of human life from the very moment of conception to natural death is THE paramount issue of our time. Abortion, euthanasia, human cloning and embryonic stem cell research are intrinsic evils – actions that are always and everywhere wrong and no circumstance can justify their use. Each is a direct attack on innocent human life."[21]

Bishop Joseph A. Galante

Camden, New Jersey

Catholics Cannot Equate Lesser Issues to Abortion.

"[T]he Church teaches that there may be circumstances under which defensive war may be necessary and just to protect innocent human life. ... Similarly, while there are virtually no instances in modern society under which the death penalty may be considered morally acceptable, the Church teaches that there may be circumstances — however rare and unlikely — under which it may be justified. ...

"Some issues, however, do not admit of exception, are never permissible, can never be supported, and must always be opposed. Abortion, which involves the direct taking of an innocent human life; euthanasia, the direct termination of the life of a person with disabilities or who is sick or dying; and *embryonic* stem cell research, where human embryos are destroyed in order to extract their cells for therapeutic purposes, are all gravely wrong and must be given special priority and weight. This is so because they rest on foundational moral principles that can never be compromised, namely, the dignity of innocent human life and the right to life.

"So, while the Church concerns itself with a broad range of issues that have serious moral implications, it also recognizes that not all issues carry equal moral weight. Certain issues have unique status and must weigh more heavily on the Catholic conscience. As Catholics, then, we do not weigh a wide range of issues against abortion and euthanasia and consider whether they cumulatively outweigh the intrinsic evil of taking an innocent life, since this intrinsic evil never can be justified. ...

"Simply put, our concern for the *dignity of the human person already born is rendered moot if we do not place first concern on the right of that person to be born.*

"Certainly, efforts to reduce the root causes of abortion by providing economic supports and assistance for low-income women and families and access to quality childcare for working mothers must be encouraged. Yet to say, 'I will address those factors that might have the benefit of reducing abortion, but will not oppose the very laws that permit it,' is not only unpersuasive, it also is an illogical and unsustainable position."[22]

Francis Cardinal George

Archbishop of Chicago

Abortion is a Defining Issue.

"[Abortion is] a defining issue not only personally but also socially. Poverty can be addressed incrementally, but the death of a child is quite final."[23]

Abortion is Not a Matter of Prudential Judgment.

Cardinal George responding to the question of whether overturning *Roe v. Wade* is a matter of prudential judgment for a Catholic:

"It can't be. If you've got an immoral law, you've got to work to change that. You've got children being killed every day. It goes on forever. That's the great scandal, and that's why there's such a sense of urgency now. There's no recognition of the fact that children continue to be killed, and we live, therefore, in a country drenched in blood. This can't be something that you start playing off pragmatically against other issues."

And to the contention that supporting better health care and anti-poverty measures is not an acceptable alternative to outlawing abortion, Cardinal George responded, "Absolutely right."[24]

Archbishop José H. Gomez

San Antonio, Texas

The Right to Life is in the Declaration of Independence.

"[A]bortion is an issue that affects all segments of our society. It represents the primary right guaranteed in our Declaration of Independence – the right to life. Unless we protect this fundamental right of each human person, at all stages of life, no other issue or liberty matters."[25]

Bishop F. Joseph Gossman

Raleigh, North Carolina

Life Comes First.

"All issues are not of equal moral worth. Life comes first."[26]

Archbishop Wilton D. Gregory

Atlanta

Without the Right to be Born, Other Issues Don't Matter.

"According to the principles of *Faithful Citizenship,* Catholics must support the just care of the poor, the rights of workers, the dignity of people who immigrate to a new nation, the conservation of the environment; we must assess the very complex economic issues, seek to provide affordable health care for people who do not enjoy that security, and foster the more humane treatment of those who are imprisoned, to list only some of the issues that we now face. However, before and prior to all of those vitally important concerns, *Faithful Citizenship* places the issue of Life itself. All of those other matters are of immense and lasting significance, yet they remain of no consequence for those who are not granted the first right – the right to be born."[27]

Bishop James V. Johnston

Springfield-Cape Girardeau, Missouri

Other Social Issues Are Not Morally Equivalent to the Destruction of Innocent Human Life.

"The bishops also point out two temptations that can distort the church's defense of human life and dignity. 'The first is a moral equivalence that makes no ethical distinctions between the different kinds of issues involving human life and dignity. The direct and intentional destruction of innocent human life from the moment of conception until natural death is always wrong and is not just one issue among many.' This means that one cannot make other social issues such as education or health care morally equivalent to the deliberate destruction of innocent human life.

"Issues such as how to provide affordable health care or better education or how to conduct and conclude a war are issues that are open to principled debate as to how they should be addressed; as they say, 'there is more than one way to skin a cat.' Life issues such as abortion, euthanasia, and embryonic stem-cell research are not in that category. These are simply always wrong in every conceivable circumstance. Not only that, they strike at the very foundational right upon which all other rights depend, the right to life.

"The second temptation the bishops cite relates to a 'misuse of necessary moral distinctions as a way of dismissing or ignoring other serious threats to human life and dignity.' Catholics cannot treat other issues related to human dignity and justice as optional."[28]

Bishop Peter J. Jugis

Charlotte, North Carolina

Other Issues Do Not Have the Same Moral Weight.

"[N]ot all moral issues have the same moral weight. Procured abortion is always intrinsically evil and can never be justified. It is a direct attack on an innocent human life. The destruction of human embryos for stem cell research is also intrinsically evil, as is euthanasia. They can never be justified because all these directly target and destroy innocent human life.

"Other moral issues do not have the same moral weight. ... [T]he death penalty may be justified in very limited instances: 'in cases of absolute necessity ... when it would not be possible otherwise to defend society ... [and today] such cases are very rare, if not practically non-existent' (Evangelium vitae, 56; cf. also CCC 2267). The Catechism reminds us that war, for instance, may also be justified under certain defined conditions (CCC 2309). But procured abortion may never be justified. Euthanasia may never be justified. Destruction of human embryos for stem cell research may never be justified. They are always intrinsically evil."[29]

Bishop David Kagan

Bismarck, North Dakota

Abortion is the Fundamental Issue.

"[T]here are some actions that are never acceptable and should not be made so by law. They include abortion, euthanasia, embryonic stem cell research, and not recognizing the unique and special role of marriage as the union of one man and one woman.

"All the other social, economic, and political issues only gain importance from the fundamental issue of the respect for the individual person and the inviolability of each person's life and God-given dignity."[30]

Pope St. John Paul II

The Right to Be Born Comes First.

"Above all, the common outcry, which is justly made on behalf of human rights – for example, the right to health, to home, to work, to family, to culture – is false and illusory if the right to life, the most basic and fundamental right and the condition for all other personal rights, is not defended with maximum determination."[31]

The Right to Be Born is the First Right.

The right to be born is "the first right, on which all the others are based, and which cannot be recuperated once it is lost."[32]

Abortion is Murder of the Most Innocent.

"Among all the crimes which can be committed against life, procured abortion has characteristics making it particularly serious and deplorable. The Second Vatican Council defines abortion, together with infanticide, as an 'unspeakable crime'... The moral gravity of procured abortion is apparent in all its truth if we recognize that we are dealing with murder and, in particular, when we consider the specific elements involved. The one eliminated is a human being at the very beginning of life. No one more absolutely innocent could be imagined. In no way could this human being ever be considered an aggressor, much less an unjust aggressor! He or she is weak, defenceless, even to the point of lacking that minimal form of defence consisting in the poignant power of a newborn baby's cries and tears."[33]

Bishop William E. Lori

Bridgeport, Connecticut

Catholic Social Teachings Are Weighted.

"Contrary to what many believe, the Church's social teaching is both consistent and broad. It includes questions on the protection of the vulnerable, including the unborn and the frail elderly, as well as questions on war and peace, labor, economics, race relations, education, the environment, and the overall just ordering of society.

"Those teachings are also weighted. The most vulnerable and innocent deserve the most protection. Hence the Church's uncompromising stand on the need to legally protect unborn human life, even at its earliest stages, and to never use it merely as a means to an end – as in embryonic stem-cell research – no matter how compelling that goal might seem. After all, if a human person does not enjoy the right to life, he or she enjoys none of the other rights that are consonant with human dignity."[34]

Archbishop William Levada

San Francisco

Abortion Has Greater Moral Weight Than Other Social Issues.

"Catholic social teaching covers a broad range of important issues, but not all moral issues have the same moral weight as abortion and euthanasia. ... Paramount among these moral principles is the sanctity of human life."[35]

Bishop Paul S. Loverde

Arlington, Virginia, and

Bishop Francis X. DiLorenzo

Richmond, Virginia

We Must Compare the Gravity of Abortion to Lesser Issues.

"[One] would need to compare the gravity of abortion against the gravity of the other considerations. And making that comparison would necessarily involve examining just how serious abortion is in terms of its very nature and in terms of its impact on members of the human family. That means we must appreciate the difference in moral gravity between policies which are intrinsically unjust (e.g., abortion, euthanasia, and the deliberate destruction of human embryos) and policies involving prudential judgments about which people of good will may disagree concerning various means of promoting economic justice, public safety, and fair opportunities for every person.[36] ...

"[T]he proper formation of conscience also means discerning the differences in moral gravity among various issues. Disregarding the right to life itself — the foundation upon which all other human rights are based and without which no other right could possibly exist — is more serious than any other human rights violation."[37]

Bishop Joseph F. Martino

Scranton, Pennsylvania

To the Unborn Child, No Other Issue Matters.

"Another argument goes like this: 'As wrong as abortion is, I don't think it is the only relevant 'life' issue that should be considered when deciding for whom to vote.' This reasoning is sound only if other issues carry the same moral weight as abortion does, such as in the case of euthanasia and destruction of embryos for research purposes. Health care, education, economic security, immigration, and taxes are very important concerns. ... However, the solutions to problems in these areas do not usually involve a rejection of the sanctity of human life in the way that abortion does. *Being 'right' on taxes, education, health care, immigration, and the economy fails to make up for the error of disregarding the value of a human life. Consider this: the finest health and education systems, the fairest immigration laws, and the soundest economy do nothing for the child who never sees the light of day.*

"Even the Church's just war theory has moral force because it is grounded in the principle that innocent human life must be protected and defended. Now, a person may, in good faith, misapply just war criteria leading him to mistakenly believe that an unjust war is just, but he or she still knows that innocent human life may not be harmed on purpose. A person who supports permissive abortion laws, however, rejects the truth that innocent human life may never be destroyed. This profound moral failure runs deeper and is more corrupting of the individual, and of the society, than any error in applying just war criteria to particular cases."[38]

Bishop Timothy A. McDonnell

Springfield, Massachusetts

Abortion is the Foremost "Social Justice Issue."

"The right to life is at the basis of everything else we do. We have to understand that. There's no either/or, abortion or social justice. Abortion is a social justice issue."[39]

Bishop William Murphy

Rockville Centre, New York

The No. 1 Issue is Abortion.

"Many issues are very important in our society today. But none of them can eclipse the centrality of human life, especially innocent human life in the womb or at the end of life. ... Above all and over all, the number one issue more fundamental and crucial than any other is abortion – that is the direct taking of innocent life."[40]

The Right to Be Born is the Foremost Issue.

"All too often — and once is too often — the Church is accused of being a 'single issue' faith community concerning public issues. A glance at the *Compendium of the Social Doctrine of the Church* as well as the U.S. bishops' statement, *Forming Consciences for Faithful Citizenship,* puts that lie to rest. So let's all agree that the Church and Church leadership are not guilty of being single issue.

"What the Church does teach is the truth that the first and foremost issue is that of human life."[41]

Archbishop John J. Myers

Peoria, Illinois

"Abortion is Not Just One Issue Among Many."

"We Catholics have made a comprehensive commitment to justice and to seeking a decent life for everyone, especially the poor and marginalized. No right, however, is more an issue of fundamental justice than the right to be born, the right to live.[42] ... Abortion is not just one issue among many."[43]

Bishop R. Walker Nickless

Sioux City, Iowa

The "Direct Taking of Life" Issues Are Non-Negotiable.

"Now, it must be admitted that not every moral evil is equally grave (CCC 1852-1854). Some issues have little effect beyond themselves; some touch on a few related issues; some are foundational to the whole structure of politics and society. The issues which have been labeled as 'non-negotiable Catholic issues' are the most grave, because they are at the foundation of all our rights and responsibilities. These are, namely, the 'life issues' of abortion, euthanasia, embryonic stem cell research, and human cloning; and the fundamental social issue of the family, which in this country today mostly means the definition of marriage. These issues are 'non-negotiable' because, if the fundamental right to life is not secure, no rights are ultimately secure. If existence is contingent upon the will of others, so too is every other human right contingent."[44]

Archbishop Edwin F. O'Brien

The Military Services

Among Moral Issues, Abortion is Preeminent.

"Our bishops' statements remind us that there are any number of moral concerns facing our electorate ... But among these and many other matters of moral concern, one subject stands out as preeminent – foundational to every other. And that is the sacred dignity of human life and the right to life itself!"[45]

Bishop Thomas Olmsted

Phoenix

Catholics May Disagree on Many Issues, But Not on Abortion.

"In 2002, the Congregation for the Doctrine of the Faith issued a document entitled, Doctrinal Note on Some Questions Regarding Participation of Catholics in Political Life, that addresses the existence of political matters in which Catholics may disagree. There are, indeed, many issues upon which Catholics may legitimately differ such as the best methods to achieve welfare reform or to address illegal immigration.

"Conversely, however, there are other issues that are intrinsically evil and can never legitimately be supported. For example, Catholics may never legitimately promote or vote for any law that attacks innocent human life.

"There are some matters, however, on which Catholics may disagree with the Church's hierarchy. In some cases, for example, a Catholic may agree with the teaching of the Church, but come to a different prudential judgment about its application.

"Examples of these issues might include an instance where someone agrees with the Church's teaching on 'just war' or 'capital punishment,' but reaches a different conclusion as to whether the facts of the situation constitute a 'just war' or the 'rare' circumstances where capital punishment may be used under Church teaching.

"It should be emphasized, however, that despite these examples, there are other issues, such as abortion or euthanasia, that are always wrong and do not allow for the correct use of prudential judgment to justify them. It would never be proper for Catholics to be on the opposite side of these issues."[46]

Cardinal Seán Patrick O'Malley

Boston

The Centerpiece of the Church's Social Teaching is the Right to Be Born.

"The church's social teaching is very coherent and extends to all aspects of economic justice, racial equality, war and peace, immigration, education, and healthcare issues. But the centerpiece of our teaching will always be the right to life."[47]

Pope Benedict XVI

(as Cardinal Joseph Ratzinger)

Not All Moral Issues Have the Same Weight.

"Not all moral issues have the same weight as abortion and euthanasia. For example, if a Catholic were to be at odds with the Holy Father [John Paul II] on the application of capital punishment or on the decision to wage war, he would not for that reason be considered unworthy to present himself to receive Holy Communion. While the Church exhorts civil authorities to seek peace, not war, and to exercise discretion and mercy in imposing punishment on criminals, it may still be permissible to take up arms to repel an aggressor or to have recourse to capital punishment. There may be a diversity of opinion even among Catholics about waging war and applying the death penalty, but not however with regard to abortion and euthanasia."[48]

Bishop Alexander K. Sample

Marquette, Michigan

Matters of Intrinsic Evil Outweigh Other Issues.

"As Catholics we are faced with a number of issues that are of concern and should be addressed, such as immigration reform, healthcare, the economy and its solvency, care and concern for the poor, and the war on terror. As Catholics we must be concerned about these issues and work to see that just solutions are brought about. There are many possible solutions to these issues and there can be reasonable debate among Catholics on how to best approach and solve them. These are matters of 'prudential judgment.' But let us be clear: issues of prudential judgment are not morally equivalent to issues involving intrinsic evils. No matter how right a given candidate is on any of these issues, it does not outweigh a candidate's unacceptable position in favor of an intrinsic evil such as abortion or the protection of 'abortion rights.'

"As *Forming Consciences for Faithful Citizenship* states:

"'The direct and intentional destruction of innocent human life from the moment of conception until natural death is always wrong and is not just one issue among many. It must always be opposed.'"[49]

Bishop Arthur Joseph Serratelli

Paterson, New Jersey

Abortion is First in the Church's Hierarchy of Issues.

"Some say Catholics are a one-issue people. This is blatantly false! The Church speaks often and at length on social justice, the global economy, the environment, capital punishment, poverty and war, as well as on respect for life. The Church's teaching is logical. The Church recognizes a hierarchy of values. Not all moral issues bear the same moral weight. We can defend our own life when attacked. We should defend the rights of others. At times the evil of war may be permitted – lamentably and always as the last resort – to guarantee and protect the rights and lives of innocent people. But the direct killing of innocent life is always wrong. Abortion, euthanasia, embryonic stem cell research and human cloning destroy the most fundamental right of all – the right to live. They are never permitted! They are intrinsically evil."[50]

Bishop Bernard W. Schmitt

Wheeling-Charleston, West Virginia

All Evils Are Not Equal, and Abortion is the Greatest Evil.

"[I] want to say, clearly and distinctly, as your brother and your Bishop, abortion is the greatest moral evil of our age. As the deliberate killing of an innocent human being, there is 'no circumstance, no purpose, no law whatsoever' that can justify or excuse abortion. (*Evangelium vitae, 62*).

"It is true that there are other evils which occupy our attention as a society, especially during an election. Euthanasia, the death penalty, war, genocide, hunger, abject poverty, discrimination, and unjust labor practices are all attacks on human dignity and the value of human life. ...

"All evils are not equal. Abortion, representing as it does an attack on the most innocent of all human life and the most sacred of all human relationships, is so grave and profound an evil that it calls all men and women of good will to action."[51]

Bishop Michael J. Sheridan

Colorado Springs, Colorado

Abortion Trumps All Other Issues.

"In the midst of what could be a difficult and confusing exercise [an upcoming election] it is very important to remember that not all issues are of equal gravity. As men and women of good will we strive to achieve true justice for all people and to preserve their rights as human beings. There is, however, one right that is "inalienable," and that is the RIGHT TO LIFE. This is the FIRST right. This is the right that grounds all other human rights. This is the issue that trumps all other issues."[52]

Bishop Larry Silva

Honolulu, Hawaii

Without Life, All Other Issues Do Not Matter.

"There are many issues to consider: war, the economy, ecology, the stability of the family, health care, education, the elimination of poverty at home and abroad. Among the many issues to be weighed, however, one issue alone far outweighs all others: the right to life. Without life, all other issues do not matter. It is the right to life that is fundamental. Abortion in a special way is an issue that we need to focus on, since it is a violation of the human rights of human beings who are so vulnerable they cannot speak for or defend themselves. It is the most widespread – and the only legal – form of domestic violence. It is a cancer that erodes our respect for one another in many different ways. It is a hidden source of anger, depression and denial for those who cannot admit what they know in their heart of hearts, that it is the deliberate taking of the life of a real human girl or boy."[53]

Bishop Richard Stika

Knoxville, Tennessee

A Catholic Cannot Be Pro-Choice.

"One cannot be pro-choice and an authentic Catholic! Simple as that. Everything else is secondary ... immigration, poverty ... these have political solutions."[54]

Bishop John M. Smith

Trenton, New Jersey

Opposition to Abortion Must Be a Priority for Catholics.

"There is a multitude of serious issues facing voters ... [W]e know that support and promotion of abortion is always wrong and can never be justified. Opposition to abortion must be a priority for Catholics who support the Church's teaching about the sacredness of life."[55]

Bishop Paul J. Swain

Sioux Falls, South Dakota

Without Life, There Are No Other Issues.

"While it is true that there are a variety of important issues affecting the quality of life in the years after birth and before death, they are meaningless if there is no life to begin with.

"Without life there are no other issues.

"This is the stark reality we as faithful Catholics should bring to our election decisions concerning candidates and referenda."[56]

Bishop James Timlin

Scranton, Pennsylvania

Abortion Takes Precedence Over Every Other Issue.

"Abortion is the issue this year and every year in every campaign. Catholics may not turn away from the moral challenge that abortion poses for those who seek to obey God's commands. They are wrong when they assert that abortion does not concern them, or that it is only one of a multitude of issues of equal importance. No, the taking of innocent human life is so heinous, so horribly evil, and so absolutely opposite to the law of Almighty God that abortion must take precedence over every other issue. I repeat. It is the single most important issue confronting not only Catholics, but the entire electorate. ...

"... I urge Catholics to focus on the real issue of this campaign, the right to life."[57]

Bishop Robert Vasa

Baker, Oregon

No Good Work Compensates for Ignoring Abortion.

"A person may work very admirably to alleviate poverty, but this does not justify ignoring the greatest poverty which is the one which fails to recognize the value of life. A person may work very admirably to promote social justice, but this does not justify turning a blind eye to the greatest injustice openly operative in our society which is the unjust deprivation of the pre-born of their most basic constitutional right, the right to life."[58]

Archbishop John Vlazny

Portland in Oregon

The Bishops' Teaching on Abortion Carries Moral Authority.

The ongoing war and terrorism in Iraq and across the Middle East are ... matters of urgent concern. [P]rudential judgment will be needed in applying moral principles to specific policy choices in this regard. The same is true in our discussions about housing, health care, immigration and other such issues. Here the judgments and recommendations of the bishops will not carry the same moral authority as do statements of universal moral teachings, such as those affecting human life."[59]

Archbishop Donald W. Wuerl

Washington, D.C.

No Other Issue Rises to This Level of Moral Certitude.

"*Forming Consciences* tells us that in the public political debate today there is no other issue that rises to this level of moral certitude. Abortion is always wrong."[60]

The U.S. Conference of Catholic Bishops

Abortion is not just "one issue among many."

"The direct and intentional destruction of innocent human life from the moment of conception until natural death is always wrong and is not just one issue among many. It must always be opposed."[61]

Abortion is an "Intrinsically Evil" Action, Superior to Other Issues.

"There are some things we must never do, as individuals or as a society, because they are always incompatible with love of God and neighbor. Such actions are so deeply flawed that they are always opposed to the authentic good of persons. These are called 'intrinsically evil' actions. They must always be rejected and opposed and must never be supported or condoned. A prime example is the intentional taking of innocent human life, as in abortion and euthanasia. In our nation, 'abortion and euthanasia have become preeminent threats to human dignity because they directly attack life itself, the most fundamental human good and the condition for all others' (Living the Gospel of Life, no. 5). It is a mistake with grave moral consequences to treat the destruction of innocent human life merely as a matter of individual choice. A legal system that violates the basic right to life on the grounds of choice is fundamentally flawed."[62]

Abortion is the Fundamental Human Rights Issue.

"At this particular time, abortion has become the fundamental human rights issue for all men and women of good will. .... For us abortion is of overriding concern because it negates two of our most fundamental moral imperatives: respect for innocent life, and preferential concern for the weak and defenseless."[63]

It is Imperative to Give Priority to Abortion.

"Among important issues involving the dignity of human life with which the Church is concerned, abortion necessarily plays a central role. Abortion, the direct killing of an innocent human being, is always gravely immoral (The Gospel of Life, no. 57); its victims are the most vulnerable and defenseless members of the human family. It is imperative that those who are called to serve the least among us give urgent attention and priority to this issue of justice."[64]

Abortion is the Preeminent Issue.

"[A]bortion and euthanasia have become preeminent threats to human dignity because they directly attack life itself, the most fundamental human good and the condition for all others."[65]

Being Right on Some Issues Doesn't Excuse Being Wrong on Abortion.

"Any politics of human life must work to resist the violence of war and the scandal of capital punishment. Any politics of human dignity must seriously address issues of racism, poverty, hunger, employment, education, housing, and health care. ... Catholic public officials are obliged to address each of these issues as they seek to build consistent policies which promote respect for the human person at all stages of life. *But being 'right' in such matters can never excuse a wrong choice regarding direct attacks on innocent human life.* ... As Pope John Paul II reminds us, the command never to kill establishes a minimum which we must respect and from which we must start out 'in order to say yes over and over again, a yes which will gradually embrace the *entire horizon of the good.'" (Evangelium Vitae, 75).*[66]

The Catholic Bishops of Kansas

Unlike Issues of Prudential Judgment, Abortion is Pure Evil.

"In some moral matters the use of reason allows for a legitimate diversity in our prudential judgments. Catholic voters may differ, for example, on what constitutes the best immigration policy, how to provide universal health care, or affordable housing. Catholics may even have differing judgments on the state's use of the death penalty or the decision to wage a just war. The morality of such questions lies not in what is done (the moral object), but in the motive and circumstances. Therefore, because these prudential judgments do not involve a direct choice of something evil and take into consideration various goods, it is possible for Catholic voters to arrive at different, even opposing judgments. ...

"A correct conscience recognizes that there are some choices that always involve doing evil and which can never be done even as a means to a good end. These choices include elective abortion, euthanasia, physician-assisted suicide, the destruction of embryonic human beings in stem cell research, human cloning, and same-sex 'marriage.' Such acts are judged to be intrinsically evil, that is, evil in and of themselves, regardless of our motives or the circumstances. They constitute an attack against innocent human life, as well as marriage and family."[67]

The Catholic Bishops of Massachusetts

Abortion is of Absolute Centrality Among Issues.

"We ... in a particular way, wish to underscore the absolute centrality of the protection of human life. Support and promotion of abortion by any candidate is always wrong and can never be justified. We will never cease to denounce abortion and euthanasia and teach all Catholics that to support those positions is to support death over life."[68]

The Catholic Bishops of New York State

The Right to Live Outweighs Other Catholic Concerns.

"[A]s the U.S. Bishops' recent document Forming Consciences for Faithful Citizenship makes clear, not every issue is of equal moral gravity. The inalienable right to life of every innocent human person outweighs other concerns where Catholics may use prudential judgment, such as how best to meet the needs of the poor or to increase access to health care for all. ... To the extent candidates reject this fundamental right by supporting an objective evil, such as legal abortion, euthanasia or embryonic stem cell research, Catholics should consider them less acceptable for public office."[69]

The Catholic Bishops of Pennsylvania

Protecting Human Life is the Preeminent Obligation of Society.

"We wish to reiterate that the intentional destruction of innocent human life, as in abortion and euthanasia, is not just one issue among many. Time and time again, we bishops have taught that the right to life is the most basic and fundamental human right and must always be defended. Intrinsic evils can never be supported.

"Catholic teaching does not treat all issues as morally equivalent. The protection of human life from conception until natural death is the preeminent obligation of a truly just society."[70]

The Catholic Bishops of Wisconsin

The Right to Live is the Most Essential of All Human Rights.

"First and foremost, the right to life of every human person – from conception to natural death – is the primary and thus most essential of all human rights."[71]

Congregation for the Doctrine of the Faith

The Right to Live is Superior to All Other Rights.

"The first right of the human person is his life. He has other goods and some are more precious, but this one is fundamental – the condition of all the others. Hence it must be protected above all others. It does not belong to society, nor does it belong to public authority in any form to recognize this right for some and not for others: all discrimination is evil, whether it be founded on race, sex, color or religion. It is not recognition by another that constitutes this right. This right is antecedent to its recognition; it demands recognition and it is strictly unjust to refuse it."[73]

Father Richard J. Neuhaus

Editor, First Things magazine

Abortion is Not One Issue Among Others.

"Is it possible to vote for any politician who persistently — publicly, defiantly and in the face of repeated pastoral efforts at reproach — continues to

179

support *Roe v. Wade?*

"Rome has made it clear that abortion is not one issue among others. It is intrinsically evil. That cannot be said of any other issue in mainstream U.S. politics today."[73]

Father Stephen F. Torraco

Associate Professor of Theology, Assumption College

Abortion and the Death Penalty Are Not Equivalent Issues.

"It is not correct to think of abortion and capital punishment as the very same kind of moral issue. On the one hand, direct abortion is an intrinsic evil, and cannot be justified for any purpose or in any circumstances. On the other hand, the Church has always taught that it is the right and responsibility of the legitimate temporal authority to defend and preserve the common good, and more specifically to defend citizens against the aggressor. This defense against the aggressor may resort to the death penalty if no other means of defense is sufficient. The point here is that the death penalty is understood as an act of self-defense on the part of civil society.

"In more recent times, in his encyclical *Evangelium Vitae,* Pope John Paul II has taught that the need for such self-defense to resort to the death penalty is "rare, if not virtually nonexistent." Thus, while the Pope is saying that the burden of proving the need for the death penalty in specific cases should rest on the shoulders of the legitimate temporal authority, it remains true that the legitimate temporal authority alone has the authority to determine if and when a 'rare' case arises that warrants the death penalty. Moreover, if such a rare case does arise and requires resorting to capital punishment, this societal act of self-defense would be a 'morally good action' even if it does have the unintended and unavoidable evil effect of the death of the aggressor. Thus, unlike the case of abortion, it would be morally irresponsible to rule out all such 'rare' possibilities *a priori,* just as it would be morally irresponsible to apply the death penalty indiscriminately."[74]

Deacon Michael Bickerstaff

Editor in Chief, The Integrated Catholic Life

Abortion is of Greater Weight Than Other Moral Wrongs.

"Opposition to abortion and euthanasia does not excuse indifference to those who suffer from poverty, violence and injustice. ... *But being 'right' in such matters can never excuse a wrong choice regarding direct attacks on innocent human life.* ... If we understand the human person as the 'temple of the Holy Spirit' – the living house of God – then these latter issues fall logically into place as the crossbeams and walls of that house. *All direct attacks on innocent human life, such as abortion and euthanasia, strike at the house's foundation.* These directly and immediately violate the human person's most fundamental right – the right to life. Neglect of these issues is the equivalent of building our house on sand.

"In our opposition to abortion, we are not excused from caring about other moral wrongs; we may not be indifferent to them. But, abortion and euthanasia are not two of many morally equivalent attacks on human dignity and life; these two direct attacks are preeminent moral threats against life; they are of a greater moral weight."[75]

Deal Hudson

Publisher and Editor, The Christian Review

Abortion is Not a Matter of a Catholic's Prudential Judgment.

"Few Catholics make the distinction between binding statements of principle and the non-binding prudential judgments by the USCCB on policy issues and its support of specific pieces of legislation before Congress. ... Catholic principles apply to all political issues but, in many cases, do not lead prudentially to only one acceptable or 'official' Catholic position. However, abortion, euthanasia, and gay marriage are matters of principle that do not admit prudential judgments, and therefore can never be supported."[76]

18

The Seamless Garment Ripped to Shreds

Catholics Must Always Vote For the Most Anti-Abortion Candidate, or Risk Their Eternal Salvation.

The previous chapter featured candid bishops, priests and others who have explicitly declared that there is a hierarchy of societal issues for Catholics and no other issue is as important as abortion because of its intrinsic evilness and its prevalence in today's world. In this chapter, we read statements from clerics stating that abortion is therefore the most important issue for a Catholic to consider when voting. (The offices cited are those held at the time of the quotation.)

Archbishop Eusebius J. Beltran

Oklahoma City, Oklahoma

"I Am Proud to Be a Single Issue Voter"

"Several years ago, I remember being criticized for urging people to vote pro-life. I was accused of being a 'single issue voter.' On reflection, that's not a bad designation. If one issue is big enough and important enough and capable of overshadowing other issues, then it should be addressed. If one issue is so fundamental that it affects every other issue, then it should be given prominence. If one issue perpetrates a grave injustice to anyone, then it has to be stopped. If one issue is a matter of life or death, then life has to be chosen. The one issue that is reflected in each of these situations is abortion. Therefore I am proud to be called a 'single issue voter' in this regard for there is no other issue as basic, as fundamental and as urgent.

"Abortion is the most serious and critical problem we are faced with today."[1]

Archbishop Raymond L. Burke

St. Louis

There is No Excuse for a Catholic to Vote for a Pro-Choice Candidate.

"The Church ... recognizes that it is sometimes impossible to avoid all cooperation with evil, as may well be true in selecting a candidate for public office. In certain circumstances, it is morally permissible for a Catholic to vote for a candidate who supports some immoral practices while opposing other immoral practices. ... But, there is no element of the common good, no morally good practice, that a candidate may promote and to which a voter may be dedicated, which could justify voting for a candidate who also endorses and supports the deliberate killing of the innocent, abortion, embryonic stem-cell research, euthanasia, human cloning or the recognition of a same-sex relationship as legal marriage. These elements are so fundamental to the common good that they cannot be subordinated to any other cause, no matter how good."[2]

In Voting There is an Order of Priority.

"We are morally bound in conscience to choose leaders at all levels of government, who will best serve the common good, 'the sum total of social conditions which allow people, either as groups or as individuals, to reach their fulfillment more fully and more easily' (*Gaudium et spes, n. 26a*). ... In considering 'the sum total of social conditions,' there is, however, a certain order of priority, which must be followed. Conditions upon which other conditions depend must receive our first consideration. The first consideration must be given to the protection of human life itself, without which it makes no sense to consider other social conditions."[3]

Voting For a Pro-Choice Candidate Cannot Be Justified.

"Some Catholics have suggested that a candidate's position on the death penalty and war are as important as his or her position on procured abortion and same-sex 'marriage.' This, however, is not true. Procured abortion and homosexual acts are intrinsically evil, and, as such, can never be justified in any circumstance.

"Although war and capital punishment can rarely be justified, they are not intrinsically evil; neither practice includes the direct intention of killing innocent human beings. In some circumstances, self-defense and defense of the nation are not only rights, but responsibilities. Neither individuals nor governments can be denied the right of lawful defense in appropriate circumstances (*cf. Catechism of the Catholic Church, nn. 2265 and 2309*). While we must all work to eradicate the circumstances which could justify either practice, we must stop the killing of innocent unborn children and the practice of euthanasia, and safeguard marriage and the family now.

"One cannot justify a vote for a candidate who promotes intrinsically evil acts which erode the very foundation of the common good, such as abortion and same-sex 'marriage,' by appealing to that same candidate's opposition to war or capital punishment.

"Some Catholics, too, have suggested that a candidate's position on other issues involving human rights are as important as his or her position on the right to life. Our Holy Father Pope John Paul II has reminded us that, in order to defend all human rights, we must first defend the right to life."[4]

Bishop Ronald W. Gainer

Lexington, Kentucky

On Abortion, Catholics Must Be Single-Issue Voters.

"We have all heard fellow Catholics say that 'I cannot be a single issue voter.' Fair enough – there are many issues on all of our minds. But consider this. If someone were to break into your home – your place of security and well-being – and hold a scalpel to your throat with the intent to kill you, I suspect that you would in that moment become a single issue person. In that instant, everything would focus on the one question: 'What must I do to survive?' Everything else immediately becomes secondary. Many of the unborn are precisely in that situation. They cannot act in their own defense. You and I must."[5]

Bishop Robert Hermann

Archdiocesan Administrator, St. Louis

Elections Are About Saving Our Children. Other Issues Take Second Place.

"More than anything else, (elections are) about saving our children or killing our children. *This life issue is the overriding issue facing each of us ... All other issues, including the economy, have to take second place to the issue of life.*"[6]

Cardinal James Hickey

Washington

One Issue Rises Above the Others.

"[T]here is one issue that rises above the others. When you vote ... I hope and pray that you will not forget the most disenfranchised citizens in this land – the unborn."[7]

Adam Cardinal Maida

Detroit

Most Importantly, Where Does the Candidate Stand on Abortion?

"[M]ost importantly, where does the candidate stand on abortion, described by the Michigan Catholic Conference as the preeminent threat to human dignity because it directly attacks life itself, the most fundamental human good and the condition for all others?"[8]

Monsignor Kevin McMahon

John Cardinal Krol Chair of Moral Theology, St. Charles Borromeo Seminary

A Candidate's Correct Stance on Other Issues Doesn't Matter.

"[A] voter who disagrees with a candidate's support for abortion or euthanasia would not be justified in voting for that candidate because the candidate favors such worthy objectives as improving education, health care, the environment, and so forth. Some mistakenly think that the pursuit of a 'greater' good constitutes a proportionate reason for performing or assisting in acts which are intrinsically evil."[9]

Archbishop John J. Myers

Newark

For Catholic Voters, Abortion is the Foremost Issue.

"As voters, Catholics are under an obligation to avoid implicating themselves in abortion, which is one of the gravest of injustices. Certainly, there are other injustices, which must be addressed, but the unjust killing of the innocent is foremost among them."[10]

Bishop Thomas Olmsted

Phoenix

Are All Issues Are Equal When Choosing a Political Candidate?

"Absolutely not! The Catholic Church is actively engaged in a wide variety of important public policy issues including immigration, education, affordable housing, health and welfare, to name just a few. On each of these issues we should do our best to be informed and to support those proposed solutions that seem most likely to be effective. However, when it comes to direct attacks on innocent human life, being right on all the other issues can never justify a wrong choice on this most serious matter."[11]

Bishop Dennis M. Schnurr

Duluth, Minnesota

A Catholic Must Always Vote Against Pro-Choice Candidates.

"As followers of Jesus Christ, we must be advocates for the weak, the fragile and the marginalized in all these issues. But advocacy on behalf of others in these situations never excuses wrong choices and attitudes regarding the direct attacks on innocent human life.

"The failure to protect and defend human life in its most vulnerable stages at life's beginning and its natural end makes suspect any claims to the 'rightness' of positions of other matters affecting the poor and powerless of the human family. One does not play with 'percentages' here. A committed and convinced Catholic is always pro-life on the issue of abortion and euthanasia, and that includes the voting booth.

"Let me repeat, there are some actions and behaviors that are always wrong; they are incompatible with our love of God and the dignity of each human person. Abortion, the direct taking of innocent human life prior to birth, is always morally wrong, as is the deliberate destruction of human embryos for any reason. Assisted suicide and euthanasia are not acts of mercy but morally wrong actions. Direct attacks on civilians and terrorist acts are always to be condemned."[12]

Bishop Joseph E. Strickland

Tyler, Texas

We MUST Vote No on Pro-Choice Candidates.

"When we choose a candidate for whatever level of public office, we MUST inquire as to their stand with regard to the life of the unborn. ... Our vote is very often the only voice we have and we MUST VOTE NO to abortion … If a candidate for whatever office callously demands the slaughter of unborn children as a so-called right and vigorously supports organizations that profit from the multi-billion dollar abortion industry, then how can any other human right they may champion be truly meaningful?"[13]

Bishop Thomas J. Tobin

Providence, Rhode Island

Okay, here's how you should vote.

"Okay, here's how you should vote. … Abortion is different (from other issues). It is always intrinsically evil. There are no circumstances that justify abortion. Its victims are innocent and defenseless, and number in the millions. Abortion is the fallacious foundation upon which the culture of death builds its ugly edifice."[14]

Father Stephen F. Torraco

Associate Professor of Theology, Assumption College

A Candidate's Wrong Position on Abortion Cannot Be Offset by Any Other Issue.

In answer to the question: *If I think that a candidate who is pro-abortion has better ideas to serve the poor, and the pro-life candidate has bad ideas that will hurt the poor, why may I not vote for the candidate that has the better ideas for serving the poor?*

"First, when it comes to the matter of determining how social and economic policy can best serve the poor, there can be a legitimate variety of approaches proposed, and therefore legitimate disagreement among voters and candidates for office. Secondly, solidarity can never be at the price of embracing a 'disqualifying issue.' Besides, when it comes to the unborn, abortion is a most grievous offense against solidarity, for the unborn are surely among society's most needful. The right to life is a paramount issue because as Pope John Paul II says it is 'the first right, on which all the others are based, and which cannot be recuperated once it is lost.' If a candidate for office refuses solidarity with the unborn, he has laid the ground for refusing solidarity with anyone."[15]

A Pro-Choice Candidate Disqualifies Himself From a Catholic's Vote.

"A candidate for office who supports abortion rights or any other moral evil has disqualified himself as a person that you can vote for.[16] ...

"[M]oral evils such as abortion, euthanasia and assisted suicide are examples of a 'disqualifying issue.' A disqualifying issue is one which is of such gravity and importance that it allows for no political maneuvering. It is an issue that strikes at the heart of the human person and is non-negotiable.

"A disqualifying issue is one of such enormity that by itself renders a candidate for office unacceptable regardless of his position on other matters. You must sacrifice your feelings on other issues because you know that you cannot participate in any way in an approval of a violent and evil violation of basic human rights.

"Key to understanding the point above about 'disqualifying issues' is the distinction between policy and moral principle. On the one hand, there can be a legitimate variety of approaches to accomplishing a morally acceptable goal. For example, in a society's effort to distribute the goods of health care to its citizens, there can be legitimate disagreement among citizens and political candidates alike as to whether this or that health care plan would most effectively accomplish society's goal. In the pursuit of the best possible policy or strategy, technical as distinct (although not separate) from moral reason is operative. Technical reason is the kind of reasoning involved in arriving at the most efficient or effective result. On the other hand, no policy or strategy that is opposed to the moral principles of the natural law is morally acceptable. Thus, technical reason should always be subordinate to and normed by moral reason, the kind of reasoning that is the activity of conscience and that is based on the natural moral law."[17]

Bishop Robert Vasa

Baker, Oregon

In Voting, Abortion is the Only Deciding Issue.

"When we have (a pro-choice candidate) ... then the other issues, in many ways, do not matter because they are already wrong on that absolutely fundamental issue. ...

"Abortion needs to be in our country a defining issue, and we ought not be afraid to make it a defining issue because when we do that we will have an end of abortion in this country."[18]

The Catholic Bishops of Pennsylvania

For a Catholic Voter, the Right to Live is More Important Than Other Issues.

"[A] voter cannot avoid considering some issues to be more important than others.

"How then does the concerned citizen rank issues? Assisting the unemployed, feeding the hungry, and providing adequate medical care for the sick and poor are crucial human rights concerns. On a broader scale, averting war and protecting human life from destruction and abuse are even more crucial. Each of these issues is important and needs to be addressed.

However, there are significant differences in the issues themselves.

"For example, while no candidates or public officials support nuclear war, they may disagree about how to avoid it. On the right to life issue, however, the disagreement is not in strategies for protecting human life, but whether some lives should be protected at all. This fact changes the way in which a candidate's position should be evaluated."[19]

The Bishops of Massachusetts

Voting For a Pro-Choice Candidate Can Be a Mortal Sin.

"[W]hen it is a matter of choosing between two (candidates), where one is pro-life and the other pro-choice, then we must always choose pro-life."[20]

Father John Trigilio, Jr.

President, Confraternity of Catholic Clergy, Co-Host, EWTN's Web of Faith

Catholics Have a Moral Obligation to Choose the Most Anti-Abortion Candidate.

"Not all moral issues are of the same moral weight. The right to life is paramount; economic, environmental, military, and social issues are secondary, if not tertiary. When the choice is between a candidate who manifests his or her pro-abortion position and a candidate who professes to be pro-life, the moral obligation is to choose life by choosing the pro-life politician.

"It is not that we are single-issue voters, but there is a proportion, a hierarchy of values in which the right to life outweighs all other concerns. The unjust killing of innocent lives is not eclipsed or overshadowed by any other concern. When there are two candidates whose stand on abortion is basically the same, then other issues can and must be brought into the equation to make a prudent vote."[21]

Father Matthew Habiger

Former President, Human Life International

Pro-Abortion Catholic Politicians Should Be Publicly Shamed.

"It is not sufficient to think that, since candidate X takes the 'right position' on other issues such as the economy, foreign relations, defense, etc. but only goes wrong on abortion, one can in good conscience, vote for him/her. *Abortion deals with the first and most basic human right, without which there is nothing left to talk about.*

"Is this too stringent a way of thinking? Is it not nuanced enough, or does it do injustice to the complexities of a pluralistic society? Consider this question in light of another issue. Would voters be understanding and nuanced in their toleration of a known racist? Or would that be sufficient reason for everyone to consider him/her unfit for public office? Why should we understand intolerance in the case of racism, but not in the case of murdering unborn babies? Abortion is not just another 'issue' – it is a matter of life and death, the great civil rights issue of our time. …

"It is a scandal that Catholic politicians vote for bills which fund or otherwise advance abortion. They should be named, publicly shamed and admonished so that they can cease their evil and return to God."[22]

Father Anthony J. Mastroeni

Adjunct Professor, Felician College and Seton Hall University

A Candidate Who is Pro-Choice is Automatically Disqualified.

"There are some political issues that represent 'non-negotiable' moral principles that do not admit of exception or compromise, for they concern intrinsically evil acts or behavior. An individual political position is either in accord with these principles or it is not. And if not, then that position runs contrary to the moral law.

"In the November [2016] election there are six non-negotiable moral issues: Abortion, Euthanasia or assisted suicide, Embryonic Stem Cell Research, Human Cloning, Homosexual Marriage, and Religious Liberty. These moral issues should disqualify any candidate who holds, promotes or protects them of any Catholic vote. Other issues, like providing health care, how to cure the immigration crisis, how to correct foreign trade deficits, do not normally involve intrinsically evil acts which are always and everywhere wrongful. Instead, they admit of a variety of political solutions on which morally prudent persons can differ. ...

"Without governmental protection against intrinsically immoral actions, the common good is gravely imperiled and left to face an uncertain future for democracy.

"As an old Russian peasant was heard to remark in 1917, 'When the country forgets God, it builds its own gallows.' Recently, a leading U.S. churchman stated in his weekly column, "Both candidates [referring to anti-abortion Donald Trump and pro-choice Hillary Clinton] are – what's the right word? – so problematic that neither is clearly better than the other" (*Catholic Standard, Philadelphia, PA, 8/12/16*). To be sure, this kind of advice is not particularly helpful because it is not evidently correct. A cursory look at the official political platforms of both parties will show a moral fault-line of differences existing between them." ...

"Certain issues must always be entered into the moral calculus of one's vote. ... Is this 'single-issue' voting? No, while I do not vote for someone solely on the basis of one issue, there are certain issues that are what we can call 'automatic disqualifiers.' Just as one would most reasonably conclude that a member of the KKK or a neo-Nazi should never hold public office because of his racism, so too any reasonable person can and should conclude that anyone who favors the killing of innocent human babies in the womb is manifestly unfit to hold any position of influence in a civilized society. Or, as the bishops put it:

"As Catholics we are not single-issue voters. A candidate's position on a single issue is not sufficient to guarantee a voter's support. Yet if a candidate's position on a single issue promotes an intrinsically evil act, such as legal abortion, redefining marriage in a way that denies its essential meaning, or racist behavior, a voter may legitimately disqualify a candidate from receiving support.

"And what about 'all the other good positions' a candidate may have, even if lacking in that one area? St. John Paul II, in *Christifideles Laici,* could not be clearer:

"'Above all, the common outcry, which is justly made on behalf of human rights – for example, the right to health, to home, to work, to family, to culture – is false and illusory if the right to life, the most basic and fundamental right and the condition for all other personal rights, is not defended with maximum determination.' (*n. 38*)

"Following on Pope John Paul's assertion, the bishops leave no doubt about Catholic social teaching on abortion and euthanasia: 'The direct and intentional destruction of innocent human life from the moment of conception until natural death is always wrong and is not just one issue among many. It must always be opposed.'

"*Faithful Citizenship* also has counsel on what to do if all candidates are equally bad on critical issues:

"'When all candidates hold a position that promotes an intrinsically evil act, the conscientious voter faces a dilemma. The voter may decide to take the extraordinary step of not voting for any candidate or, after careful deliberation, may decide to vote for the candidate deemed less likely to advance such a morally flawed position and more likely to pursue other authentic human goods. In making these decisions, it is essential for Catholics to be guided by a well-formed conscience that recognizes that all issues do not carry the same moral weight and that the moral obligation to oppose policies promoting intrinsically evil acts has a special claim on our consciences and our actions. These decisions should take into account a candidate's commitments, character, integrity, and ability to influence a given issue.'"[23]

19

Conscience Isn't What You Think, Or What You Think

Wayward Catholic citizens, intentionally or neglectfully, often rationalize the act of voting for pro-choice politicians by citing the Church's teaching that "man has the right to act in conscience and in freedom so as personally to make moral decisions," as the *Catechism* sets out.[1] They thereby find all kinds of ways, "in conscience," to justify their sinful votes: "He's great on immigration" or "She wants to help the poor" or "He's such an anti-war crusader." Of course, these may be laudable positions, but none surpass the moral gravity of abortion, and none, the Church teaches, excuse voting for the candidate who is not the most anti-abortion. Still, many Catholics use the *Catechism's* "conscience" precept as a rationale, a loophole, for immoral voting behavior.

It is true that if a Catholic were to seek the meaning of "conscience" in any given dictionary, he might find something like this: "an inner feeling used as a guide to discern the rightness or wrongness of a person's own behavior." Thus do many Catholics rely merely on such an internal "feeling," one that is informed only by preexistent knowledge, when they vote. But, from a Catholic perspective, that definition of "conscience" is so deficient as to be thoroughly incorrect. Your conscience must be properly formed – that is, *informed* – by the Church's teaching before you can morally rely on it. To act without doing so is, itself, a sin of omission that can lead to the mortal sin of voting for a candidate who is not the one most opposed to abortion.

So corrupted has the Catholic Church's authentic definition of "conscience" become that the anti-Catholic, rabidly pro-abortion group, "Catholics for Choice," has as its motto, "In Good Conscience."

But bishops and priests have roundly made clear that you cannot "vote your conscience" until it is correctly formed by authoritative teaching, i.e., what the Catholic Church teaches.

• "Before following our conscience, we must form it in accord with the voice of God," said Bishop Thomas Olmsted of Phoenix, in a 2006 interview. "Our conscience is not the origin of truth. Truth lies outside us. It exists independent of us and must be discovered through constant effort of mind and heart. ... Conscience receives the truth revealed by God and discerns how to apply that truth to concrete circumstances. ... The education of conscience is indispensable for human beings who are subjected to negative influences and tempted by sin to prefer their own judgment and to reject authoritative teachings." But that they must do."[2]

• "If the candidate about whom you have strong feelings or opinions is pro-abortion," wrote Father Stephen F. Torraco, Ph. D in his esteemed work, *A Brief Catechism for Catholic Voters*, "then your feelings and opinions need to be corrected by your correctly informed conscience, which would tell you that it is wrong for you to allow your feelings and opinions to give lesser weight to the fact that the candidate supports a moral evil."[3]

• "Although we must all follow our consciences," said Bishop John J. Myers, "the task of conscience is not to create moral truth but to *perceive* it. It is quite possible for an individual to perceive the moral reality of a particular situation erroneously. Such a person may be *sincere*, but he or she is *sincerely wrong*."[4]

• "Often we hear people claim that they are making decisions in accord with conscience even when those decisions defy the natural law and the revealed teachings of Jesus Christ," wrote Bishop Michael J. Sheridan in a 2004 pastoral letter. "This is because of a widespread misunderstanding of the very meaning of conscience. For many, conscience is no more than personal preference or even a vague sense or feeling that something is right or wrong, often based on information drawn from sources that have nothing to do with the law of God. The right judgment of conscience is not a matter of personal preference, nor has it anything to do with feelings. It has only to do with objective truth."[5] The referenced "objective truth" is the Church's dictate that a Catholic must vote for the candidate who is least supportive of abortion.

• "Conscience is NOT the same as opinions or feelings." wrote Father Anthony J. Mastroeni. "It is an act of the intellect judging the rightness or wrongness of an act or omission. Feelings come from another part of the human soul; they come and go and should be governed by the intellect and will. Also, conscience is not the same as an opinion because its judgment is based upon the intellect's understanding of the natural moral law, inherent in human nature, or the divinely revealed moral law, such as the Ten Commandments. These are not opinions we invent, but rather they are discovered either by reason's understanding of the human person, or they are revealed by God. Conscience then is the echo within the human person of objective, moral truth; and our opinions – if they are to be taken seriously by anyone other than ourselves – need to be in harmony with objective truth, and not the other way around. As Catholics, we are fortunate to have the Church's Magisterium to help guide and form our conscience. Among other truths, that Magisterium teaches us that, 'A well-formed Christian conscience does not permit one to vote for a political program or an individual law which contradicts the fundamental contents of faith and morals.'"[6]

• "The Church teaches the primacy of conscience, but also emphasizes that one's conscience must be properly formed in light of the Gospel and Church teaching," said Bishop Joseph A. Galante. "In other words, conscience is not simply a feeling, a preference, or a matter of doing what one thinks is right. It has an objective dimension, since it rests on truth, truth that remains valid and unchanging. ... Because conscience can be clouded by sin, confusion or ignorance, it can be mistaken. For this reason, we must work continuously to form our conscience by becoming informed about issues and entering ever more deeply into prayer, Scripture and Church teaching, guided by the Holy Spirit."[7]

• The common misunderstanding about voting one's conscience was demonstrated by an article that was published in 2008 about the USCCB's *Forming Consciences for Faithful Citizenship.* In a letter to the editor of *The Trenton Times,* Trenton, New Jersey Bishop John M. Smith chided the newspaper for misinterpreting the teaching of the Church, noting that the article's headline, "Vote Your Conscience," was "a serious oversimplification that undermines the core message of (the bishops') statement." Smith wrote "that this requires serious engagement and commitment and that it does not begin or end at the polling booth." The USCCB document, he said, even tells Catholics how to form their consciences, "beginning with a 'willingness and openness to seek the truth and what is right' through the study of sacred scripture and the *Catechism of the Catholic Church* ... And yet, nowhere in the article is the need to form one's conscience ever addressed. Instead, readers are led to believe that they should vote on the basis of what they 'think' or 'feel.' There is no reference to this active process Catholics are instructed to perform."[8]

Any Catholic voter who relies solely on his own feelings or opinions that are not consistent with Church teaching is not voting with an informed conscience. Archbishop John Donoghue of Atlanta made this point quite succinctly: "You have an erroneous conscience if you think there is some case in which you can vote for a pro-abortion candidate. You're wrong as far as Church teaching is concerned, because you are guilty of 'cooperating with the evil' of abortion."[9]

Bishop Myers is just as definitive: "The Church's moral teaching provides specific norms for the formation of the Christian conscience ... The specific norms taught by the Church in this area are not mere optional proposals ... For a Catholic to refuse, knowingly and willingly, to form his or her conscience in accord with these authoritative norms is to withhold part of his or her heart, mind, and soul from union with Christ and His Church. Such people exclude themselves, in important respects, from Christian life and the Catholic community."[10]

A Catholic's conscience is not his own. It is subject to acceptance of the teachings of the Catholic Church. Then it is his obligation to vote in a manner consistent with those teachings.

20

Bishops Warn: Your Vote Can Be a Mortal Sin

This is America. Land of the free. The right to vote as one pleases is sacrosanct.

So very true, as a *constitutional* right. But is it a *Catholic* right? Certainly, a Catholic has the same civil rights as any other citizen, but he is bound by a higher authority to exercise that right in accordance with Church teaching. Many Catholics ignore this moral requirement, out of sheer ignorance, itself, or they use the fraudulent "seamless garment" construct as a pretext for voting immorally. Therefore, in these times of watered-down doctrine and pervasive relativism in the Church, Catholics often waltz into the voting booth believing that they can vote for whomever they please. They do not believe that their vote could ever be sinful, and especially not mortally sinful.

This is not a lightweight matter, although it is treated as such by liberal or negligent bishops and priests who, by their laxity, refute the fundamental notion that there is a hierarchy of sinfulness, including when a citizen votes. Otherwise, wouldn't they be earnestly seeking to instruct their parishioners of this Church teaching? Wouldn't they be preaching this urgent truth in order to save the souls in their care? For whatever reason that these clerics fail to communicate this teaching, they are wrong in not doing so.

Catholic teaching holds that, in any given election, not voting for the most anti-abortion candidate can be a mortally sinful act.

Given that abortion constitutes the greatest genocide in the history of mankind, the failure of so many Catholic bishops and priests to warn their sheep of their voting responsibility is a self-mockery of their ordinations. Their sole obligation under those holy orders is to lead the souls for whom they are responsible to Heaven. In this one moment of eternity, they have the opportunity to take the most basic threshold step of that singular duty – saving Catholic souls by teaching them that their eternal salvation can hang in the balance when they vote. But, instead, they treat this genocide as just another moral issue and thereby lead them astray.

Which Catholic churchmen are, instead, boldly declaring this teaching that you probably never have heard, i.e., that voting incorrectly can be a mortal sin? Well, plenty of them, and some are quoted below. Indeed, as noted in a 2014 article by Howard Kainz at TheCatholicThing.org, "For the last two decades, a number of bishops have warned not only politicians but individual voters that they should not receive communion without confession, after voting for [candidates who support] abortion rights – including Bishops Burke of St. Louis, Wenski of Orlando (now Miami), Sheridan of Colorado Springs, Maher of San Diego, Weigand of Sacramento, and Cardinals Law and O'Malley of Boston."[1] And plenty more surely agree with them, but are not inclined to be as outspoken. (Their timidity is not a valid excuse – evangelizing is their job.) But why should you believe these churchmen instead of the "seamless garment" priests and bishops who dissent from this teaching?

Well, first of all, there's abundant substantiation for their pronouncements in the statements of popes, such as John Paul II and Benedict XVI, as well as in the *Catechism of the Catholic Church*. And if that isn't persuasive enough, isn't the potential consequence of which they speak, i.e. eternity in hell, sufficient to take these authorities at their word? This is where the logic of Pascal's Wager is operative. Why take the risk that voting contrary to this teaching isn't a mortal sin when so many bishops have said that it is? Moreover, isn't it perfectly logical that genocide is more important in God's eyes than policies on lesser issues, like immigration or health care? With so much warning from such credible sources, why would any Catholic risk dying and then having to explain to God Almighty why he didn't favor saving lives over merely improving lives? (Or would God find his choice so damnable that He wouldn't even give this soul the time to explain?)

This is what every Catholic must learn and practice: Voting incorrectly can be a mortal sin. Who says so? The successors to Christ's apostles, to whom He gave sole authority to teach on matters of faith and morals. Their statements are below, with some astute concurrences from priests thrown in. (The offices cited are those held at the time of the quotation.)

Bishop Thomas J. Paprocki

Springfield, Illinois

Voting for a candidate who favors abortion "makes you morally complicit and places the eternal salvation of your own soul in serious jeopardy."

Prior to the election in November of 2012, Bishop Paprocki produced a video wherein he warned Catholics that the act of voting for a candidate who favors abortion jeopardizes their salvation.

"Again, I am not telling you which party or which candidates to vote for or against, but I am saying that you need to think and pray very carefully about your vote, because a vote for a candidate who promotes actions or behaviors that are intrinsically evil and gravely sinful makes you morally complicit and places the eternal salvation of your own soul in serious jeopardy."[2]

Bishop Michael J. Sheridan

Colorado Springs, Colorado

Any Catholics who vote for candidates who stand for abortion "jeopardize their salvation."

In May of 2004, Bishop Sheridan told his flock very directly that anyone who votes for a politician that advocates for abortion disqualifies himself for Holy Communion. Here is the essence of his pastoral letter:

"There must be no confusion in these matters. Any Catholic politicians who advocate for abortion, for illicit stem cell research or for any form of euthanasia ipso facto place themselves outside full communion with the Church and so jeopardize their salvation. Any Catholics who vote for candidates who stand for abortion, illicit stem cell research or euthanasia suffer the same fateful consequences. It is for this reason that these Catholics, whether candidates for office or those who would vote for them, may not receive Holy Communion until they have recanted their positions and been reconciled with God and the Church in the Sacrament of Penance."[3]

Bishop David L. Ricken

Green Bay, Wisconsin

To vote for a candidate who opposes the Catholic Church's teaching on abortion "could put your own soul in jeopardy."

Just prior to the 2012 election, Bishop Ricken wrote the following to Catholics in his diocese:

"I would like to review some of the principles to keep in mind as you approach the voting booth to complete your ballot. ... These are areas that are 'intrinsically evil' and cannot be supported by anyone who is a believer in God or the common good or the dignity of the human person. They are: abortion, euthanasia, embryonic stem cell research, human cloning, homosexual 'marriage' ... To vote for someone in favor of these positions means that you could be morally complicit with these choices which are intrinsically evil. ... This could put your own soul in jeopardy."[4]

Archbishop Charles J. Chaput

Denver

If you vote for a candidate who supports abortion, "should you go to confession? The answer is yes."

In June 2008, Archbishop Chaput wrote the following after being disingenuously "quoted" by a group called "Catholics for Obama '08":

"In the United States ... abortion is an acceptable form of homicide... If you vote this way [for a candidate that supports or promotes abortion], are you cooperating in evil? And if you know you are cooperating in evil, should you go to confession? The answer is yes."[5]

Bishop Robert W. Finn

Kansas City-St. Joseph

Is voting for a candidate who supports abortion a grave sin? Bishop Finn warned of eternal consequences:

"Despite hardship, beyond partisanship, for the sake of our eternal salvation: This we should never do."

From an October 2008 interview with radio personality Hugh Hewitt:

Bishop Finn: "I just don't think there's any question that in all of Church teaching that the life issues, particularly the protection of unborn children against the crime of abortion, has to be our greatest priority. This is an ongoing slaughter of 4,000 children every single day for the last 35 years. And if we don't do anything about it, we bear a lot of responsibility. If we support and promote persons who have pledged to extend it and intensify the slaughter, then we bear a great responsibility with them."

Hewitt: When you say bear a great responsibility, does that rise to the level, in the eyes of the Church teaching, to grave sin?

Bishop Finn: I think it is, of course. ... we're talking about the willful destruction, direct destruction of a human life. ... [Y]ou can't support a person who wants to go to complete full-scale war against the unborn. ... I think that they (Catholic voters) have to see their apostolic mandate to do what they can to support human life. ... People have to realize that they will be held accountable for these important decisions before God."

Hewitt: *"When you say they will be held accountable for their votes, do you mean that it could cost someone their eternal soul?"*

Bishop Finn: *"Well, of course. ...[T]hese people who get elected, they don't just arrive all on their own. We elect them. We, you and I, support them or we don't. And so we have some participation in that. Now, someone wrote to me and said well, you know, I voted for Obama, I'll repent later. And well, I hope that God does change a heart if they feel that they've made a terrible mistake and have to repent. But it's much more important and vital that we make the right decision when it's before us."*[6]

In that same month, Bishop Finn wrote an article titled "Can a Catholic Vote in Support of Abortion" in the diocesan newspaper, wherein he said a Catholic cannot vote for pro-choice candidates because they ask *"us to be participants in their own gravely immoral act. This is something which, in good conscience, we can never justify. Despite hardship, beyond partisanship, for the sake of our eternal salvation: This we should never do."*[7]

Bishop Kevin Farrell

Dallas, and

Bishop Kevin Vann

Fort Worth

To vote for a candidate who supports the intrinsic evil abortion would be to cooperate in the evil and, therefore, morally impermissible. It may affect each individual's salvation.

"[W]e cannot make more clear the seriousness of the overriding issue of abortion ... it is the defining moral issue. ... To vote for a candidate who supports the intrinsic evil of abortion or 'abortion rights' when there is a morally acceptable alternative would be to cooperate in the evil – and, therefore, morally impermissible. ... [A]s stated in (the USCCB's) Forming Consciences for Faithful Citizenship, *the decisions we make on these political and moral issues affect not only the general peace and prosperity of society at large, but also may affect each individual's salvation."*[8]

Bishop Robert J. Carlson

Sioux Falls, South Dakota

Opposition to abortion binds every Catholic under pain of mortal sin and admits of no exceptions.

In August 2004, Bishop Carlson issued the following statement titled, "On Catholic Teaching on Abortion and Political Beliefs":

"Opposition to abortion binds every Catholic under pain of mortal sin and admits of no exceptions. ... [Y]ou cannot vote for a politician who is pro-abortion when you have a choice and remain a Catholic in good standing. ... Life is 'the issue,' because every other right is dependent upon it. Understand that this is not simply one bishop's opinion, but is the truth as revealed to us through the church founded by Christ."[9]

Bishop Daniel Jenky

Peoria, Illinois

Voters "who callously enable the destruction of innocent human life in the womb' ... 'are objectively guilty of grave sin."

Just prior to the 2012 election, Bishop Jenky required that the following letter be personally read at the weekend Masses by each celebrating priest in his diocese:

"Today, Catholic politicians, bureaucrats, and their electoral supporters who callously enable the destruction of innocent human life in the womb also thereby reject Jesus as their Lord. They are objectively guilty of grave sin.

"For those who hope for salvation, no political loyalty can ever take precedence over loyalty to the Lord Jesus Christ and to his Gospel of Life."[10]

The Bishops of Kansas

A Catholic would commit moral evil if he were to vote for a candidate who takes a permissive stand on those actions that are intrinsically evil, such as abortion, when there is a morally-acceptable alternative.

On August 15, 2006, the four bishops of Kansas issued a statement, titled "Moral Principles for Catholic Voters." The following month, the Kansas document was endorsed by the bishops of Colorado.

"[T]here are some choices that always involve doing evil and which can never be done even as a means to a good end. These choices include elective abortion, euthanasia, physician-assisted suicide, the destruction of embryonic human beings in stem cell research, human cloning, and same-sex 'marriage.' Such acts are judged to be intrinsically evil ... [I]t is a correct judgment of conscience that we would commit moral evil if we were to vote for a candidate who takes a permissive stand on those actions that are intrinsically evil when there is a morally-acceptable alternative."[11]

Archbishop Alfred C. Hughes

New Orleans

Pro-choice candidates "should not partake of Holy Communion" ... Citizens

210

who vote for them "share in responsibility for this grave evil."

In a 2004 pastoral letter titled, "Co-Responsibility for Public Policy," Archbishop Hughes said that a Catholic participates in "grave evil" by voting for pro-choice politicians.

"When Catholic officials openly support the taking of human life in abortion, euthanasia or the destruction of human embryos, they are no longer faithful members in the Church and should not partake of Holy Communion. Moreover, citizens who promote this unjust taking of human life by their vote or support of such candidates share in responsibility for this grave evil."[12]

Archbishop Raymond Burke

St. Louis

Catholics who support pro-choice candidates participate in a grave evil ... It is a serious sin.

In a 2004 interview with *The St. Louis Review*, Archbishop Burke said, *"It's not right to support candidates who are for abortion ... [C]atholics who support such pro-abortion candidates participate in a grave evil ... It is a serious sin ... They must show a change of heart and be sacramentally reconciled or refrain from receiving Holy Communion."*[13]

Bishop Samuel J. Aquila

Fargo, North Dakota

A Catholic who cooperates with evil puts his soul in jeopardy of salvation.

In a 2004 sermon, Bishop Aquila said that Catholics who cooperate with evil by, for example, supporting abortion rights "bring judgment upon themselves." Many Catholic clerics have explicitly stated that supporting a pro-abortion or pro-choice candidate constitutes cooperating with evil.

211

"[J]esus Christ has warned clearly within the Gospel that hell is a reality and that we are free to choose it. Catholics who separate their faith life from their professional and social activities are putting the salvation of their souls in jeopardy. They risk the possibility of hell. Any Catholic who stands for a law of man, most especially one which is objectively evil, before a law of God, puts his or her soul in jeopardy of salvation for they cooperate with a real evil."[14]

Humberto Cardinal Medeiros

Archbishop of Boston

Those who vote for pro-abortion lawmakers share in deadly sin.

In a letter read to all Catholics in the archdiocese just prior to the 1980 Democratic presidential primary, Cardinal Medeiros said that citizens who vote *"for those lawmakers ... who make abortions possible by law"* share in the guilt for a *"horrendous crime and deadly sin."*[15]

Archbishop Javier del Rio Alba

Arequipa, Peru

In 2011, Archbishop Rio Alba stated that "[V]oting for a candidate who supports abortion is a mortal sin."

"A Catholic can never cast his vote for a candidate that we know is in favor of abortion ... who is in favor of all that is against the good of man and, of course, against the teachings of our Holy Catholic Church. In this, dear brothers, we must be very firm."[16]

"Catholics can never cast their vote for a candidate who by word or deed says he will support abortion."[17]

Father Stephen F. Torraco

Associate Professor of Theology, Assumption College

"To vote for a candidate ... with the knowledge that the candidate is pro-abortion ... the voter sins mortally."

In his definitive work, *A Brief Catechism for Catholic Voters*, Father Torraco answers the question: Is it a mortal sin to vote for a pro-abortion candidate?

"Except in the case in which a voter is faced with all pro-abortion candidates ... a candidate that is pro-abortion disqualifies himself from receiving a Catholic's vote. This is because ... abortion is intrinsically evil and cannot be morally justified for any reason or set of circumstances. To vote for such a candidate even with the knowledge that the candidate is pro-abortion is to become an accomplice in the moral evil of abortion. If the voter also knows this, then the voter sins mortally."[18]

Father Matthew Habiger

Former President, Human Life International

To vote for a candidate who favors abortion "is a sin, and must be repented."

As president of Human Life International, Father Habiger wrote in 1999, *"It is a scandal that Catholic politicians vote for bills which fund or otherwise advance abortion. They should be named, publicly shamed and admonished so that they can cease their evil and return to God. To vote for such a candidate is to willfully participate in that candidate's choices and deeds. It is a sin, and must be repented."*[19]

Father Jay Scott Newman

St. Mary's Catholic Church, Greenville, South Carolina

Persons who vote for a pro-abortion politician "should not receive Holy Communion until and unless they are reconciled to God in the Sacrament of Penance."

Shortly after the 2008 election, Father Newman wrote the following to his parishioners:

"Voting for a pro-abortion politician when a plausible pro-life alternative exists constitutes material cooperation with intrinsic evil, and those Catholics who do so place themselves outside of the full communion of Christ's Church and under the judgment of divine law.

"Persons in this condition should not receive Holy Communion until and unless they are reconciled to God in the Sacrament of Penance, lest they eat and drink their own condemnation."[20]

Father Joseph Illo

Star of the Sea Church, San Francisco

Catholics who vote for a pro-abortion candidate should "go to confession before receiving communion."

Like Father Newman, Father Illo counseled his parishioners after the 2008 election: *"If you are one of the 54% of Catholics who voted for a pro-abortion candidate, you were clear on his position and you knew the gravity of the question, I urge you to go to confession before receiving communion. Don't risk losing your state of grace by receiving sacrilegiously."*[21]

Father Anthony J. Mastroeni

Adjunct Professor, Felician College and Seton Hall University

Anyone who knowingly votes for a candidate who promotes such abortion commits mortal sin.

In *Latin Mass* magazine, Father Mastroeni wrote the following in an article titled, "Voting Your Catholic Conscience":

"Some things always and everywhere are morally wrong. There can never be justification for directly and deliberately taking innocent human life: abortion, destruction of human embryos, human cloning, euthanasia ... Therefore, anyone who knowingly votes for a candidate who promotes such evils is a formal cooperator in these evils and, consequently, commits grave or mortal sin. Moreover, not to vote for a candidate for whom there is reasonable hope that such evils will be eradicated, or at least seriously limited, is also to be a formal cooperator in evil by omission; that is, not doing what we reasonably can do."[22]

Bishop Kevin Doran

Elphin, County Roscommon, Ireland

Catholics who voted to allow abortion should go to confession.

On May 28, 2018, Bishop Doran, of Elphin, said that Catholics who voted "yes" on Ireland's pro-abortion referendum committed a mortal sin and should go to confession if they wish to receive Holy Communion. He told those Catholics that *"you should consider coming to confession, where you would be received with the same compassion that is shown to any other penitent."*[23]

21

Step-by-Step: How to Vote So You Don't Go to Hell

How does a Catholic vote in such a way so as to avoid eternal damnation? (Bet you never thought you'd have to ask that question.)

Well, it's an extraordinarily simple, four-step process that has nothing to do with what most Catholics are taught or believe about "voting Catholic." Bishop Robert F. Vasa used the analogy of a farm combine to explain it: The first sieve in the combine disposes of the largest refuse, just as the first step discards pro-choice candidates.[1]

Step One: The Catholic voter must first inform his conscience about the mortal sinfulness of voting for a candidate who supports any one of the intrinsic evils of abortion, euthanasia, embryonic stem cell research, homosexual "marriage," human cloning, or opposing religious freedom, if there is no alternative candidate who is better on these issues. (And he does have a duty to so inform his conscience.)

Step Two: He must vote for the candidate who is least supportive of any one or more of these evils.

Step Three: If all candidates are equally bad, or equally good, he can vote for whichever he wishes, based on his own assessment of which would, as Father Stephen F. Torraco prescribed, be "most likely to limit the evils of abortion or any other moral evil at issue."[2]

Step Four: If, and only if, the Catholic voter cannot discern that one candidate would be most likely to limit such evils, then he should base his vote on which candidate best reflects Catholic values on matters that are not intrinsically evil, i.e., matters of prudential judgment.

This is the sequential process authorized by the bishops, though it seems no one of them has articulated it so concisely. Steps One and Two have been thoroughly covered in other areas of this book. It is Steps Three and Four that we now address.

As to Step Three, it is a matter of degree. As a threshold matter, Bishop Vasa said, "The conditions under which an individual may be able to vote for a pro-abortion candidate would apply only if all the candidates are equally pro-abortion."[3] Bishop Robert Finn wrote that "we are often faced with 'imperfect candidates.'" He said that where two candidates are permissive on abortion, "we should choose the candidate whose position will likely do the least grave evil, or whose position will do the most to limit the specific grave evil of abortion."[4]

Bishop Robert Hermann said, "If there were two candidates who supported abortion, but not equally, we would have the obligation to mitigate the evil by voting for the less-permissive candidate."[5] The bishops of Kansas issued a joint statement in 2006, instructing voters that "when there is no choice of a candidate that avoids supporting intrinsically evil actions, especially elective abortion, we should vote in such a way as to allow the least harm to innocent human life and dignity. We would not be acting immorally therefore if we were to vote for a candidate who is not totally acceptable in order to defeat one who poses an even greater threat to human life and dignity."[6]

Bishop Earl Boyea echoed those sentiments, including two of the six contemporary intrinsic evils in his statement. *"[W]hen there is no choice of a candidate that avoids supporting intrinsically evil actions, especially elective abortion or embryonic stem-cell research, we should vote in such a way as to allow the least harm to innocent human life and dignity," he wrote in 2008. "We would not be acting immorally, therefore, if we were to vote for a candidate whose positions on these issues are not totally acceptable in order to defeat one who poses an even greater threat to human life and dignity."*[7]

Cardinal James A. Hickey posed this question that the Catholic voter should ask himself: "[A]s each of us makes a prudential judgment in voting for a new president, we need to ask which candidate will offer even a measure of protection for the unborn. Who is more likely to pierce through the rhetoric and politics of choice in the clear realization that abortion is always a choice to destroy an utterly innocent and defenseless human being?"[8]

Archbishop Raymond Burke concurred, with a reminder of the long view. "A Catholic who is clear in his or her opposition to the moral evil of procured abortion could vote for a candidate who supports the limitation of the legality of procured abortion," he wrote in 2004, "even though the candidate does not oppose all use of procured abortion, if the other candidate(s) do not support the limitation of the evil of procured abortion. Of course, the end in view for the Catholic must always be the total conformity of the civil law with the moral law, that is, ultimately the total elimination of the evil of procured abortion."[9]

Father Torraco said that the rule given to Catholic politicians by Pope St. John Paul II applies to Catholic voters as well. "[W]hen it is not possible to overturn or completely abrogate a pro-abortion law," John Paul wrote, "an elected official, whose absolute personal opposition to procured abortion was well known, could licitly support proposals aimed at limiting the harm done by such a law and at lessening its negative consequences at the level of general opinion and morality. This does not in fact represent an illicit cooperation with an unjust law, but rather a legitimate and proper attempt to limit its evil aspects." Torraco added, "Logically, it follows from these words of the Pope that a voter may likewise vote for that candidate who will most likely limit the evils of abortion or any other moral evil at issue."[10]

As an example of proper moral voting to limit evil, Monsignor Kevin McMahon offers an example: "[W]hen presented with one candidate who is pro-abortion, and another who is both pro-abortion and pro-euthanasia, a voter may conclude that he could prevent more evil by voting for the pro-abortion candidate who does not promote euthanasia as well. This would be similar to a politician's support for imperfect legislation."[11]

Virtually any candidate who is anti-abortion is almost certain to be anti-euthanasia also. But a Catholic voter could, possibly, hypothetically, in an alternate universe, be faced with the unlikely choice of one candidate who is anti-abortion but not anti-euthanasia versus a second candidate who is anti-euthanasia but not anti-abortion. A logical application of McMahon's rule would be for the Catholic voter to assess which candidate would cause less intrinsic evil. Given the far greater number of abortions in the United States, compared to the number of euthanasia murders, the lesser harm would surely be caused by the first candidate, and he should receive the Catholic's vote.

Is all of this "limiting" a matter of choosing the lesser evil? On that unimportant, though purely academic question, bishops have varied, if only semantically. But it's an interesting question, nonetheless. "Recall the traditional Catholic principle of choosing the lesser evil," observed Bishop Vincent De Paul Breen, of the Diocese of Metuchen. "When faced with two options, neither of which is entirely good, one may choose the lesser evil. This enables us to give morality a voice and to vote for whoever will best promote our Christian concerns."[12]

But Archbishop Burke again saw it less a finite decision, and more a mere offensive blow in the ongoing battle against abortion. "A Catholic may vote for a candidate who, while he supports an evil action, also supports the limitation of the evil involved, if there is no better candidate," he wrote in 2004. "For example, a candidate may support procured abortion in a limited number of cases but be opposed to it otherwise. In such a case, the Catholic who recognizes the immorality of all procured abortions may rightly vote for this candidate over another, more unsuitable candidate in an effort to limit the circumstances in which procured abortions would be considered legal. Here the intention of the Catholic voter, unable to find a viable candidate who would stop the evil of procured abortion by making it illegal, is to reduce the number of abortions by limiting the circumstances in which it is legal. This is not a question of choosing the lesser evil, but of limiting all the evil one is able to limit at the time."[13]

Step 4 in this winnowing process is triggered only when the Catholic voter sincerely concludes that all of the candidates are precisely the same on abortion and euthanasia. This could mean, strictly theoretically, that the candidates are equally pro-abortion or equally anti-abortion. In this scenario, a Catholic is left to consider the many remaining moral issues where his own prudential judgment, providing it conforms to Catholic teaching, may be used to select a candidate.

Drawing on the language of the USCCB's document, *Forming Consciences for Faithful Citizenship,* Bishops Kevin Farrell of Dallas and Kevin Vann of Fort Worth explained that if "both candidates running for office support abortion or 'abortion rights,' a Catholic would be forced to then look at the other important issues and through their vote try to limit the evil done."[14] Bishop Vasa elaborated on this instruction, using an example where the candidates are equally pro-abortion. In that case, he explained, "you begin to screen for the other issues and make a conscientious decision to vote for this pro-abortion candidate because his positions on these other issues are more in keeping with good Catholic values. It doesn't mean that you in any way support or endorse a pro-abortion position, but you take a look in that context at the lesser of two evils."[15] Or, as Cardinal Burke said, "limiting all the evil one is able to limit at the time."[16]

An unfortunate choice, yes, but Catholics have a moral duty, as we shall see in the next chapter, to vote for *somebody,* contrary to what many churchmen preach and laymen believe.

22

Not Voting Can Also Be a Mortal Sin

W hy is it a sin for a Catholic to not vote, even if there's not a good candidate on the ballot?

Answer: There will always be one candidate who is preferable to the others, even if microscopically. A Catholic can never "sit this one out." To do so is at minimum offensive to God and could even imperil one's eternal salvation. "Voting is a civic duty which would seem to bind at least under venial sin whenever a good candidate has an unworthy opponent," wrote Father Heribert Jone in his highly esteemed 1929 book, *Moral Theology*. "It might even be a mortal sin if one's refusal to vote would result in the election of an unworthy candidate."[1]

The sinful gravity of not voting was illustrated by the message of Pope Pius XII to the priests in Rome when the Communists vowed to take control of the Italian government as the 1948 elections approached. "It is your right and duty to draw the attention of the faithful to the extraordinary importance of the coming elections, and to the moral responsibility which follows from it for all those who have the right to vote," Pius wrote. "Without doubt the Church intends to remain outside and above all political parties, but how could it be possible to remain indifferent to the composition of a parliament to which the Constitution gives the power to legislate in matters which concern so directly the highest religious interest, and the condition of the life of the Church in Italy itself? ... Consequently it follows: That in the present circumstances it is strictly obligatory for whoever has the right, man or woman, to take part in the elections. He who abstains, particularly through indolence or from cowardice, thereby commits a grave sin, a mortal offense."[2]

A grave sin. A mortal offense. Those terrifying words should not have failed to send every eligible Catholic in Italy to either the voting booth or the confessional. Thus does it remain for any Catholic today – the matter of voting is a two-pronged act fraught with eternal danger, i.e., failing to vote, in itself, or voting contrary to Church teaching. Either can be a mortal sin.

Bishops in quite recent times have repeated this teaching of a moral "obligation," "duty" and "responsibility."

"Catholic citizens have a serious moral obligation to exercise their right to vote," said Lansing, Michigan Bishop Earl Boyea before the election of 2008.[3] "Every Catholic has an obligation to participate in the political process," said Archbishop Samuel J. Aquila, of Denver, a month before the 2016 election. That same week, Bishop David Kagan of Bismarck, North Dakota told his flock that "each Catholic citizen has that privilege and duty to participate in our nation's governing by the exercise of our constitutional right to vote in national, state and local elections."[4] And in their "2008 Election Year Statement," the bishops of Florida said, "As Catholics, we are called to carry the values of the Gospel and the sacredness of human life into the public square. These dual responsibilities to faith and citizenship are at the heart of what it means to be a Catholic in a free and democratic nation."[5]

Many other bishops have declared that Catholics have a moral duty to vote:

• In October 2000, just before the presidential election, the bishops of Massachusetts said that Catholics must exercise their "moral obligation" to vote and to acknowledge the "absolute centrality" of the protection of human life (meaning primarily abortion and euthanasia) when choosing candidates.[6]

• "Some may be discouraged by the particular candidates available; others feel that none adequately represents all of our concerns, especially our commitment to the right to life from the moment of conception until natural death. However, by *not* voting, we cede control of our nation to those who lack or oppose our moral commitments. Recall the traditional Catholic principle of choosing the lesser evil; when faced with two options, neither of which is entirely good, one may choose the lesser evil. This enables us to give morality a voice and to vote for whoever will best promote our Christian concerns." – *Bishop Vincent De Paul Breen, Diocese of Metuchen, October 18, 2000*[7]

• "As Catholics we are morally obligated to pray, to act, and to vote to abolish the evil of abortion in America, limiting it as much as we can until it is finally abolished. ... The Church teaches that all Catholics should participate as 'faithful citizens' in the public square, especially through our voice in the voting booth, and that we have the responsibility to treat the decision for whom we will vote for with profound moral seriousness." – *Bishop Kevin Farrell, Bishop of Dallas, and Bishop Kevin Vann, Bishop of Fort Worth, October 8, 2008*[8]

• "Because we have a moral obligation to vote, deciding not to vote at all is not ordinarily an acceptable solution to" the dilemma of having to choose among candidates who are equally unacceptable on abortion and the five other intrinsic evils. – *Catholic Bishops of Kansas, 2006*[9]

• "Simply put, faithful citizenship refers to our duty as Catholics to be full participants in the public square in order to make our nation and the world a better and more just place. With this duty comes the responsibility to exercise our right to vote and to be engaged in the political process." – *Catholic Bishops of New York State, September 2008*[10]

• "For Catholics, voting ought not to be seen as just an option or a privilege but a duty." – *Catholic Bishops of Illinois, October 2006*[11]

• "[T]he Church teaches that we have an obligation, in justice, to vote, because the welfare of the community depends upon the persons elected and appointed to office. ... I must point out that the Catholic who chooses not to vote at all, when there is a viable candidate who will advance the common good, although not perfectly, fails to fulfill his or her moral duty, at least, in the limitation of a grave evil in society." – *Archbishop Raymond L. Burke, Diocese of St. Louis, October 2004*[12]

• "We are citizens of the United States, and we have a responsibility as disciples to help form our society. So, to vote is the first message." – *Bishop Gerald Kicanas, Bishop of Tucson, 2008*[13]

• "The lay faithful are never to relinquish their participation in public life." – *Pope John Paul II*[14]

• "As Catholics we have a duty to bring our faith and values into the public square in order to build a just society." – *Archbishop Alex J. Brunett, Diocese of Seattle*[15]

The *Catechism of the Catholic Church,* itself, teaches that "Submission to authority and co-responsibility for the common good make it morally obligatory ... to exercise the right to vote."[16] In his essay, "Voting Your Catholic Conscience," Father Anthony J. Mastroeni says that failure to exercise that right "can be a serious dereliction of that moral responsibility which requires us to promote and secure the common good of our fellow citizens.

"Not to vote in November (2016), as some otherwise devout Catholics intend to do because neither candidate attracts them or is perfect enough, is to put oneself in a very morally precarious position causing a less worthy candidate to be elected. Usually there is no candidate who represents a perfect score on all the issues operating in an election, and it is sobering to recall that the last Perfect Candidate stood on the portico of Pontius Pilate while a poll was taken, and Jesus lost." Mastroeni likened a non-voting Catholic to a resident of New Orleans in 2007, "riding out Katrina in your house near a levee on Lake Pontchartrain while refusing to take safe refuge in a school gym just because it doesn't have all the amenities of a five-star hotel."[17]

Bishop James V. Johnston of Springfield-Cape Girardeau, Mo. noted what is ultimately at stake for each Catholic who is eligible to vote. "Most Americans learn from an early age that voting is a civic duty. However, many Americans do not realize that voting is fundamentally a moral act. Like other moral actions in our lives, it is a choosing for which we will each be accountable before God."[18]

23

How Trump Overcame the Catholic Intelligentsia

As the 2016 campaign began, the mainstream media's consensus was that Donald Trump's ribald coarseness would, with no doubt whatsoever, so offend Catholics (among others) that even his anti-abortion and pro-Christian declarations could only be perceived as half-hearted and more likely disingenuous altogether.

But by late winter, with Trump's GOP nomination nearly in hand, some Catholic notables were beginning to panic.

"His campaign has already driven our politics down to new levels of vulgarity," thundered a March 2016 written appeal to "Our Fellow Catholics" from 37 professors and pundits, a group that included conservatives like Kate O'Beirne, former Washington editor of *National Review,* and Robert Royal, founder of the Faith and Reason Institute. "His appeals to racial and ethnic fears and prejudice are offensive to any genuinely Catholic sensibility. He promised to order U.S. military personnel to torture terrorist suspects and to kill terrorists' families – actions condemned by the Church and policies that would bring shame upon our country.

"And there is nothing in his campaign or his previous record that gives us grounds for confidence that he genuinely shares our commitments to the right to life, to religious freedom and the rights of conscience, to rebuilding the marriage culture, or to subsidiarity and the principle of limited constitutional government."

The statement ended with a plea to support one of the other Republican candidates "who are far more likely than Mr. Trump to address these concerns."[1]

Who could blame the signers of this document for their state of alarm in March of 2016? Based on all that was known at the time, it was understandable. And although he had lately been professing that he was "very pro-life," Trump had said on a 1999 broadcast of NBC's "Meet the Press" that he was "very pro-choice." On the single-most important issue for Catholics, Donald Trump couldn't be trusted.

One of the signers, Dr. Chad Pecknold, a theology professor at The Catholic University of America, went so far as to call Trump "a false friend to the working class, and an enemy to the unborn,"[2] both of which betrayed an innocent and widely-shared ignorance about the mercurial Mr. Trump. Setting aside the question of what a "false friend" actually is, it was precisely the working class, including the Catholics in that class, that would elect him. After his inauguration, Trump would exhibit no signs of abandoning that segment of Americans.

And "an enemy to the unborn"? Notwithstanding Trump's pro-choice comments made in the past, Pecknold and others gave the candidate no benefit of the doubt for his professed conversion on the issue, a change of heart caused by the tale of two personal friends who decided not to abort their baby. Indeed, on his very first day in office, Trump would sign a ban on federal money destined for foreign organizations that perform or provide information about abortions. Three months later, he would sign legislation that stopped federal funding for Planned Parenthood and other abortion providers. And he would go on to nominate two conservative Supreme Court justices in Neil Gorsuch and Brett Kavanaugh, and a host of other conservative appointees.

But in the spring of 2016, none of this had yet happened, and ominous warnings continued to issue amid Trump's reassuring rhetoric. "A Trump presidency would be a disaster for life, the family, and religious freedom," said Stephen White, a fellow at the Ethics and Public Policy Center in Washington, D.C.[3] Father Thomas Petri, academic dean at the Dominican House of Studies, also in Washington, D.C., cautioned that Catholics "must be careful to understand the very grave and immoral positions that Trump espouses both politically and in his personal life."[4]

Pecknold finally cut to the chase: "The evidence is overwhelming that no Catholic who desires to be informed by the Church's teaching can vote for Donald Trump."[5]

Well, that was a reasonable sentiment during the primary season, when there were at least a dozen other Republican candidates who seemed more genuinely in line with Catholic values than Trump, but it would not be true when the reality of the general election hit – and his sole opponent was narrowed to one: Hillary Clinton, who, in this new age of rank candor, would soon be heard brazenly disparaging Catholic doctrine, itself.

Trump vs. Clinton. It was then that the 2016 election changed for Catholics who were faithful to the core teachings of the Church.

"The choice then is crystal-clear," deduced Catholic writer Dave Armstrong. "Either radically leftist, child-killing justices from Hillary, who will dominate the court for at least a generation, or the pro-life conservatives that Trump has said he would appoint."

There has never been an ideal presidential candidate for a Catholic, Armstrong said. "The Church allows us to vote for folks who aren't totally in line with Catholic teachings" ... "It doesn't follow that I agree with every jot and tittle of what (Trump) stands for, nor does voting for him imply that, as Catholic social teaching regarding voting makes clear. He was my 15th choice of the original GOP primary candidates."

Armstrong drew an historical analogy to illustrate that the life issue – that is, abortion, euthanasia and embryonic stem cell research – is the pivotal criterion for Catholics. "Yes, I'm a Catholic," he said. "I vote for the candidate who is pro-life, or at least more pro-life than the other person. If I were in Germany in 1932, I would have voted for the guy who didn't hate Jews and didn't want to kill them. Some considerations are far more important than others."

Therefore, said Armstrong, "I have no trouble voting for Trump at all. He is clearly the superior choice in this scenario."[6]

Many Catholics adopted – or acquiesced to – this same logic as it became clear that the choice now came down to Trump or Clinton. For some, it was a matter of choosing the least-worst option, because Trump was exceedingly repulsive in so many ways. But on the life issue, the one that should matter most for Catholics, Trump at least propounded the better policy, no matter what he might truly believe in his heart. He became the best available hope.

This was true even with a Catholic on the Democratic ticket, because as the summer went on Democratic vice presidential candidate Tim Kaine's adherence to authentic Catholic doctrine would be increasingly called into question. The scrutiny peaked in September when Kaine clumsily tried to reconcile his support for homosexual marriage with his Catholicism.

"[M]y church ... teaches me about a creator in the first chapter of Genesis who surveys the entire world, including mankind, and said it is very good," Kaine told attendees on Sept. 10 at the national dinner for the Human Rights Campaign, which lobbies for the homosexual agenda. "Pope Francis famously said 'Who am I to judge?' and to that I want to add, 'Who am I to challenge God for the beautiful diversity of the human family?' I think we're supposed to celebrate it, not challenge it."[7]

Kaine's mutilation of Genesis, and his prediction at the dinner that the Catholic Church would someday approve of homosexual marriage, touched off an onslaught of criticism, including a profound correction three days later from his own bishop, Francis DiLorenzo, of the Diocese of Richmond, Va., who retorted that "despite recent statements from the campaign trail, the Catholic Church's 2,000-year-old teaching to the truth about what constitutes marriage remains unchanged and resolute."[8]

The Rev. Kevin Bezner, a deacon of the Ukrainian Catholic Eparchy of St. Josaphat in Parma, Ohio, wrote on The Christian Review's website that he wished DeLorenzo had called for Kaine to either denounce his views and repent or choose to be excommunicated. Bezner said Kaine was predicting the impossible, as the Church "has no authority to change its teaching on marriage or homosexuality because these teachings come from Jesus Christ,

God. The truth is that homosexuality is not part of God's 'beautiful diversity.' Homosexuality is the result of man's weakness, his inability in some cases but in many cases his outright rejection of God's order."

Bezner said that Kaine, who attended a boys Catholic high school, "is the perfect product of Jesuit formation" and that if he actually understood Genesis, he would know that it "provides us with the foundation for our understanding of man and woman as complementary partners and so why traditional marriage, and not same-sex or any other type of false marriage, is part of God's plan."

Bezner therefore concluded that a vote for the Clinton-Kaine ticket was a vote against the Catholic Church and Christianity and, therefore, "a vote against Jesus Christ and God's law."[9]

Meanwhile, with polls in September still indicating that Trump was lagging with Catholics, veteran Catholic political strategist Deal Hudson formed a 34-member Catholic advisory group to persuade the faithful that Trump was, in fact, their candidate. Members included such notables as former U.S. Senator Rick Santorum; Matt Schlapp, chairman of the American Conservative Union; Father Frank Pavone, founder of Priests for Life; longtime conservative activist Richard Viguerie; Congressmen Steve Chabot and Mike Kelly; Kansas Gov. Sam Brownback; Tom Monaghan, founder of Ave Maria University (and Domino's Pizza); Former Oklahoma Gov. Frank Keating; and Joseph Cella, founder of the National Catholic Prayer Breakfast who had been one of the signers of the anti-Trump "Appeal to Our Fellow Catholics" letter just six months earlier.

Virtually all of them had favored a Republican candidate other than Trump prior to Trump's securing of the nomination. Now it was either him or Hillary, and they dug up enough virtue in Trump to hold their noses and publicly back him.

"If you look at the totality of Mr. Trump's positions," Cella said, "such as preserving and protecting religious liberty, the sanctity of human life, providing an uplifting and empowering economic agenda and opening wide the opportunity for school choice, particularly to Hispanics and African Americans in urban areas, the difference couldn't be more stark on these core issues between Mr. Trump and Hillary Clinton."[10]

The actual effect of this group, or the mere establishment of it, was immeasurable, 1) in the sense that it may have had a significantly positive influence on the campaign, or 2) in the sense that there were simply no metrics to measure it, or 3) in both senses. But coincidentally or otherwise, the conversation as to the Catholic vote began to change at about the time of the group's inception. Indeed, a spate of articles began appearing in the final weeks before the election positing the stark question of whether it was moral at all for Catholics to support the 2016 Democratic ticket.

It was the same question that orthodox Catholic leaders had been submitting for months.

At CatholicVote.com, Lori Ann Watson drew from the *Catechism* to explain "Why Catholics Can't Vote for Hillary – Even Once. Ever. For Any Reason." Noting the Church's incontrovertible teaching that abortion is a grave moral evil, as declared in CCC paragraph 2271, she then spelled out what this means for every Catholic:

"The Church … warns us against cooperation in the sins of others," she wrote in her Oct. 7 essay. "Paragraph 1868 of the Catechism says, 'Sin is a personal act. Moreover, we have a responsibility for the sins committed by others when we cooperate in them:

'– by participating directly and voluntarily in them;

'– by ordering, advising, praising or approving them;

'– by not disclosing or not hindering them when we have an obligation to do so;

'– by protecting evil-doers.'

"Each voter who casts a ballot for Clinton will (if Clinton is elected) enable her to expand the evil of intentional killing, and these voters will fail to do all that they can to hinder her goals."

Watson went on to delineate the difference between "prudential judgment" and "non-negotiable" issues for the Catholic voter: "Even those who like Clinton's stance on another issue are called to put that issue behind abortion and euthanasia on the priority list. The Church's instruction to the faithful regarding things such as poverty and immigration bears the tone of an exhortation, not a specific mandate; it calls us to serve as we are able. ...

"The Church's teaching in regards to poverty and immigration conveys a sense of urgency, but it's founded on a certain level of conditionality; She calls us to give all we can, but there is no across-the-board 'you must do *this*; you must not do *that*' imperative. Life issues are different: there is a very clear line, and crossing it is a grave sin. Pro-life issues *do* outweigh social justice issues. It's not ideal to have to choose between the two, but if we're faced with that choice, life wins.

"Voting for someone who promotes abortion and euthanasia is a cooperation in the deaths of innocent human lives. Don't cooperate with someone who promotes death. Don't vote for Hillary Clinton."[11]

Also in early October, Thomas D. Williams, Ph. D, who teaches philosophical ethics at the University of St. Thomas in Rome, called out the illogicality of the well-worn "personally opposed" trope that Kaine and many Catholic politicians use to bifurcate their religious identity from any evil actions their "political selves" might take – as if God grants them such license upon paying the filing fee for elective office.

"Being personally opposed to abortion," Williams wrote, "is like being personally opposed to racism or wife-beating. You can't just 'opt-out' while supporting other people's right to do harm. As one writer noted, 'Don't like abortion? Don't have one!' is as silly as saying, 'Don't like rape? Don't rape anyone!'"[12]

Williams, who is also a permanent research fellow at the Center for Ethics and Culture at the University of Notre Dame, cited Pope St. John Paul II's condemnation of the "personally opposed" justification. The legal toleration of abortion, John Paul wrote in 1995, "can in no way claim to be based on respect for the conscience of others, precisely because society has the right and the duty to protect itself against the abuses which can occur in the name of conscience and under the pretext of freedom."[13]

And then came the Oct. 11 bombshell, when WikiLeaks released internal Clinton campaign emails that lambasted Catholics, their beliefs and their Church. The emails described "the systematic thought and severely backwards gender relations" of the Catholic Church. Another message between campaign officials nakedly suggested using contraception as a wedge issue to capture more of the Catholic vote. In retrospect, the leaked emails may have proved the pivotal factor for then-undecided Catholic voters in the 2016 presidential campaign. The blowback to the Clinton campaign internal emails was immediate and thunderous:

– The emails illustrated "the open anti-Catholic bigotry of her senior advisers, who attack the deeply held beliefs and theology of Catholics."14 – Joseph Cella, Founder of the National Catholic Prayer Breakfast.[14]

– "For someone to come and say, 'I have a political organization to change your church to complete my political agenda or advance my agenda,' I don't know how anybody could embrace that." –Raymond Arroyo, EWTN television host.[15]

– "Long before Hillary Clinton called millions of Americans a 'basket of deplorables,' her top campaign advisers and liberal allies openly mocked Catholics, Southerners and a host of other groups." – *The Washington Times*[16]

– "For 30 years Hillary Clinton has been openly hostile to practicing Catholics. Now her staff is caught calling Catholics 'backwards' in emails seething with disdain." – Kellyanne Conway, political commentator and Trump campaign official.[17]

– "It's no secret that progressive elites despise religion, but it's still striking to see their contempt expressed so bluntly as in the leaked email chains that include Clinton campaign chairman John Podesta." –*The Wall Street Journal*[18]

– "Yesterday, I stopped short of asking Hillary Clinton to fire John Podesta, her campaign chairman. In light of the latest Wikileaks revelations, she has no choice but to cut all ties with this man. The man is hell bent on creating mutiny in the Catholic Church and must therefore be fired." – Bill Donohue, president of The Catholic League for Religious and Civil Rights[19]

The looming threat to authentic Catholic doctrine in a Clinton/Kaine administration spurred an unprecedented level of commentary from bishops and priests as well. Denver Archbishop Samuel J. Aquila laid out the parties' differences in black and white for his flock, declaring that the 2016 Democratic Party platform "is aggressively pro-abortion, not only in funding matters, but in the appointment of only those judges who will support abortion and the repealing of the Helms Amendment, which prevents the U.S. from supporting abortion availability overseas. Conversely, the Republican party platform is supportive of the Hyde Amendment (which prohibits federal tax dollars from being used for abortion) and just this year strengthened its support for life by calling for the defunding of Planned Parenthood, banning dismemberment abortion and opposing assisted suicide."[20]

Likewise, in a letter read at all Sunday Masses in his diocese before election day, Bishop William Murphy of the Diocese of Rockville Centre, New York, said that "support of abortion by a candidate for public office, some of whom are Catholics, even if they use the fallacious and deeply offensive 'personally opposed but…' line, is reason sufficient unto itself to disqualify any and every such candidate from receiving our vote."[21] Naturally, he caught some flak from liberal Catholics for saying it, particularly from known radicals like Father Thomas Reese, a longtime writer for liberal publications including the utterly dissident *National Catholic Reporter*.

In the Fall 2016 issue of *Latin Mass* magazine, Father Anthony J. Mastroeni made the case against the Democratic ticket simply by quoting directly from the respective party platforms: [22]

Differences in the Republican and Democrat Platforms

Republican Platform

"The Constitution's guarantee that no one can 'be deprived of life, liberty or property' deliberately echoes the Declaration of Independence's proclamation that 'all' are 'endowed by their Creator' with the inalienable right to life. Accordingly, we assert the sanctity of human life and affirm that the unborn child has a fundamental right to life which cannot be infringed. We support a human life amendment to the Constitution and legislation to make clear that the Fourteenth Amendment's protections apply to children before birth" [p. 13]. "We oppose the use of public funds to perform or promote abortion or to fund organizations, like Planned Parenthood, so long as they provide or refer for elective abortions or sell fetal body parts rather than provide healthcare" [p. 13]. "We support the appointment of judges who respect traditional family values and the sanctity of innocent human life" [p. 13].

"We condemn the Supreme Court's ruling in *U.S. v. Windsor,* which wrongly removed the ability of Congress to define marriage policy in federal law. We also condemn the Supreme Court's lawless ruling in *Obergefell v. Hodges* ... In *Obergefell,* five unelected lawyers robbed 320 million Americans of their legitimate constitutional authority to define marriage as the union of one man and one woman" [p. 11].

Democratic Platform

"We believe that every woman should have access to quality reproductive health care services, including safe and legal abortion – regardless of where she lives, how much money she makes, or how she is insured. We believe that reproductive health is core to women's, men's, and young people's health and wellbeing ... We will continue to oppose – and seek to overturn – federal and state laws and policies that impede a woman's access to abortion, including by repealing the Hyde Amendment" [p. 37]. "We will continue to stand up to Republican efforts to defund Planned Parenthood health centers, which provide critical health services to millions of people" [p. 37]. "We will appoint judges who... will protect a woman's right to safe abortion..." [p. 25].

"Democrats applaud last year's decision by the Supreme Court that recognized LGBT people – like every other American – have the right to marry the person they love. But there is still much work to be done" [p. 19].

The distinction between the two platforms was so stark that the most artful sophist would struggle to distort it.

Father Peter Stravinskas was more specific in a sermon preached at New

York's Church of the Holy Innocents on Sunday, Oct. 16:

"How do the two principal parties compare on issues traditionally of great import to Catholics? The one party has never had stronger positions on all the "non-negotiables" of Catholic social teaching, while the other party has never had more radical positions in total opposition to Catholic social teaching. ...

"So, what is one to do in this current election cycle? Many of you have logically asked your priests what they are going to do – and you have a right to know that. So let me say this: I could never support Hillary Clinton and the radically leftist program of her party. I am reasonably comfortable with the Republican platform (especially as that relates to the right to life, traditional marriage, parental freedom of choice in education and religious liberty), but distinctly uncomfortable with its standard-bearer due to his brashness and very spotty record as a would-be conservative.

"That said, I know for sure where Clinton will lead the country because of the consistent trajectory she has pursued her entire life. And how can we ignore the latest revelations about her staff mocking Catholic morality and even seeking to incite the laity to rebel against their bishops' teaching? I hope that Donald Trump has had a genuine conversion and/or that the people with whom he will surround himself will be able to move him into right paths, particularly in regard to the critically important task of appointing solid justices to the Supreme Court."[23]

Like so many other Catholics (and non-Catholics), Father Stravinskas would not so much pull the lever for Donald Trump as to pull it against Hillary Clinton.

And others in the Church Militant also began kicking into high gear in the weeks prior to the election.

Two days after the Stravinskas sermon, Archbishop Joseph Naumann, of Kansas City in Kansas, issued a bruising assessment of Tim Kaine, who had attended a Jesuit high school located just a few miles from Naumann's chancery office. "Unfortunately, the vice-presidential debate revealed that the Catholic running for the second highest office in our land is an orthodox member of his party," Naumann wrote, "fully embracing his party's platform, but a cafeteria Catholic, picking and choosing the teachings of the Catholic Church that are politically convenient."[24]

At The Christian Review website on Oct. 24, Father Gerard Lessard wrote, "What good could be greater than human life created in the image of God? Therefore, I will tolerate unintended and unforeseen evils, if they should ensue, to choose the greatest good."[25] In Donald Trump, the priest would allow for unforeseen evils. In Donald Trump, he would choose the greater good – or at least the lesser evil.

And thus did Donald Trump triumph among Catholics, at least according to exit polls that showed a 52% to 45% margin over Clinton.[26] Mark Gray, a political scientist at Georgetown University's Center for Applied Research in the Apostolate, later said his research showed that Clinton had actually won Catholics. But even he allowed that "I don't think we will ever really definitively know," and that the Catholic vote may have been a "toss up."[26]

Still, even the *possibility* that Trump may have won Catholics was traumatizing enough to liberal members of the Church, those who wouldn't allow the trifling matter of magisterial teaching to interfere with their personal discernment in the voting booth. Maybe some of them found justification in the widely-reported eruption of Father Jack Plotkowski of Des Plaines, Ill., who, shortly before election day, allegedly shouted in the sanctuary of St. Zachary Church, "I don't care who hears it. Anyone voting for Trump is going to hell. It's a mortal sin."[27] A rationale from Father for his audacious construal of God's justice could not be found. That, however, is not the case with the many assertions to the contrary, made by the priests, bishops, cardinals and popes quoted herein, which are amply supported by Church teaching.

The faithful at large seemed to accept the preponderance of clerical objections to the Clinton/Kaine ticket. Perhaps American Catholics had had enough of the twisting and churning of Church teaching, especially on abortion, and welcomed a clear message of authentic Church doctrine. For some, the last straw may have been when the rebellious and fraudulently named "Catholics for Choice" took out full-page ads in September, calling for public funding of abortion, an action that was immediately and strenuously denounced by Cardinal Timothy Dolan, chairman of the U.S. bishops' committee on pro-life activities.[28]

To Catholic commentator Matt C. Abbott, writing a couple of days after the election, it appeared "that many Catholics – with the help of a dedicated pro-life movement – are finally beginning to see through that ugly 'seamless garment' embraced and promoted by a number of clergy and religious over the last 30 years."[29] The "seamless garment" philosophy is a heretical deceit used by liberal Catholics to justify voting for pro-choice candidates.

In a *New York Post* column a few weeks after the election, George Mason University law professor Frank Buckley said Catholics shared a "Catholic sensibility" with Trump's supporters, even the non-Catholics among them. Catholics, he said, rejected the politics of division promulgated by the Democratic Party, citing especially Clinton's call for the American legal system to reform "deep-seated cultural codes, religious beliefs and structural biases" to ensure access to abortion. And "when the choice was put to the Democratic presidential candidates," Buckley wrote, "they all picked Black Lives Matter over All Lives Matter, with the exception of Jim Webb." Buckley, who served as a Trump speechwriter, said Catholic voters were also swayed by the call to patriotism embedded in Trump's "Make American Great Again" campaign slogan. "Catholics aren't the prisoners of political ideology," Buckley said. "They're looking for policies that speak to the concerns of ordinary Americans, things that work, not abstract theories."[30]

Hence, the rise of Trump. He gave hope to those Americans who felt estranged from new cultural trends. "Hope," of course, is a popular, if overworked, term in presidential politics. Bill Clinton was "The Man From Hope" (he was born in Hope, Arkansas). The title of Barack Obama's pre-2008 campaign book was titled, *The Audacity of Hope.* But as much as those two Democrats may have given hope to their respective constituencies, so did Trump give hope to his.

Among them was Deacon Bezner, who at The Christian Review website undoubtedly spoke for many Catholics in enumerating his reasons for being "filled with hope" after the election of Donald Trump. "I am filled with hope," he said,

- "... because among the greatest losers of this election nationally are abortion and Planned Parenthood; same-sex marriage, the transgender agenda, and the falsely named Human Rights Campaign; President Obama and the forced payment for contraception through Obamacare; the biased and disgraced national media; many Wall Street elites; Hollywood elites; and political correctness."
- "... because Mr. Trump has Mike Pence of Indiana as vice president. And I believe that he will be a strong and helpful guide for Mr. Trump."
- "... because I take Mr. Trump at his word and believe that he will appoint Supreme Court Justices who will uphold the Constitution and traditional Christian and American morality."
- "... because in its exit poll results Fox News reports that 81 percent of white evangelicals, 60 percent of Protestants, 52 percent of Catholics, 61 percent of Mormons, and 55 percent of other Christians voted for Trump."
- "... because never before have I witnessed so many Catholic priests and bishops speak so clearly about the moral teachings of the Catholic Church, how to rightly vote your conscience, and why the policies of Hillary Clinton, Tim Kaine, and the Democratic Party are unacceptable to those who truly live their faith."
- "... because unlike many among them I believe that Mr. Trump and his administration will work for African Americans, who have suffered so much as a result of the anti-life policies of the Democratic Party."

Bezner recounted the courage of a young priest who had recently been serving in his first parish assignment. This priest refused to cease forcefully explaining to parishioners why the policies of Hillary Clinton, Tim Kaine and the Democratic Party were morally wrong, in the face of constant intimidation from a powerful local priest who dissented from Church doctrine on intrinsic evils. But the young priest would not be silenced. He knew what the Church truly teaches about non-negotiable issues versus those that are a matter of prudential judgment. He'd had enough of doctrinal equivocating, evasion and doublespeak.[31]

And so, apparently, had a majority of Catholic voters in the presidential election of 2016.

24

The "Catholic Ticket"? Not the One With the Catholic

The 2016 Republican nomination of Donald Trump for president presented the orthodox Catholic cognoscenti with a challenge. The aforementioned open letter from dozens of prominent scholars, many of whom were unabashed conservatives, called Donald Trump "manifestly unfit to be president of the United States."

An interpretation – and clear endorsement – of the letter by an anonymous author for the Catholic News Agency recited the common Catholic objections to Trump's personal and public moral transgressions, about which few would argue: his vulgarity, his sexual escapades, his misogyny, his proposal to ban Muslims from entering the U.S., his advocacy for imposing the death penalty for murderers of a police officers, and his acceptance of torturing terrorists.[1] The CNS writer went on to quote Professor Chad Pecknold's assertion that Trump was also a "false friend" to the working class, would restrict religious liberty, and should be seen as "an enemy to the unborn, racial and religious minorities and the dignity of the human person generally."

While many Catholics were wary of Trump early on, the CNS article had a clear anti-Trump agenda. Particularly egregious was CNS's castigating tone, one that ushered its interpretation into the realm of absurdity by irrelevantly quoting the grave moral acts listed in the bishops' *Faithful Citizenship* document, most of which Trump had not been known to commit or even favor: "Racism and other unjust discrimination, the use of the death penalty, resorting to unjust war, the use of torture, war crimes, the failure to respond to those who are suffering from hunger or a lack of health care, pornography, redefining civil marriage, compromising religious liberty, or an unjust immigration policy ...."

Despite the ceaseless barrage of accusations from his enemies, Donald Trump is unequivocally not racist. This need not be proven here. It's just a hollow, inane barb thrown at him from the Left based on his non-liberal policies. Trump's acceptance of the death penalty for murderers is not out of the ordinary for American public officeholders, nor entirely contrary to Catholic doctrine. Whether Trump has resorted to any "unjust war" has not at all been objectively determined, and certainly could not have been pre-judged before he was elected. He has not imposed torture, committed war crimes, promoted pornography (despite alleged past dalliances with that industry – we all have sins in our past) or failed to respond to those who are hungry or needing health care. And he has most certainly been an advocate for traditional marriage and religious liberty.

So what about that other niggling issue? You know ... abortion, which Trump said he opposed. On that topic the CNS writer, believing that he was speaking for the letter signers, again engaged in prejudgment. How? Well, he just decided that he didn't believe Trump, noting that "several major pro-life groups had questioned Trump's commitment to the pro-life cause." That was quite true early on. Many abortion opponents, including this author, preferred other Republican candidates before Trump emerged as the frontrunner in the winter of 2016. But for the remainder of the primary and general election campaigns, he did not waver in his staunch anti-abortion stance.

In short, CNS largely and deliberately mischaracterized the content of the letter, adding alarming suggestions simply to "juice" the original document signed by the 37 prominent American Catholics. The actual letter had been a reasonable response to the Republican candidate field at the time it was written. These were no minor signers, and they were hardly a band of liberals. On March 7, 2016, the date of the letter, anti-abortion advocates such as these were solidly unconvinced that Donald Trump, the womanizing, fast-living, egocentric billionaire, could have somehow become one of their own. They were much more comfortable with any one of the other known anti-abortion candidates, like Ben Carson, Ted Cruz, Marco Rubio or Rick Santorum. Anyone but Trump. But it soon became clear that The Donald would be the GOP standard-bearer, and his anti-abortion rhetoric was better welcomed. With Hillary Clinton as the only other choice, the anti-abortion groups began, somewhat reluctantly, to line up behind their unexpected presidential nominee.

The overriding defect in the CNS article wasn't that it shamelessly embellished the group's letter with clear disdain for Donald Trump. It was that it conspicuously danced around the U.S. bishops' clear teaching on issues of intrinsic evil vis-à-vis issues of prudential judgment. Trump's announced opposition to abortion was swiftly and unfairly discredited, and the focus then shifted to his perceived shortcomings on issues of lesser priority, i.e., issues of prudential judgment. The CNS article thus tacitly acknowledged that abortion is the most important issue for Catholics to consider, but in the case of Donald Trump it placed the emphasis on lesser issues. Trump deserved to be taken at his word, if even reservedly.

Had CNS decided to publish an article that comported with the bishops' teaching, it would have acknowledged the bishops' hierarchy of Catholic voting criteria with the same zest as it recited Trump's record of personal moral turpitude. Irrespective of Trump's history as a lout, the hierarchy of Catholic issues construct has primacy. It overrides personality and personal history. Donald Trump was taking the correct position on the issue at the top of that hierarchy, the issue that was dispositive for a Catholic voter in the 2016 presidential election, but the CNS writer refused to give him credit for it.

CNS thus took liberties with the stratification of issues that its own corporate parent, the USCCB, had established. How are rank-and-file Catholics supposed to trust the bishops' teaching if a division of the

USCCB, itself, doesn't? In making voting decisions, are Catholics allowed to cavalierly skip past the abortion question, as the CNS writer did? No, they are not, and to do so would be to adopt the false teaching of the seamless garment, in which all issues are of the same moral weight.

CNS should, of course, have taken Trump at his word, just as it presumably would have done for all of the other anti-abortion candidates. Once it had reported, without the snarky asides, that Trump was, in fact, an anti-abortion advocate, the analysis could have continued with his stance on matters of prudential judgment, the process of evaluation that is taught by the bishops.

Had Trump voiced as much advocacy for abortion as his opponent, Hillary Clinton, the Catholic voter would have been left to judge which candidate would have offered the best chance for the reduction, if not eradication, of abortion. For example, even a pro-abortion candidate might, without enthusiasm, sign an anti-abortion bill into law if doing so somehow worked to his political advantage. As Cardinal James A. Hickey said, "[W]e need to ask which candidate will offer even a measure of protection for the unborn."[2] In other words, a candidate need not be "pure" on the issue in order to win the anti-abortion vote. Rather, he need only exhibit the greater likelihood of enacting anti-abortion public policy. And that's this issue that a Catholic must first consider in the voting booth.

Today, the odds of a particular candidate failing to distinguish himself in this manner are long, especially because of the influence that the substantial anti-abortion voting bloc wields. One candidate will surely emerge as the one to most likely help enact anti-abortion legislation. And as the bishops collectively and individually have declared, abortion is *the* Catholic issue of our time and therefore must be the first to be weighed in voting. Yes, there are, of course, five other intrinsic evils in play today – euthanasia, embryonic stem-cell research, homosexual "marriage," human cloning and religious freedom – and the candidates' positions on those issues must be considered alongside abortion. But, as the bishops have said, the sheer magnitude of the abortion genocide makes it the paramount intrinsic evil for a Catholic voter.

And so it is not unreasonable or untrue to say that Catholic voters must indeed be, by this deduction, single-issue, i.e., dominant-issue voters today, at least on their first review of the candidates. We have shown that, as a practical matter, the bishops' teaching is that abortion is truly a litmus test, pragmatically the *only* test, for selecting a candidate for whom to vote. Everything else is secondary. Collectively, the bishops ensconce this teaching deeply into their scholarly (and currently too diplomatic) discourse, but many exemplary bishops have retrieved it and made it crystal clear.

Catholics must, effectively, be single-issue voters because of the outsize status of abortion today. Abortion is the greatest moral outrage in history – far greater than the Nazi holocaust, Mao's extermination of up to 45 million of his own countrymen or Stalin's murder of 60 million fellow Russians. Yet, day-by-day abortion continues. More than any other issue today, it demands the concerted political focus of Catholics. To analogize: If a Catholic had the power to vote against a policy that would result in another holocaust, would he not make that the singular basis for his vote?

It's not that the other non-negotiable intrinsic evils are *less* evil than abortion. It's that abortion – the mass murder of innocent children – has become an unprecedented genocide and demands immediate political remedy. The other intrinsic evils – euthanasia, embryonic stem-cell research, homosexual "marriage," human cloning and opposing religious freedom – are just as abominable, but these don't murder, involve the annihilation of human beings, at least on the monstrous scale that abortion does.

Veteran Catholic political scholar and activist Deal Hudson argued that Catholics who vote according to Church teaching are effectively single-issue voters only because they must be *dominant*-issue voters. "Opposition to abortion," he writes, "binds every Catholic on pain of mortal sin; it admits of no exceptions. There is no question, then, that as the dominant issue, a politician's position on abortion qualifies him or her for the Catholic vote. From the perspective of the Church, not all the policy positions taken by candidates are of equal importance. Catholics, by understanding themselves as dominant-issue voters, can preserve the hierarchy of values at the core of Church teaching while not ignoring the legitimate spectrum of issues important to political consideration.

"Furthermore, by understanding the dominance of life issues, Catholics will overcome their confusion about the difference between moral principle and prudential judgment. Unlike the admonition against abortion, most of the general principles proposed in Church teaching can be implemented in a variety of ways; it's simply a mistake to assume—as the Left often does—that one kind of implementation is more 'Catholic' than another."[3]

Had Trump and Clinton not differed in their expressed stances on abortion, the other intrinsic evils that are in play today would still have tipped the scales in Trump's favor for correct Catholic voting. If it had (theoretically) remained a draw between Trump and Clinton on all six of those high-priority issues, the Catholic voter would next look to lesser moral issues that are matters of prudential judgment, i.e., the voter's own determination of which candidate best represents the Catholic view. On these issues, the Catholic voter would be free to vote as he wishes. But here's the sticking point: it rarely progresses to this level of scrutiny of the candidates. Why? Because the six specific issues of higher priority – those involving intrinsic evil – must first be considered before any issues of personal prudential judgment. In any given election, even if all of the candidates are precisely the same on abortion, they will surely not be precisely the same on euthanasia, embryonic stem-cell research, homosexual "marriage," human cloning or religious freedom.

But what if each candidate scores a "Catholic" rating on the same number of these intrinsic-evil issues, but not on the same specific issues? For example, Candidate A is good only on abortion, embryonic stem-cell research and euthanasia, and Candidate B is good only on abortion, human cloning and religious freedom? Well, then the voter can make a decision based on the likelihood of one candidate modifying his position on the other intrinsic-evil issues. If there is no such apparent likelihood, then the voter can take into account the candidates' respective positions on the lesser moral issues, those of prudential judgment. But well before the comparative analysis would get this far, all but one candidate would most likely be eliminated. One of the candidates will probably be better on abortion and, if not, one will surely have emerged better on at least one of the other five issues of intrinsic evil. For a Catholic, choosing the right candidate is determined at the level of the intrinsic evils. It almost never comes down to issues of personal prudential judgment.

Donald Trump may have checked nearly all of the boxes that the March 2016 letter signers presented for his disqualification. And yes, prior to his nomination, other Republican candidates had better track records on opposing abortion. But thereafter it would have been wrong for any Catholic to reject Trump on the basis of his apparently newfound anti-abortion stance, no matter its believability. Catholicism embraces redemption. Hillary Clinton was a diehard pro-choice candidate, and her running mate was a seamless-garment, pro-choice Catholic. Donald Trump, on the other hand, was at least *saying* he was anti-abortion, and he thus became the correct choice in the Catholic process for evaluating candidates.

And by his actions in office, from appointing judges to enacting policies, he would indeed become the most anti-abortion president in American history.

Endnotes

Chapter 1
A Teaching Fatally Ignored

1. *Catechism of the Catholic Church* (CCC), 2nd. ed., 888.
2. Guttmacher Institute estimate for 2017.
3. Patty Maguire Armstrong, "The Catholic Vote: What Should it be? What will it be?," *The Remnant* newspaper, October 23, 2012, https://www.remnantnewspaper.com/Archives/2012-1031-patti-mjm-catholic-vote.htm
4. U.S. Conference of Catholic Bishops, *Forming Consciences For Faithful Citizenship – Part I – The U.S. Bishops' Reflection on Catholic Teaching and Political Life,* no. 23.
5. Cardinal Joseph Ratzinger (later Pope Benedict XVI), "Worthiness to Receive Holy Communion: General Principles," Private letter to Cardinal Theodore McCarrick, July 2004.
6. Peter Kreeft, *Fundamentals of the Faith: Essays in Christian Apologetics,* Ignatius Press, 1988.
7. Ibid.
8. Pope Benedict XVI, at the funeral of Cardinal Joachim Meisner, July 15, 2017.

Chapter 2
Does a Catholic Voting Bloc Even Exist?

1. George J. Marlin, *The American Catholic Voter,* St. Augustine's Press, 2004, p. 37;

2. Mark Summers, "Onward Catholic Soldiers: The Catholic Church During the Civil War," Acton.org, December 21, 2011.

3. Marlin, p. 187.

4. Ibid., p. 174.

5. Ibid., p. 231.

6. Ibid., p. 261.

7. Archbishop Charles Chaput, Diocese of Denver, "Political Responsibility," October 28, 2000.

8. Marlin, p. xx.

9. Ibid., pp. 311-312.

Chapter 3
His Greatest Seduction: The Kennedy Capitulation

1. Michael O'Brien, *John F. Kennedy's Women, The Story of a Sexual Obsession,* Now and Then Reader, LLC, 2011.

2. Chaput, Address at Houston Baptist University, March 3, 2010, http://romereturn.blogspot.com/2010/03/archbishop-charles-chaput-at-houston.html

3. Mark S. Massa, S.J., "A Catholic for President? John F. Kennedy and the 'Secular' Theology of the Houston Speech, 1960," *Journal of Church and State 39 (1997),* pp. 297-317.

4. Armstrong.

5. "Jefferson's Wall of Separation Letter," https://www.usconstitution.net/jeffwall.html

6. Daniel L. Dreisbach, "The Mythical 'Wall of Separation': How a Misused Metaphor Changed Church-State Law, Policy, and Discourse," Heritage.org, June 23, 2006.

7. Chaput.

8. Marlin, pp. 255-256.

9. Ibid., p. 260.

10. Chaput, "Political Responsibility."

11. Marlin, p. 261.

12. Ibid., pp. 234-235.
13. Ibid., p. 235.
14. Ibid., p. 237.
15. Ibid., pp. 275-276.
16. Ibid., p. 282.
17. Massa.
18. Armstrong.
19. Chaput, "Let's Make a Deal: Catholic Conscience and Compromise," *Denver Catholic Register,* September 22, 2004.
20. Chaput, "Political Responsibility."

Chapter 4
The JFK Aftermath: Suddenly Like Everyone Else

1. Marlin, p. xvii.
2. John Zmirak, "Where Do Pro-Choice Catholic Democrats Like Joseph Biden and Nancy Pelosi Come From?," Stream.org, April 28, 2016.
3. Ibid.
4. Ibid.
5. Marlin, pp. 270-271.
6. Father Peter M.J. Stravinskas, Homily preached at the Church of the Holy Innocents, October 16, 2016.
7. Marlin, pp. 291-293.
8. Ibid., pp. 294-295.
9. Ibid., pp. 296-297.
10. Gregory Allen Smith, Politics in the Parish, pp. 181-182, Georgetown University Press, 2008.
11. Marlin, pp. 301-303.
12. Ibid., p. 306, 323.
13. https://cara.georgetown.edu/presidential%20vote%20only.pdf
14. Pew Research Center, https://www.pewresearch.org/fact-tank/2016/11/09/how the-faithful-voted-a-preliminary-2016-analysis/

Chapter 5
The Anti-Antiabortion Democratic Party

1. Marlin, pp. 301-303.

2. Ramesh Punnuru, *The Party of Death: the Democrats, the Media, the Courts, and the Disregard for Human Life;* Regnery Publishing, 2006.

3. Marlin, pp. 296-297.

4. Charles Camosy, "Democrats Could Destroy the GOP – If Only They Would Welcome Antiabortion Liberals," washingtonpost.com, March 21, 2016.

5. Ibid.

6. Philip Pullella, "Pope warns Catholic politicians who back abortion," Reuters, May 9, 2007. https://www.reuters.com/article/us-pope-abortion/pope-warns-catholic-politicians-who-back-abortion-idUSN0932690220070509?mod=related&channelName=worldNews

7. Bishop Arthur J. Serratelli, "Pro-Choice vs. Communion," Catholic Exchange, June 20, 2007. https://catholicexchange.com/pro-choice-vs-communion

8. Ibid.

9. James Antle, III, "Who are the Pro-Life Democrats?," *Catholic World Report,* May 14, 2011.

10. "Democrats Weigh Deemphasizing Abortion as an Issue," *New York Times,* December 24, 2004.

11. "Howard Dean: I Don't Think There's Room for Prolifers in the Democratic Party," townhall.com, March 7, 2017.

12. Antle.

13. Ibid.

14. Ibid.

15. Father Anthony J. Mastroeni, S.T.D., J.D., "Voting Your Catholic Conscience," *Latin Mass* magazine, Fall 2016, p. 61.

16. Ibid.

17. Archbishop Samuel J. Aquila, "Voting as a Catholic in 2016," Denver-Catholic.org, October 5, 2016.

18. Mastroeni.
19. Edmund Kozak, "WikiLeaks: Podesta and Left-Wing Activist Plot 'Catholic Spring,'" LifeZette.com, October 12, 2016.
20. Ibid.
21. Ibid.
22. Amy Moreno, "Growing Backlash From Catholic Church Against Clinton Campaign," truthfeed.com, October, 14, 2016.
23. Ibid.
24. Ibid.
25. Stravinskas.
26. Moreno.
27. Ibid.
28. Marlin, pp. 301-303.
29. Father Kevin Bezner, "A Vote for Clinton/Kaine is a Vote Against Christianity," thechristianreview.com, September 15, 2016.

Chapter 6
The Untaught Catholic Voter

1. Bishop George L. Thomas, Helena, "Political Year Offers Opportunity to Renew Our Efforts to Build a Culture of Life," *The Montana Catholic,* October 15, 2004.
2. Pew Research Center, "Public Opinion on Abortion," August 29, 2019. https://www.pewforum.org/fact-sheet/public-opinion-on-abortion/
3. Russell Shaw, "A Question for Catholics Before They Head to the Voting Booth," *OSV Newsweekly,* December 10, 2015.
4. Ibid.
5. CCC, 1816.
6. Father Dwight Longenecker, "The Catholic Beach House," January 17, 2019. https://dwightlongenecker.com/the-catholic-beach-house/
7. Bishop Robert J. Carlson, "Statement On Catholic Teaching on Abortion and Political Beliefs," August 2004.
8. Bishop Robert Hermann, "Bishop Asks Catholic Voters to 'Save Our

Children!'" *St. Louis Review*, October 10, 2008.

9. Aquila.

10. Bishop Robert Vasa, "Modern Look at Abortion Not Same as St. Augustine's," *The Catholic Sentinel*, September 5, 2008.

11. Bezner.

12. Mastroeni.

13. Bishop Emeritus Rene Henry Gracida, Statement, "On the 2004 Presidential Questionnaire," August 10, 2004. https://www.priestsfor-life.org/magisterium/bishops/04-08-10gracida.htm

14. Marlin, p. 339.

15. Ibid.

Chapter 7
A "Fallen Away" Opportunity

1. "Catholics' Church Attendance Resumes Downward Slide," Gallup, Inc., April 9, 2018.

2. Armstrong.

3. Catherine Harmon, "Church-attendance numbers tell a different story," *Catholic World Report*, November 7, 2012. https://www.catholic-worldreport.com/2012/11/07/church-attendance-numbers-tell-a-different-story/

4. Steven Wagner, "The Catholic Political Identity," *Crisis* magazine, November 1, 1998.

5. Ibid.

Chapter 8
America's Mythical "Law": Separation of Church and State

1. *Constitution of the United States*, https://constitutionus.com/#billofright-spreamble

2. Dreisbach.

3. Ibid.

4. Chaput, Address at Houston Baptist University, March 3, 2010, http://romereturn.blogspot.com/2010/03/archbishop-charles-chaput-at-houston.html

5. Bishop Samuel J. Aquila, *New Earth* diocesan newspaper, November 2008.

6. Bishop Thomas Olmsted, Zenit.org, October 15, 2006.

7. Chaput, "Public witness and Catholic citizenship," October 18, 2012, *http://www.priestsforlife.org/library/5805-public-witness-and-catholic-citizenship*

8. Mastroeni.

9. Ibid.

10. Cardinal James Francis Stafford, Address at Catholic University of America, November 13, 2008.

11. Paul A. Fisher, *Behind the Lodge Door: The Church, State and Freemasonry in America,* TAN Books, October 17, 1991.

12. Olmsted, *Catholics in the Public Square,* 2006.

13. Eusebius J. Beltran, "Vote Pro-Life!," *The Sooner Catholic,* November 6, 1994.

14. Bishop William E. Lori, *Church and State, Part 1,* September 2004.

15. Serratelli, "Catholic Politicians Criticize Pope," http://www.priestsfor-life.org/magisterium/bishops/07-06-19-arthur-serratelli.htm

16. Bishop Joseph A. Galante, "Faithful Citizenship: Living in a way worthy of the Gospel," October 2008.   http://www.priestsfor-life.org/magisterium/bishops/galante-faithful-citizenship.htm

17. Bishop William Murphy, LifeSiteNews, November 2, 2016. https://www.life-sitenews.com/news/bishop-murphy-catholic-voters-obliged-to-reject-abortion-supporters-candida

18. United States Conference of Catholic Bishops (USCCB), *Forming Consciences for Faithful Citizenship,* Part I, 11.

19. Ibid., Part I, 9.

20. Stravinskas.

21. Chaput, "Faith and Patriotism," October 22, 2004. http://www.priests-forlife.org/magisterium/bishops/04-10-22chaput.htm

22. Ibid.

23. Lori.

24. Chaput.

25. Archbishop José H. Gomez, "We Cannot Ignore the Life Issues," October 2008. http://www.priestsforlife.org/magisterium/bishops/08-10-29-gomez.htm

26. Aquila, Homily delivered at the Legislative Mass, Cathedral of the Holy Spirit, Bismarck, North Dakota, January 18, 2007. http://www.priestsforlife.org/magisterium/bishops/07-01-18-aquila.pdf

Chapter 9
Yes, I Am Trying to Impose My Beliefs on You

1. *Gaudium et Spes,* 43.

2. Galante.

3. Bishop Thomas J. Tobin, "Without a Doubt – My R.S.V.P. to Rudy Giuliani," *Rhode Island Catholic,* May 31, 2007. http://thericatholic.com/stories/my-rsvp-to-rudy-giuliani,123?

4. Chaput.

5. Chaput, "Political Responsibility."

6. Chaput, "Let's Make a Deal: Catholic Conscience and Compromise," *Denver Catholic Register,* September 22, 2004.

7. Bishop Edward P. Cullen, "The Concerned Citizen," *The A.D. Times,* October 26, 2000.

8. Ibid.

9. Pope Francis, *Evangelii Gaudium,* 183

Chapter 10
For Better or Worse, the Bishops Are Still in Charge

1. CCC, 862.

2. Ibid., 888.

3. Ibid., 890.

4. Ibid., 892.

5. Ibid., 895.

6. Ibid., 1558

7. "Priest Gives Pulpit to Homosexual Partners to Share 'Witness' Story Prior to Mass," LifeSiteNews, January, 17, 2019.

8. Bishop Thomas Wenski, "Politicians and Communion," *Orlando Diocese News,* May 3, 2004.

9. Archbishop Timothy M. Dolan, "How Can Anyone Be Silent on This Key Civil Rights Question?," *Milwaukee Journal Sentinel,* September 28, 2008.

10. Mary Stadnyk, "Bishop John Smith of Trenton, NJ blasts hypocrisy of 'pro-choice' Catholic politicians," *The Monitor* (Catholic Diocese of Trenton), March 31, 2004.

Chapter 11
The Bishops Fiddle While Rome's Church Burns

1. Deal Hudson, "A Texas Archbishop Slaps Down 'Catholics for Choice!,'" *The Christian Review,* September 13, 2016.

2. Bishop Joseph E. Strickland, "The Absurdity of Catholics for Choice," *Bishop's Blog,* September 13, 2016. https://www.bishopstrickland.com/blog/post/the-absurdity-of-catholics-for-choice

3. Kathryn Jean Lopez, "Aborting Church: Frances Kissling and Catholics for a Free Choice," *Crisis* magazine, April 1, 2002.

4. "Statement from Archbishop Jerome Hanus in Response to Comments Made by Sister Michelle Nemmers at Democratic Rally in Dubuque, Iowa," October 31, 2004. https://www.priestsforlife.org/magisterium/bishops/04-10-31hanus.htm

5. Bishop Alexander K. Sample, Marquette, Michigan, "A Needed Clarification," Faith Matters, October 17, 2008. https://www.priestsforlife.org/magisterium/bishops/sample-clarification.htm

6. Lisa Bourne, "Dissident Catholic Nun: NARAL Leader's Abortion Story 'Touching and Compelling,'" LifeSiteNews, August 1, 2016.

7. Sample.

8. "Cdl. Cupich's rationales for not taking canonical action against prominent pro-abortion Catholic politicos are as unconvincing as ever," In the Light of the Law, A Canon Lawyer's Blog, June 14, 2019. http://www.allowcopy.com/open/?url=https:%5C/%5C/canon-lawblog.wordpress.com%5C/2019%5C/06%5C/14%5C/cdl-cupichs-rationales-for-not-taking-canonical-action-against-prominent-pro-abortion-catholic-politicos-are-as-unconvincing-as-ever%5C/

9. Ed Condon, "Excommunicate Cuomo," *First Things,* January 29, 2019. https://www.firstthings.com/web-exclusives/2019/01/excommunicate-cuomo

10. Edward N. Peters, "On excommunicating Andrew Cuomo for heresy," *Catholic World Report,* January 31, 2019. https://www.catholicworldreport.com/2019/01/30/on-excommunicating-andrew-cuomo-for-heresy/

11. Ibid.

Chapter 12
"I'm Personally Opposed to Abortion, and Any Law Against It"

1. CCC, 2272-2273.

2. Catholic Bishops of Pennsylvania, "Personal Participation: The Key to a Just Society," October 1984.

3. Bishop Donald W. Trautman, "Reflections on the U.S. Bishops' Statement, Living the Gospel of Life," Speech at the Rose Dinner, Washington, D.C., January 22, 1999.

4. Father Stephen F. Torraco, Ph.D, *A Brief Catechism for Catholic Voters,* EWTN, 2002.

5. *Gaudium et Spes* 43.

6. Bishop David Ricken, "A Letter to Catholic Politicians and Public Officials on the Subject of Abortion and the Law," *The Wyoming Catholic Register,* August 2004.

7. Olmsted.

8. Ricken.

9. Serratelli, "Politics and Logic," October 26, 2004. https://bishopser-ratelli.rcdop.org/news/politics-and-logic

10. Bishop Michael J. Sheridan, Pastoral Letter on "The Duties of Catholic Politicians and Voters," May 1, 2004.

11. Archbishop Henry J. Mansell, "Religious Convictions and Public Policy," *The Catholic Transcript, June 2004*

12. Tobin.

13. Galante.

14. Bishop Lawrence E. Brandt, Pastoral Letter, "Integrity and the Political Arena," Aug. 10, 2004.

15. Bishop F. Joseph Gossman, Respect Life Homily, Oct. 3, 2004.

16. Marlin, p. 301.

17. Bishop John J. Myers, Pastoral Statement, "The Obligations of Catholics and the Rights of Unborn Children," June 1990. https://www.tandfon-line.com/doi/abs/10.1080/00243639.1990.11878066

18. Tobin.

19. Ibid.

20. Trent Horn, "The inconsistency of 'Personally Opposed but Still Pro-Choice,'" *Catholic Answers* magazine, July 25, 2016.

21. Ibid.

22. Pope John Paul II, *The Gospel of Life* (71).

23. Myers.

24. Tobin.

Chapter 13
Joe & Nancy Wrestle With God Almighty

1. Bishop Francis Malooly, Letter to the Editor, "Catholic Church Has Made No Exception Regarding Abortion Since Ancient Times," *The News Journal,* October 26, 2008.

2. Vasa.

3. Cardinal Justin F. Rigali and Bishop William E. Lori, Statement on

House Speaker Nancy Pelosi's comments on NBC's Meet the Press on August 24, 2008.

4. Malooly.

5. Father John Connery, S.J., *Abortion, The Development of the Roman Catholic Perspective,* Loyola University Press, 1977.

6. CCC, 2271

7. Bishop R. Walker Nickless, Pastoral Letter, "Understanding the Issues and What's at Stake," August 2008. https://www.ewtn.com/catholicism/library of-sioux-city-corrects-pelosi-3797

8. Myers.

9. Malooly.

10. Vasa.

11. David G. Bonagura, Jr., "Dear Bishops, Now is the Time," *Crisis* magazine, September 16, 2008.

12. Chaput, speech sponsored by ENDOW (Educating on the Nature and Dignity of Women), October 17, 2008.

13. Archbishop Edwin O'Brien, "The Way of Life," *The Catholic Review,* October 2008.

14. Malooly.

15. Judie Brown, "Pro-abortion Catholic Politicians: An Avoidable Crisis," all.org, August 9, 2016.

16. Ibid.

17. Ibid.

18. Thomas D. Williams, Ph. D, "Tim Kaine's Catholic Problem," Breitbart.com, Oct. 5, 2016.

19. Ibid.

20. Bishop Blase Cupich, Statement Read at Masses November 2-3, 2002.

21. Bishop Edward B. Scharfenberger, "Statement in Response to Recent Planned Parenthood Rallies," February 13, 2017.

22. Ibid.

23. Chris Churchill, "Churchill: Bishop scolds Catholic Politicians who stood with Planned Parenthood," *Albany Times Union,* February 15, 2017.

24. Ibid.

25. "Bishop bars Patrick Kennedy from Communion over abortion," CNN.com, November 23, 2009. https://www.cnn.com/2009/POLI-TICS/11/22/kennedy.abortion/index.html

26. "Vatican Office Says No Communion for Pro-Abortion Obama Nominee Sebelius," LifeNews.com, March 13, 2009.

27. JD Flynn and Matt Hadro, "Biden communion denial was required by diocesan policy," Catholic News Agency, October 30, 2019.

28. Archbishop John F. Donoghue, Bishop Robert J. Baker, Bishop Peter J. Jugis, "Worthy to Receive the Lamb: Catholics in Political Life and the Reception of Holy Communion," August 4, 2004.

29. USCCB, *Living the Gospel of Life,* no. 32.

30. Ibid.

31. USCCB, *Catholics in Political Life,* June 18, 2004.

32. USCCB, *Living the Gospel of Life,* no. 23.

33. Bishop Lawrence E. Brandt, "Integrity and the Political Arena," August 10, 2004.

34. Ibid.

35. Philip Pullella, "Pope Warns Catholic Politicians Who Back Abortion," Reuters, May 9, 2007.

36. Steven Ertelt, "Pope Francis: Pro-Abortion Politicians Ineligible for Communion," LifeNews.com, May 7, 2013.

37. Ibid.

38. *Code of Canon Law,* no. 915.

39. Ertelt.

40. William E. May, "Legislative efforts in the United Sates to prohibit 'partial-birth abortion,'" Catholic News Agency, https://www.catholic-newsagency.com/resources/abortion/partial-birth-abortion/legislative-efforts-in-the-united-states-to-prohibit-partial-birth-abortion

41. Richard W. Stevenson, "Bush Signs Ban On a Procedure For Abortions," *New York Times,* November 6, 2003.

42. Sacred Congregation for the Doctrine of the Faith, "Declaration on Procured Abortion," November 18, 1974.

43. Pope John Paul II, *Evangeliium Vitae*, no. 7.
44. Philip F. Lawler, *The Faithful Departed, The Collapse of Boston's Catholic Culture,* 2010, Encounter Books, p. 82.
45. Ibid., p. 85.
46. Ibid.
47. Ricken, "Life: The Social Justice Issue of Our Time," *The Compass* newspaper, October 17, 2008.
48. "Kansas City archdiocese breaks ties with Girl Scouts," Catholic News Agency, May 5, 2017.
49. Donald R. McClarey, "Pro-Abort Catholic Politicians and the Church," *The American Catholic,* September 9, 2009.
50. Ibid.

Chapter 14
Catholic Doctrine According to Alfred

1. ConnecticutCatholicCorner.blogspot.com, June 19, 2016.
2. Anne Hendershott, Ph. D, "Catholic Groups Publish 'Pope Francis' Voter Guide," CatholicWorldReport.com, June 17, 2016.
3. Ibid.
4. Ibid.
5. Ibid.
6. Ibid.
7. Ibid.
8. Deacon Terry Barber, Sunday Bulletin of Sacred Heart Catholic Church, Lacey, Washington, April 24, 2016.
9. Sisters of the Precious Blood, *Grassroots* newsletter, June 2016.
10. Sisters of St. Francis, "Stepping Into the Voting Booth," Sisters of St. Francis of Philadelphia, Congregational E-News, November 1, 2016.
11. USCCB, *Forming Consciences for Faithful Citizenship*, no. 37.
12. Ibid., no. 42.
13. "Faithful Citizenship Opportunities," *St. John's Parish Newsletter,* October 2, 2016.

14. Father Jerome McKenna, "The Pastor's Corner," Sunday Bulletin of St. Paul of the Cross Roman Catholic Church, Atlanta.

15. Hendershott.

16. Ibid.

17. Ibid.

18. Ibid.

19. Michael Sean Winters, "USCCB: 'Faithful Citizenship' Trainwreck," ncronline.org, November 16, 2015.

20. Ibid.

21. Ibid.

22. Alex Smith, "Bishop Finn Condemns National Catholic Reporter," KCUR.org, https://www.kcur.org/post/bishop-finn-condemns-national-catholic-reporter-0#stream/0, February 4, 2013.

23. Andrew Gans, "14th Annual GLAAD Media Award Winners Include The Goat and Zanna, Don't!," Playbill.com, April 8 2003. http://www.playbill.com/article/14th-annual-glaad-media-award-winners-include-the-goat-and-zanna-dont-com-112515

24. Kevin J. Jones, "Inside a dubious LGBT media guide to Pope Francis' visit," Catholic News Agency, September 11, 2015. https://www.catholic-newsagency.com/news/inside-a-dubious-lgbt-media-guide-to-pope-francis-visit-43140

25. "Editorial: No reconciling the irreconcilable when it comes to marriage," *National Catholic Reporter,* July 1, 2014. https://www.ncron-line.org/news/politics/editorial-no-reconciling-irreconcilable-when-it-comes-marriage

26. "Editorial: Our persons of the year for 2015," *National Catholic Reporter,* December 28, 2015. https://www.ncronline.org/news/people/editorial-our-persons-year-2015

27. Bill Donohue, "Pope Francis Says Gay Couples Are Not a Family," CNS News, https://www.cnsnews.com/commentary/bill-donohue/pope-francis-says-gay-couples-are-not-family, June 18 2018.

28. *National Catholic Reporter.*

Chapter 15
The Holey Seamless Garment

1. Marlin, pp. 299-300.
2. Camosy.
3. Camosy, "Yes, Catholics May Vote for Bernie Sanders," *National Catholic Register,* ncronline.org, Feb. 9, 2016.
4. Father Dwight Longenecker, "Can a Catholic Vote for Bernie Sanders?," patheos.com, February 3, 2016.
5. Camosy.
6. Ratzinger.
7. Jimmy Evans, "Don't Be Misled, Catholics Are Paragraph 22 People: Bishop Vasa on Forming Consciences for Faithful Citizenship," fratres.wordpress.com, October 21, 2008.
8. Archbishop Elden F. Curtiss, Omaha, Nebraska, "Deciding the Issues That Are Most Important to Us," November 1, 2008.
9. Chaput.
10. Father Chris Heath, "Conscience Formation," https://www.stthomas-more.net/Resources/Documents/CONSCIENCE%20FORMA-TION.pdf
11. Bishop Kevin Farrell and Bishop Kevin Vann, Joint Statement to the Faithful of the Dioceses of Dallas and Fort Worth, October 8, 2008.
12. Archbishop Joseph F. Naumann, Kansas City in Kansas, and Bishop Robert W. Finn, Kansas City-St. Joseph, Joint Pastoral Letter, "Our Moral Responsibility as Catholic Citizens," September 12, 2008.
13. Myers, "A Voter's Guide: Pro-Choice Candidates and Church Teaching," September 7, 2004.
14. Bishop Paul S. Loverde and Bishop Francis X. DiLorenzo, "Election Letter: Voting With a Well-Formed Conscience," October 2008.
15. Myers.
16. Deacon Michael Bickerstaff, "Is it Morally Permissible to Vote for a Pro-Abortion Candidate?," IntegratedCatholicLife.org, October 21, 2012.

17. John-Henry Westen, "Bishop Vasa: Pro-abortion Candidates are 'Disqualified' – Clarifies *Faithful Citizenship*," LifeSiteNews.com, September 12, 2008.

18. Lori, *Church and State, Part 2,* October 2004.

19. Donoghue, "On Conscientious Voting," September 16, 2004.

20. Farrell and Vann.

21. Camosy.

22. Gallagher.

23. Camosy.

Chapter 16
Clerics All Dolled Up in Their Seamless Garment

1. Hudson, "The Major Confusion of Catholic Voters – When a Catholic Can Differ With the Bishops," *The Christian Review,* July 5, 2016.

2. CatholicCulture.org, November 9, 2016.

3. Matt C. Abbott, "Trump Won the Catholic Vote," American-Thinker.com, November 11, 2016.

4. Tim Staples, "The Catholic Vote," Catholic.com, February 23, 2016.

5. Carlson.

6. USCCB, *Forming Consciences for Faithful Citizenship*, no. 37.

7. Ibid., no. 40.

8. Ibid.

9. USCCB, *Living the Gospel of Life*, no. 22.

10. Ibid.

11. John L. Allen, Jr., "Synod: Interview With Cardinal Francis George," National Catholic Reporter Conversation Cafe, October 15, 2008.

Chapter 17
The Seamless Garment Torn Apart

1. Aquila.

2. Aquila, *New Earth* diocesan newspaper, November 2008.

3. Aquila, Homily given at the Cathedral of St. Mary, Fargo, North Dakota, October 19, 2008.

4. Bishop Raymond J. Boland and Bishop Robert W. Finn, Pastoral Letter, October 7, 2004.

5. Bishop Earl Boyea, "How Shall I Cast My Vote?," October 2008.

6. Brandt.

7. Archbishop Daniel M. Buechlein, "Forming Our Consciences as We Prepare to Vote," October 2008.

8. Bishop Raymond L. Burke, Pastoral Letter, January 10, 2004.

9. Carlson.

10. Chaput, "On the Courage to be Christian," August 2008.

11. Chaput, "Faith and Patriotism," October 22, 2004.

12. Chaput, "How to Tell a Duck From a Fox – Thinking With the Church as We Look Toward November," April 14, 2004.

13. Chaput, "American and Catholic: Thoughts on Responsible Citizenship," October 11, 2000.

14. Chaput, "Election 2016: U.S. Bishops on Voting," ncregister.com, October 25, 2016.

15. Cullen.

16. "Archbishop Curtiss Issues Pro-Life Voting Statement," catholic.org, October 2008.

17. Archbishop Elden F. Curtiss, Pastoral Letter, "We Are Pro-Life People in a Pro-Life Church," September 2000.

18. Curtiss, "Deciding the Issues That Are Most Important to Us."

19. Bishop Thomas G. Doran, "Easy or Not, It is Time to Choose Rightly and Stand for the Truth and Against Intrinsic Evil," *The Observer*, October 24, 2008.

20. Farrell and Vann.

21. Bishop Ronald W. Gainer, October 2008.

22. Galante.

23. Francis Cardinal George, October 2000.

24. Allen.

25. Gomez, "Voters Must Know Stances on Life Issues," *San Antonio Express-*

News, October 29, 2008.

26. Gossman.

27. Archbishop Wilton D. Gregory, "What I have Seen and Heard," *The Georgia Bulletin,* October 30, 2008.

28. Bishop James V. Johnston, "Bishop's Column, Prudence and Preparing to Vote," October 3, 2008.

29. Jugis, Homily, August 9, 2004.

30. Bishop David Kagan, "Guide to Catholic Voting," October 7, 2016.

31. Pope John Paul II, *Christifideles Laici,* no. 38.

32. Torraco.

33. Pope John Paul II, *Gospel of Life,* no. 58.

34. Lori, *Church and State, Part I.*

35. Lori, *Church and State, Part II.*

36. Loverde and DiLorenzo.

37. Loverde and DiLorenzo, "Participating Faithfully in the Political Process", October 28, 2009.

38. Bishop Joseph F. Martino, Pastoral Letter for Respect Life Sunday, October 5, 2008.

39. Bishop Timothy A. McDonnell, "Real to Reel" program, WWLP-22 television.

40. Bourne, "New York Bishop: Catholics Shouldn't vote for Pro-Abortion Candidates. Period." LifeSiteNews, November 2, 2016.

41. "Abortion and Other Issues in an Election Year," *The Long Island Catholic,* August 27, 2008.

42. Myers, Pastoral Statement, "The Obligations of Catholics and the Rights of Unborn Children," June 1990.

43. Myers, "Sincerely in the Lord," October 17, 2000.

44. Nickless.

45. O'Brien, Pastoral Letter on Voting, October 1, 2000.

46. Olmsted.

47. Cardinal Seán Patrick O'Malley, Post on the cardinal's blog, October 31, 2008.

48. Ratzinger.

49. Sample.

50. Serratelli.

51. Bishop Bernard W. Schmitt, "Bishop Calls Abortion 'Greatest Evil of Our Age,'" October 20, 2004.

52. Sheridan.

53. Bishop Larry Silva, Pastoral Letter, *Catholic Hawaii*, October 19, 2008.

54. Bishop Richard Stika, Post on Twitter, July 5, 2019.

55. Bishop John M. Smith, Pastoral Letter, November 5, 2000.

56. Bishop Paul J. Swain, Statement on Elections, October 31, 2008.

57. Bishop James C. Timlin, "The Ballot and the Right to Life," Fall 2000.

58. Vasa, "Modern Look at Abortion Not Same as St. Augustine's," *The Catholic Sentinel*, September 5, 2008.

59. Archbishop John Vlazny, Portland in Oregon, "Political Responsibility Among Catholics," *The Catholic Sentinel*, October 2008.

60. Archbishop Donald W. Wuerl, Washington, D.C., "Continuing Reflections on Forming Consciences for Faithful Citizenship: The Teaching of Christ," September 2008.

61. USCCB, *Forming Consciences for Faithful Citizenship*, no. 28.

62. Ibid., no. 22.

63. National Conference of Catholic Bishops, "Resolution on Abortion," November 7, 1989.

64. USCCB, "Pastoral Plan for Pro-Life Activities: A Campaign in Support of Life," 2001.

65. USCCB, *Living the Gospel of Life*, no. 32.

66. *Evangelium Vitae*, no. 75.

67. Bishops of Kansas, "Moral Principles for Catholic Voters," 2006.

68. Bernard Cardinal Law, Archbishop of Baltimore; Bishop Thomas Dupre, Springfield, Massachusetts; Bishop Sean O'Malley, Fall River, Massachusetts; Bishop Daniel Reilly, Worcester, Massachusetts, "Faithful Citizenship in Massachusetts," October 20, 2000.

69. Catholic Bishops of New York State, "Our Cherished Right, Our Solemn Duty," September 2008.

70. Catholic Bishops of Pennsylvania, "A Call to Faithful Citizenship and

Respect for Life," October 2008.

71. Catholic Bishops of Wisconsin, "A Letter to Catholics in Wisconsin on Faithful Citizenship," August 2010.

72. Congregation for the Doctrine of the Faith, *Declaration on Procured Abortion (1974)*, no. 11.

73. Father Richard J. Neuhaus, "More Catholic Bishops Speak Out on Communion, Abortion and Voting," LifeNews.com, September 21, 2004.

74. Torraco.

75. Bickerstaff.

76. Hudson.

Chapter 18
The Seamless Garment Ripped to Shreds

1. Beltran.

2. Burke, St. Louis, Pastoral Letter, "On Our Civic Responsibility for the Common Good," October 1, 2004.

3. Ibid.

4. Ibid.

5. Gainer, Faithful Citizenship Statement, October 28, 2008.

6. Hermann.

7. Cardinal James Hickey, "Faithful Citizenship," *Catholic Standard*, October 26, 2000.

8. Adam Cardinal Maida, Letter to the Archdiocese, October 5-6, 2002.

9. Monsignor Kevin McMahon, "Politics, Abortion and Communion," 2006.

10. Myers, Pastoral Statement, "A Time for Honesty," May 5, 2004.

11. Olmsted.

12. Bishop Dennis Schnurr, "October a Time to Reflect on Human Dignity," October 1, 2008.

13. Strickland.

14. Tobin, "Okay, Here's How You Should Vote," *Rhode Island Catholic*,

October, 2008.

15. Torraco.

16. Ibid.

17. Ibid.

18. Westen.

19. Catholic Bishops of Pennsylvania, "Personal Participation: The Key to a Just Society," October 1984.

20. Catholic Bishops of Massachusetts, October 20, 2000.

21. Abbott, "Noted Priest: Come November, Catholics Should Vote For...," RenewAmerica.com, April 16, 2012.

22. Father Matthew Habiger, "Sin to Vote for Pro-Abortion Politicians?," EWTN.com, 1999.

23. Mastroeni.

Chapter 19
Conscience Isn't What You Think, Or What You Think

1. CCC, 1782.

2. Olmsted, in an interview about his booklet, *Catholics in the Public Square,* 2006.

3. Torraco.

4. Myers.

5. Sheridan.

6. Mastroeni.

7. Galante.

8. Bishop John M. Smith, Letter to the editor of *The Trenton Times,* August 2008.

9. "More Catholic Bishops Speak Out on Communion, Abortion and Voting," LifeNews.com, September 21, 2004.

10. Myers.

Chapter 20
Bishops Warn: How You Vote Can Be a Mortal Sin

1. Howard Kainz, "Can There Be Mortal Sin in Voting?," TheCatholic-Thing.org, July 23, 2014.

2. Bishop Thomas J. Paprocki, The-American-Catholic.com, September 27, 2012.

3. Sheridan.

4. Ricken, "An Important Moment," TheCatholicExchange.com, November 5, 2012.

5. Chaput, "Thoughts on 'Roman Catholics for Obama,'" FirstThings.com, June 4, 2008.

6. "Clarity From Kansas City Bishop Finn On A Catholic's Duty In The Voting Booth," Hugh Hewitt interview in October 2008, posted at PriestsForLife.com.

7. Finn, "Can a Catholic Vote in Support of Abortion?," *The Catholic Key,* October 14, 2008.

8. Farrell and Vann.

9. Carlson.

10. Bishop Daniel Jenky, Letter read at all diocesan weekend Masses, November 3-4, 2012.

11. Bishops of Kansas, "Moral Principles for Catholic Voters."

12. Archbishop Alfred Hughes, "Co-Responsibility for Public Policy," diocesan newspaper, January 14, 2004.

13. Burke, "Archbishop Burke to Release Pastoral Letter Stressing Priority of Abortion Issue," CatholicNewsAgency.com, July 14, 2004.

14. Aquila, Sermon at Cathedral of St. Mary, April 24, 2004.

15. Lawler, p. 62.

16. "Peruvian Archbishop says it is a 'mortal sin' to vote for pro-abortion, pro-gay candidates," Reuters, GMANewsOnline, March 30, 2016.

17. "Catholics Should Not Vote For Pro-Abortion Candidates, Explains Peruvian Archbishop," Catholic News Agency, February 17, 2011.

18. Torraco.

19. Habiger.

20. Duncan, "Father Jay Scott Newman's Original Letter on Voting for Barack Obama," Zimbio.com, November 17, 2008.

21. "Father Joseph Illo: 'God Requires This of Me,'" all.org, December 9, 2008.
22. Mastroeni.
23. "Irish Bishop Calls 'Yes' Voters on Abortion Referendum to Come to Confession," CatholicNewsAgency.com, May 29, 2018.

Chapter 21
Step-by-Step: How to Vote So You Don't Go to Hell

1. Westen.
2. Torraco.
3. Westen.
4. Finn.
5. Hermann.
6. Bishops of Kansas.
7. Boyea.
8. Hickey.
9. Burke, St. Louis, Pastoral Letter, "On Our Civic Responsibility for the Common Good," October 1, 2004.
10. Torraco.
11. McMahon.
12. Bishop Vincent De Paul Breen, October 18, 2000.
13. Burke.
14. Farrell and Vann.
15. Westen.
16. Burke.

Chapter 22
Not Voting Can Also Be a Mortal Sin

1. Father Heribert Jone, *Moral Theology,* Mercier Press, 1929, 1955.
2. Father Titus Cranny, *Catholic Principles on the Obligation of Voting*, The Catholic University of America Press, 1952.

3. Boyea.

4. Kagan.

5. Bishops of Florida, "2008 Election Year Statement – Vote With a Properly Formed Conscience in Order to Defend Human Life and Protect Dignity," September 2008.

6. Grace D. MacKinnon, "Voting Pro-Life," CatholicEducation.org, October 2002.

7. Breen.

8. Farrell and Vann.

9. Bishops of Kansas.

10. Bishops of New York State.

11. Bishops of Illinois, "Elections, Conscience, and the Responsibility to Vote," October 2006.

12. Burke.

13. Bishop Gerald Kicanas, Tucson, "Synod, Interview With Bishop Gerald Kicanas," Conversation Café, October 13, 2008.

14. Pope John Paul II, *Christifideles Laici*, no. 42.

15. Archbishop Alex J. Brunett, "Compassion or Lethal Rx?," *Catholic Northwest Progress*, October 9, 2008.

16. CCC, 2240.

17. Mastroeni.

18. Johnston.

Chapter 23
How Trump Overcame the Catholic Intelligentsia

1. Robert P. George and George Weigel, "An Appeal to Our Fellow Catholics," NationalReview.com, March 7, 2016.

2. "Can a Catholic in Good Conscience Vote For Trump?," CatholicNewsAgency.com, March 16, 2016.

3. Ibid.

4. Ibid.

5. Ibid.

6. Dave Armstrong, "How Can a Catholic Vote for Trump?!!?," Patheos.com, May 28, 2016.

7. Kailani Koenig, "Tim Kaine Predicts Catholic Church Will Change Views on Same-Sex Marriage," nbcnews.com, September 11, 2016.

8. "Catholic Marriage Won't Change, Tim Kaine's Bishop Says," *National Catholic Register,* September 14, 2016.

9. Bezner.

10. David Sherfinski and Bradford Richardson, "Trump Forming Catholic Advisory to Help Woo Bloc," thewashingtontimes.com, September 22, 2016.

11. Lori Ann Watson, "Why Catholics Can't Vote for Hillary – Even Once. Ever. For Any reason," CatholicVote.org, October 7, 2016.

12. Thomas D. Williams, Ph. D, "Tim Kaine's Catholic Problem," Breitbart.com, October 5, 2016.

13. Pope John Paul II, *Evangelium Vitae,* no. 71.

14. Edmund Kozak, "WikiLeaks: Podesta and Left-Wing Activist Plot Catholic Spring," lifezette.com, October 12, 2016.

15. Amy Moreno, "Growing Backlash From Catholic Church Against Clinton Campaign," truthfeed.com, October 14, 2016.

16. Ibid.

17. Ibid.

18. Ibid.

19. Ibid.

20. Aquila, "Voting as a Catholic in 2016," DenverCatholic.org, October 5, 2016.

21. "Bishop: Support for Abortion Should 'Disqualify' Candidates," newsday.com, October 30, 2016.

22. Mastroeni.

23. Stravinskas.

24. Archbishop Joseph F. Naumann, "Our Choices End Where Another's More Fundamental Right Begins" (pastoral letter), October 18, 2016.

25. Rev. Gerard Lessard, "There's No Need to Choose the Lesser Evil in This Election – St. Thomas Aquinas," thechristianreview.com, October

24, 2016.

26. Matt C. Abbott, "Trump Won the Catholic Vote," americanthinker.com, November 11, 2016.

27. "New Data Suggest Clinton, Not Trump, Won Catholic Vote," america-magazine.com, April 4, 2017.

28. Abbott.

29. Claire Chretien, "Cardinal Dolan blasts 'Catholics for Choice' ad campaign as 'deceptive,'" lifesitenews.com, September 15, 2016.

30. Abbott.

31. Frank Buckley, "Catholic Surprise: Another Way Trump is Remaking the GOP," *New York Post, December* 20, 2016.

32. Bezner, "The Victory of the Unlikely Donald Trump Fills Me With Hope," thechristianreview.com, November 9, 2016.

Chapter 24
The "Catholic Ticket"? Not the One With the Catholic

1. "Can a Catholic in Good Conscience Vote For Trump?," Catholic-NewsAgency.com, March 16, 2016.

2. Hickey.

3. Hudson, "Dominant-Issue Voters," Catholicity.com, https://www.catholicity.com/commentary/hudson/00218.html

CPSIA information can be obtained
at www.ICGtesting.com
Printed in the USA
LVHW090026080920
665299LV00008B/76/J

9 781734 792508